HIDDEN IN PLAIN VIEW:

REFUGEES LIVING WITHOUT PROTECTION IN NAIROBI AND KAMPALA

Human Rights Watch
New York • Washington • London • Brussels

ISBN: 1-56432-281-5
Library of Congress Control Number: 2002114404

Cover photos:

An Ethiopian refugee rests June 20 2001, outside the offices of the United Nations High Commission for Refugees in the outskirts of Nairobi where he has been camped for weeks awaiting processing of his papers. Photo by George Mulala. (c) 2001 Reuters Limited

Room in Kampala, Uganda housing approximately sixty Somali refugees. Alison Parker/Human Rights Watch

Addresses for Human Rights Watch
350 Fifth Avenue, 34th Floor, New York, NY 10118-3299
Tel: (212) 290-4700, Fax: (212) 736-1300, E-mail: hrwnyc@hrw.org

1630 Connecticut Avenue, NW, Suite 500, Washington, D.C. 20009
Tel: (202) 612-4321, Fax: (202) 612-4333, E-mail: hrwdc@hrw.org

2nd Floor, 2-12 Pentonville Road London N1 9HF, UK
Tel: (44 20) 7713 1995, Fax: (44 20) 7713 1800, E-mail: hrwuk@hrw.org

15 Rue Van Campenhout, 1000 Brussels, Belgium
Tel: (2) 732-2009, Fax: (2) 732-0471, E-mail: hrwbe@hrw.org

Web Site Address: http://www.hrw.org

Listserv address: To subscribe to the Human Rights Watch news e-mail list,
send a blank e-mail message to subscribe@igc.topica.com. with "subscribe hrw-news" in the body of the message (leave the subject line blank).

Human Rights Watch is dedicated to
protecting the human rights of people around the world.

We stand with victims and activists to prevent
discrimination, to uphold political freedom, to protect people from
inhumane conduct in wartime, and to bring offenders to justice.

We investigate and expose
human rights violations and hold abusers accountable.

We challenge governments and those who hold power to end
abusive practices and respect international human rights law.

We enlist the public and the international
community to support the cause of human rights for all.

HUMAN RIGHTS WATCH

Human Rights Watch conducts regular, systematic investigations of human rights abuses in some seventy countries around the world. Our reputation for timely, reliable disclosures has made us an essential source of information for those concerned with human rights. We address the human rights practices of governments of all political stripes, of all geopolitical alignments, and of all ethnic and religious persuasions. Human Rights Watch defends freedom of thought and expression, due process and equal protection of the law, and a vigorous civil society; we document and denounce murders, disappearances, torture, arbitrary imprisonment, discrimination, and other abuses of internationally recognized human rights. Our goal is to hold governments accountable if they transgress the rights of their people.

Human Rights Watch began in 1978 with the founding of its Europe and Central Asia division (then known as Helsinki Watch). Today, it also includes divisions covering Africa, the Americas, Asia, and the Middle East. In addition, it includes three thematic divisions on arms, children's rights, and women's rights. It maintains offices in New York, Washington, Los Angeles, London, Brussels, Moscow, Tashkent, Tblisi, and Bangkok. Human Rights Watch is an independent, nongovernmental organization, supported by contributions from private individuals and foundations worldwide. It accepts no government funds, directly or indirectly.

ACKNOWLEDGEMENTS

This report was written by Alison Parker, acting director of refugee policy at Human Rights Watch. The report is based on field research in Kenya conducted by Alison Parker from April 2, 2002 to April 6, 2002 and from April 16, 2002 to April 24, 2002. It is also based on field research in Uganda conducted by Alison Parker and Juliane Kippenberg, Human Rights Watch Africa Division NGO liaison, from April 7, 2002 to April 16, 2002. Additional research assistance was provided by Ruth Allen, Karen Barnes, and David Burkoff, interns to the refugee policy program. Rachael Reilly, refugee policy director; Peter Takirambudde, director of the Africa Division; Binaifer Nowrojee, counsel to the Africa Division, Juliane Kippenberg, Africa Division NGO liaison, Jemera Rone, senior researcher, Suliman Baldo, senior researcher, Alison des Forges, senior researcher, Michael Bochenek, counsel to the Children's Rights Division; Widney Brown, advocacy director of the Women's Rights Division; Ian Gorvin, consultant to the Program Office, and Jim Ross, senior legal advisor, edited the report. Production assistance was provided by Solome Lemma, associate to the refugee policy division, Veronica Matushaj, photo editor; and Patrick Minges, publications director.

Human Rights Watch would like to thank the Leonard H. Sandler Fellowship Program, the Oak Foundation, and the Ford Foundation for their generous support of this project. Human Rights Watch is also indebted to UNHCR, Goal, the Jesuit Refugee Service, the Refugee Consortium of Kenya, the Refugee Law Project, government officials, and numerous private citizens of Nairobi and Kampala who generously assisted us in the course of our field research.

Most of all, we would like to thank the one hundred and fifty courageous refugees who shared their stories with us for this report.

TABLE OF CONTENTS

"I have no place to go—I am just like the air blowing around, no place to stay…"

(refugee boy in Kampala, Uganda)

"I said that I am a UNHCR mandate refugee. The officer said, "What is that?" and he started beating me with a stick."

(refugee man in Nairobi, Kenya)

INTRODUCTION

SUMMARY

On the night of April 17, 2002, two Rwandan children aged nine and ten were murdered at a "secure residence" run by the Office of the United Nations High Commissioner for Refugees (UNHCR) in Nairobi, Kenya. Their throats were slit by an assailant. Their forty-three-year-old mother was also injured. The Rwandans had been placed in the facility because of the inter-ethnic nature of the family, and because the mother is related to the former president of Rwanda, Juvenal Habyarimana. The residence is under twenty-four-hour security protection, surrounded by a high fence, visitors are not permitted, and asylum seekers or refugees cannot leave the residence without permission. The family's application for resettlement to Australia had been mired in delay for some eleven months, despite the fact that their lives were at risk. The attack occurred one day after their case had been accepted by Australia for resettlement.

Few refugees living in Nairobi or Kampala, Uganda, have cases that are as high profile as this Rwandan family's. However, many are facing a similar plight—having escaped to these cities from persecution, refugees are met with further insecurity, something they hoped they had left behind. The very actors who are tasked under international law with protecting them put refugees' lives at risk: host governments, UNHCR, and the international community, including resettlement governments are all to blame for the terrible conditions and danger that urban refugees live with in Nairobi and Kampala. The extent and urgency of the problems are in plain view for those who care to look. However, there is little incentive to address the needs of urban refugees because the governments of Kenya and Uganda have policies that require that refugees live in camps. As a result, refugees who are in the city are neglected, and the abuses they face rarely come to light.

Refugees, just like other impoverished residents of Nairobi and Kampala, live in overcrowded and often squalid living conditions in the poorest neighborhoods. Refugees may not be poorer than Kenyans or Ugandans, but they must struggle for survival without the legal status or networks of friends and family that citizens have. Some are forced to sleep on the streets, leaving them vulnerable to violence and illness. Since very few relief agencies are able to assist them, food is scarce and medical treatment is difficult to obtain. Those who require counseling or medical care because they are victims of torture are forced to negotiate labyrinthine referral systems, and many simply go without treatment.

1

Not only do refugees face serious challenges to their social and economic survival, they are also at great risk from a lack of protection for their physical safety: in both countries there are serious shortcomings with the determination procedures used to decide whether a person should be recognized as a refugee and afforded protection (in Kenya, the refugee status determination is run by UNHCR; in Uganda it is done jointly by UNHCR and the government). In Nairobi, the determination system is dysfunctional because it subjects asylum seekers[1] to lengthy delays, during which they are vulnerable to ongoing abuse. The system is also marred by an overwhelming sense of futility, since the outcome of the process – a letter recognizing a particular individual's status – is routinely ignored and even destroyed by Kenyan police during arrests and roundups of foreigners that occur on a daily basis.

In Uganda, the government's role in the conflicts and politics of the Democratic Republic of Congo (DRC), Rwanda, and Sudan makes asylum seekers who come from those countries fearful of the system. While delay plagues the status determination system in Nairobi from day one, asylum seekers in Kampala only experience delays if their cases are particularly complex or the government is suspicious of the applicant. Yet it is often these complex or allegedly "suspicious" cases that require the most urgent attention.

Refugees' physical security is at risk especially before they have their status assessed, but even afterwards the risk remains. Individuals may suffer from extortion, harassment, beatings, arbitrary arrest, detention, and/or sexual violence, all at the hands of the Kenyan or Ugandan police or military. It is the responsibility of the government to prevent such abuses, and since state actors are the perpetrators, the state is directly responsible for providing redress. But when the perpetrator of the abuse, for example the Kenyan or Ugandan police, is the same party to whom a victim must turn for help and redress, complaints are rarely voiced.

Many asylum seekers or refugees in Nairobi and Kampala are also trailed, threatened, or assaulted by agents from their home countries. Refugees who suffer such abuse are often left with only one option: seeking urgent resettlement in a third country. Despite the urgency, these refugees are often faced with refusal or bureaucratic delay.

Refugees or asylum seekers in Nairobi or Kampala with security or assistance problems often do not know where to turn for help. When the police or governments of Kenya or Uganda fail them, and when UNHCR is

---

[1] This report will use the term "asylum seeker" when referring to an individual who has not yet had his or her status as a refugee assessed, on either a *prima facie* or an individual basis. *See* note 18, below, for a description of *prima facie* status. The term "refugee" will be used to refer to those who have had their status so assessed.

unresponsive, they may seek help from non-governmental organizations (NGOs) such as the Refugee Law Project in Kampala or the Refugee Consortium of Kenya in Nairobi. Despite government and UNHCR resistance, a small number of humanitarian agencies provide some assistance to the most needy urban refugees. The help is just a drop in the ocean, however, and these agencies can do little to protect refugees from violent attacks, or to intervene in status determination systems that are controlled by UNHCR or, in the case of Uganda, the government.

Human Rights Watch recommends that UNHCR, the governments of Kenya and Uganda, and donor governments implement their responsibilities to protect and assist refugees and asylum seekers living in urban areas by, *inter alia*: regularizing the legal status of urban refugees, improving the status determination systems in both Nairobi and Kampala, preventing and responding to the insecurity and ongoing human rights violations that so many asylum seekers and refugees living in urban areas face, improving the quality of and access to assistance in Nairobi and Kampala, rejecting improper use of secondary movement policies, and ameliorating problems with resettlement and UNHCR's urban refugee policy. The details of these recommendations are set forth below.

METHODS

This report is based on a mission to Kenya and Uganda that Human Rights Watch undertook during April 2002, and prior and subsequent research. In Nairobi and Kampala interviews were conducted with one hundred and fifty refugees and asylum seekers. Sometimes refugees from a particular country of origin are well organized, and several interviews were obtained by working with these refugee networks. However, we were conscious not to leave out the views or experiences of any major sub-group within a nationality (such as people of varying economic backgrounds, ages, genders, ethnicities, or political persuasions). Therefore, in other instances, Human Rights Watch researchers sought introductions from schools, doctors, humanitarian, or faith-based organizations, or by walking around in the neighborhoods where refugees live. International NGO and U.N. agency staff and the staff of local Kenyan and Ugandan NGOs were also interviewed.

Interviews with refugees were conducted in private settings – either in the offices of a humanitarian organization, in a different neutral location, or in refugees' shelters. In one case, a Human Rights Watch researcher was able to interview an imprisoned refugee in one of Nairobi's police stations. A Human Rights Watch researcher also visited Kakuma refugee camp in Kenya and conducted several interviews with refugees living there in their tents or mud-and-thatch huts.

Most of the testimonies reproduced in this report are the result of confidential in-depth interviews that lasted, on average, one to one-and-a-half hours. While we sought as much information as possible from each interview, the well-being of the interviewee was always paramount and some interviews were cut short as a result. Interviews were conducted in English or French when possible, and with the assistance of an interpreter – usually a friend or relative of the refugee – when necessary. In a few cases, particularly when a Human Rights Watch researcher was gathering information about a general subject that did not require confidentiality, such as regarding living conditions in either Nairobi or Kampala, refugees were interviewed in small groups.

Human Rights Watch researchers also made use of whatever additional evidence could be gathered to substantiate refugees' stories. Examples of such evidence include: press accounts or interviews with other refugees or officials substantiating facts; documents issued by governments and U.N., or humanitarian agencies; scars or other markings evidencing physical violence, or photographs.

In Uganda, government officials and police officers in Old Kampala police station were interviewed. In Kenya, several police officers were interviewed in the stations and jails where they work. Human Rights Watch sought meetings with the government of Kenya to discuss its responsibility to protect urban refugees on several occasions.[2]   Less than twenty-four hours before our departure from the country, the government informed Human Rights Watch that a meeting would not be granted unless a U.S.$300 research permit was purchased. When a Human Rights Watch researcher refused to pay for such a permit, the interview was denied.[3]   A Human Rights Watch researcher also invited the government of Kenya to respond in writing to some of our concerns. To date no response has been received.   A fifty-minute meeting eventually occurred between Human Rights Watch and representatives of the government of Kenya in Geneva in late September 2002.

The names of all refugees, NGO, and U.N. agency staff have been changed or withheld to protect their privacy, security, or positions.

---

[2] Human Rights Watch sought meetings with the government of Kenya twice by fax, three times through telephone contacts and four times through in-person visits to the Ministry of Home Affairs.
[3] Human Rights Watch discussion with Assistant to the Permanent Secretary, Ministry of Home Affairs, Nairobi, Kenya, April 23, 2002.

RECOMMENDATIONS

To the Government of Kenya
To create a domestic legal framework for refugees

- The **Kenyan Government** should revise and adopt its 1994 Refugee Bill so that it fully implements the Kenyan government's responsibilities under the 1951 Refugee Convention and the OAU Refugee Convention.
- Until comprehensive legislation is adopted, refugees living in camps or urban environments in Kenya should be afforded in law or administrative practice the rights granted to them under the Refugee Convention, primarily the rights to be protected against refoulement, to have equal access to the courts, to engage in wage-earning employment, to engage in self-employment (such as agriculture), the right to elementary education, and to access other forms of education.

To address the problems with camp confinement

- Refugees should be permitted freedom of movement consistent with Article 26 of the Refugee Convention and Article 12 of the ICCPR. Until those standards are met, the **Kenyan Government** should at a minimum provide, by statute or administrative regulation, permission for the following categories of refugees to leave refugee camps on a voluntary basis:
    i) individuals with serious security problems in the camps;
    ii) individuals in need of medical care only available in urban centers;
    iii) individuals who have been living in a refugee camp for an excessive length of time, such as three years or more, and for whom alternative permanent solutions in the foreseeable future appear unlikely;
    iv) individuals who are in need of educational opportunities not available in the camps; and
    v) individuals with family members who are residing legally outside of the camp.
- Standard procedures should be put in place for applications under these five exceptions to be brought before an impartial decision-maker. All recognized refugees, whether *prima facie* or individually recognized, should be allowed to apply for permission to leave the camps.

To address protection problems when asylum seekers and refugees first arrive in Nairobi and its environs

- The **Ministry of Home Affairs** should set up temporary reception sites for asylum seekers and refugees, including those who have transferred from camps, providing them with safe shelter for at least the first two weeks that they are in Nairobi. These temporary sites could be appropriate places for UNHCR to identify at-risk individuals.

To address police harassment of asylum seekers and refugees in Kenya

- The **Kenyan Police** should be instructed to recognize and respect asylum seeker and refugee documentation.
- The **Kenyan Police Department** should provide training in refugee law to serving members of the police force, and it should incorporate refugee protection and law into the police academy curriculum for all new officers.

To provide adequate reporting mechanisms for security or police harassment problems

- The **Kenyan Police** should facilitate the filing of official police reports by asylum seekers and refugees regarding security threats. Copies of these reports should be sent to UNHCR as a matter of standard operating procedure.
- The **Kenyan Government** should put in place procedures that allow asylum seekers and refugees to safely make complaints about police involvement in harassment and corruption to an independent and impartial ombudsman. Copies of these reports should be sent to UNHCR as a matter of standard operating procedure. Disciplinary action must be taken against officers guilty of such behavior. A guarantee for the security of the complainant against any potential reprisals must be made and adhered to.

To address insufficient asylum seeker and refugee documentation

- The **Ministry of Home Affairs** should provide asylum seekers, refugees, and their family members with identity documentation during each stage of the status determination process that acknowledges their permission to reside in Nairobi, and that is jointly signed by the government of Kenya and UNHCR.

To address the problem of refoulement
- The **Kenyan Judiciary** should institute training for magistrates on international refugee law, particularly non-refoulement, and develop a standard inquiry during deportation proceedings for determining fear of persecution upon return.
- The **Kenyan Police** should be trained to inquire into the *prima facie* or individualized refugee status of those in custody, and to contact UNHCR where appropriate.
- The **Kenyan Police** should allow asylum seekers or refugees in their custody to be transported to UNHCR's offices in Nairobi.

To the Government of Uganda
To address the lack of a domestic legal framework for refugees
- The **Ugandan Government** should adopt its 2001 Refugee Bill in accordance with the Refugee Convention and the OAU Refugee Convention.
- Until comprehensive legislation is adopted, refugees living in camps or urban environments in Uganda should be afforded in law or administrative practice the rights granted them under the Refugee Convention, primarily the rights to be protected against refoulement, to have equal access to the courts, to engage in wage-earning employment, to engage in self-employment (such as agriculture), to elementary education, and to access other forms of education.

To address the problems with camp confinement
- Refugees should be permitted freedom of movement consistent with Article 26 of the Refugee Convention and Article 12 of the ICCPR. Until those standards are met, the **Ugandan Government** should at a minimum provide, by statute or administrative regulation, permission for the following categories of refugees to leave refugee camps on a voluntary basis (as it already does on an informal basis for all categories except iv, below):
    i) individuals with serious security problems in the camps;
    ii) individuals in need of medical care only available in urban centers;
    iii) individuals who agree to be self-sufficient;
    iv) individuals who have been living in a refugee camp for an excessive length of time, such as three years or more, and for whom alternative permanent solutions in the foreseeable future appear unlikely;

v) individuals who are in need of educational opportunities not available in the camps; and

vi) individuals with family members who are residing legally outside of the camp.

- Standard procedures should be put in place for applications under these six exceptions to be brought before an impartial decision-maker. All recognized refugees, whether *prima facie* or individually recognized, should be allowed to apply for permission to leave the camp.

To address problems in the refugee status determination system

- The **Ugandan Government** should allow independent legal representatives or UNHCR protection staff to represent asylum seekers (and not merely observe the proceedings) before the Special Branch, the Refugee Eligibility Committee, and during appeals.

- Relations between the country of origin and Uganda should not influence the standards applied or procedures followed in a particular asylum seekers' case. Instead, the **Ugandan Government** should ensure that its criteria for transfer to the Special Branch and Refugee Eligibility Committee are transparent, and its staff decides cases based on the facts presented and in accordance with the 1951 Refugee Convention and the OAU Refugee Convention.

- The **Office of the Prime Minister** and the **Special Branch** should immediately cease using randomly chosen interpreters from among the refugee community at all stages of the determination process. Professional interpreters should be hired for each of the commonly spoken languages during determinations. If funds for interpreters are not available, then they should be sought from donor governments (see also the recommendations to donor governments, below).

To address protection problems when asylum seekers and refugees first arrive in Kampala and its environs

- The **Office of the Prime Minister** should set up temporary reception sites for asylum seekers and refugees, providing them with safe shelter for at least the first two weeks that they are in Kampala. These temporary sites could be appropriate places for UNHCR to identify at-risk individuals.

To address the problem of secondary movement policies

- The **Ugandan Government** should not apply secondary movement policies to a refugee in Uganda who was compelled to move because of specific protection or security problems in his or her previous country.

To provide adequate reporting mechanisms for security problems

- The **Ugandan Police** should facilitate the filing of official police reports by asylum seekers and refugees regarding security threats. Copies of these reports should be sent to UNHCR as a matter of standard operating procedure.
- An **independent and impartial Ombudsman** should investigate security incidents in which the Ugandan camp commandants, police, or military are implicated. Copies of all incident reports should be sent to UNHCR. Disciplinary action or prosecution must be taken against officers found responsible for such behavior. A guarantee for the security of the complainant against any potential reprisals must be made and adhered to.

To address the problem of real or perceived bias by the government of Uganda

- The **Office of the Prime Minister** should build confidence among asylum seekers in the confidentiality of the status determination process through public announcements on radio and visits to refugee communities, informing asylum seekers about the process. As a subset of these efforts, Uganda should build public awareness in the Somali community of the importance of registering with the police in Old Kampala, and of obtaining refugee status.
- The **Ugandan Government** should ensure that the Joint Verification Commission does not impede the rights of asylum seekers to fair and confidential assessment of their asylum claims

To address the problem of refoulement

- The **Ugandan Judiciary** should institute training for magistrates on international refugee law, particularly non-refoulement, and develop a standard inquiry during deportation proceedings for determining fear of persecution upon return.
- The **Ugandan Police** should be trained to inquire into the *prima facie* or individualized refugee status of those in custody, and to contact UNHCR where appropriate.

To United Nations High Commissioner for Refugees (UNHCR)
To address gaps in UNHCR's urban refugee policies

- UNHCR should adopt the Evaluation and Policy Analysis Unit's clear recommendation to re-write and re-issue its 1997 *Policy on Refugee in Urban Areas*, focusing in more detail on methods for providing adequate protection and assistance to refugees living in urban areas. The revised policy should avoid generalizations, derogatory depictions, or incorrect assumptions about urban refugees (such as that they are "irregular movers") that undermine efforts to address their protection concerns.

- UNHCR should revise its other policies and guidelines (e.g. during the planned revision of its *Guidelines on Refugee Children* in 2004) to address the specific protection and assistance problems facing asylum seekers and refugees in urban areas.

- UNHCR should systematically gather statistics about the numbers of refugees living in urban environments in Kenya and Uganda.

To address the lack of a domestic legal framework for refugees

- UNHCR should continue to encourage the governments of Kenya and Uganda to adopt domestic refugee legislation. It should also assist in the drafting process to ensure that the laws fully implement all governmental obligations towards asylum seekers and refugees under refugee and other forms of human rights law.

To address problems in the UNHCR-run refugee status determination system in Nairobi

- UNHCR should provide all asylum seekers with written information in their own language on: i) the legal standards to be applied; ii) a realistic indicative timetable for each stage of the determination process; and iii) when applicable, detailed reasons for rejection. For purposes of accountability, both the asylum seeker and the officer conducting the interview should sign this written information indicating that it was transmitted and received.

- UNHCR should post a notice board indicating by case number as made known to each asylum seeker (individual identities should not be disclosed) the progress of processing for each asylum seeker's file. If confidentiality concerns still prevent being able to post individualized tracking systems aligned with each asylum seekers' case number, then at least a generalized tracking system should be posted, indicating the progress of all files submitted on a given day.

- UNHCR offices should have adequate personnel and resources so that status determinations are fair and efficient, keeping in mind the particular difficulties and needs of applicants.

To address the problem of secondary movement policies
- UNHCR should not apply secondary movement policies to a refugee who was compelled to move because of specific protection or security problems in his or her previous country.

To address problems in the refugee status determination system in Kampala
- UNHCR in Kampala should immediately cease using randomly chosen interpreters from among the refugee community during its interviews. Professional interpreters should be hired for each of the commonly spoken languages during determinations.

To address the problem of refoulement
- One officer at UNHCR in Nairobi and Kampala should be identified to receive notices on asylum seekers or refugees who have been taken into the custody of the military or police and may face refoulement, and should respond to these referrals expeditiously.

To address the problems with camp confinement
- UNHCR should urge the two governments to provide for exceptions to the camp confinement policies in domestic law or regulation, and should revise its own policy on urban refugees.

To address protection problems when asylum seekers and refugees first arrive in the capital cities
- UNHCR and the governments of Kenya and Uganda should set up temporary reception sites for asylum seekers and refugees, providing them with safe shelter for at least the first two weeks that they are in Nairobi or Kampala. These temporary sites could be appropriate places for UNHCR to identify at-risk individuals.
- UNHCR in Nairobi should engage the services of an implementing partner NGO to work in the registration sheds at the Branch Office in Nairobi to register and adequately identify all unaccompanied and separated children, women heads of household, and other individuals in need of specialized care or assistance during their first visit to the office. UNHCR in Kampala should provide the same services through its implementing partner, InterAid. After such registration and

identification, all such asylum seekers or refugees should then be immediately referred to assistance and shelter programs.

- UNHCR should deploy a team of staff members to rotate through the various neighborhoods housing refugees in Nairobi and Kampala in order to identify at risk individuals who may not have reached UNHCR's offices, and in order to intervene in urgent protection problems in the community, including at local police stations.

To address protection and assistance problems faced by asylum seeker and refugee children

- UNHCR should work to ensure access to education for all refugee children, regardless of their location within a host country, and to the greatest extent possible given resource constraints.
- In addition to registering refugee or asylum seeker children during their first contact with the office, UNHCR should ensure that refugee children within its protection areas in camps or housed in secure accommodations in urban areas have access to education.
- Unaccompanied and separated refugee children who cannot be placed in appropriate foster care, but who are living in secure accommodations should have separate appropriate housing facilities or separated parts of housing facilities.

To address concerns about inadequate medical referrals in Nairobi

- UNHCR in Nairobi should engage the services of an implementing partner NGO to work in the registration sheds at the branch office to examine and treat medical cases on the spot and make same-day referrals to either: i) an NGO medical clinic for treatment; or ii) a hospital for urgent care. The policy should allow referrals to be made for both asylum seekers and refugees.
- To the extent possible, victims of torture and sexual violence should be identified during their first visit to UNHCR in Nairobi through the use of an implementing partner NGO engaged to assist in registering asylum seekers or refugees. However, since it will not be possible to identify all those in need in the public environment of the registration sheds, every asylum seeker or refugee should be handed a set of written (in all major relevant languages) directions to an implementing partner's offices where screening of torture victims and victims of sexual violence can be conducted in a private setting and where those in need of care can begin to be assisted immediately – well before the individual appears before a protection officer for a status determination

interview. Referrals to psychotherapeutic treatment should also be available to other asylum seekers or refugees who need or request it.

To address concerns about inadequate medical referrals in Kampala
- UNHCR in Kampala should increase the capacity of InterAid to offer quality medical treatment to all asylum seekers and refugees. Referrals to hospitals should be made on the spot; however, if an individual seeks treatment in a hospital for an urgent illness over the weekend or at a time when referrals from InterAid are not available, she should be reimbursed for her duly certified costs even if she did not receive an InterAid referral.
- Referrals to a psychotherapeutic treatment center in Kampala should be made for all victims of torture and sexual violence, and for other refugees who might need or request such treatment, after the initial intake interviews with InterAid.

To address security problems
- UNHCR in Nairobi and Kampala should establish a larger number of secure residences to house asylum seekers and refugees with security problems. Asylum seekers and refugees should be carefully vetted for potential security conflicts before they are housed in the same facility. Separate accommodation, or at least separate buildings and rooms lockable from the inside should be provided for unaccompanied and separated women and children.
- UNHCR should designate an officer to review all complaints (submitted by police, NGO partners, or refugees themselves) of security concerns affecting refugees and to take one or a combination of several immediate protection actions, depending on the nature and severity of the problem: i) give the individual the option to participate in a periodic check-in program at UNHCR's offices, so that if he or she does not appear, action can be taken; ii) assist the individual in filing an official police report; iii) permit the individual to relocate to a refugee camp, settlement, or another town or village where he or she believes his or her security to be at a lesser risk; iv) refer the individual to UNHCR-run safe accommodation; v) refer the individual for resettlement consideration (using expedited procedures when necessary); vi) provide the individual with relocation assistance to another UNHCR office in another country within the region.
- UNHCR in Kampala should pay particular attention to the security problems faced by refugees fleeing from Rwanda and the portions of

the DRC that were controlled by Uganda, in the latter case since they may be under the control of the same authorities responsible for their original persecution. UNHCR should consider referring these cases on to another country for status determination and access to resettlement procedures.

To address resettlement delays and inefficiencies
- UNHCR should put in place resettlement referral officers in both the Kampala and Nairobi UNHCR offices to prepare files of individuals for resettlement.
- UNHCR should un-freeze regular resettlement referrals from UNHCR Nairobi as a matter of urgency.
- UNHCR should process all Nairobi branch office backlogged files as a matter of urgency. If UNHCR is unable to process these files because of staffing limitations, the governments that had conditionally approved these cases for resettlement should designate embassy staff or deploy appropriately trained staff to re-vet these files immediately.
- UNHCR should allow NGO personnel to send suggested cases for resettlement to the designated resettlement officers in Kampala and Nairobi, utilizing a standard referral form and applying mutually agreed-upon threshold criteria for referral.

To the United Kingdom and Rwandan Governments
- The U.K. and Rwandan Government should ensure that the Joint Verification Commission does not impede the rights of asylum seekers to fair and confidential assessment of their asylum claims.

To Donor Governments
- Donor governments should link some of the funding through the New Partnership for Africa's Development (NEPAD) to development initiatives that address the human rights and development needs of refugees, including those living in urban areas.
- Donor governments should adequately fund protection and assistance programs in Kenya's and Uganda's refugee camps.
- Donor governments should increase support for UNHCR and NGOs to provide protection, housing, food, education, and medical assistance to asylum seekers and refugees living in Kampala and Nairobi.
- Donor governments should fund UNHCR and/or NGOs to provide safe accommodation, or at a minimum, adequate locks for the doors of the

shelters of unaccompanied and separated children and women heads of household.

- Donor governments should fund targeted training programs for magistrates and police officers on refugee and other forms of human rights law.
- Donor governments should emphasize ensuring fair treatment of asylum seekers and refugees with security problems, particularly those from Rwanda and from Ugandan-controlled portions of the DRC when considering bilateral or multilateral lending to Uganda.
- Donor governments should emphasize police anti-corruption initiatives and benchmarks in all bilateral and multilateral lending to Kenya.
- Donor governments should seek improvements in UNHCR-run or government-run status determination processes, focusing in particular upon funding programs that seek to: provide information to asylum seekers and refugees and increase the transparency of the process; increase trained staff; provide trained interpreters; and improve the quality and efficacy of identity documentation issued to asylum seekers and refugees.
- Donor governments should adequately fund a streamlined referral system to the existing psychotherapeutic treatment program for torture victims and victims of sexual violence in Nairobi, and should adequately fund a referral and treatment program for torture victims and victims of sexual violence in Kampala. Assistance should be given in order to make psychotherapeutic treatment available to all other asylum seekers and refugees who need or request it.

To Governments in Countries of Resettlement
- Governments should allow NGO personnel to send suggested cases for resettlement simultaneously to UNHCR and to embassy personnel, utilizing a standard referral form and applying mutually agreed-upon threshold criteria for referral. If a government expresses interest in a case sent in this manner to its embassy, it should liaise with UNHCR to ensure that UNHCR processes the file expeditiously.
- Governments with resettlement cases caught in the Nairobi office backlog should designate embassy staff or deploy appropriately trained staff to re-vet these files immediately.
- Governments should put in place expedited referral procedures for high-risk cases. In the case of the United States, the existing such procedures should be brought into active use.

BACKGROUND: REFUGEES LIVING IN NAIROBI AND KAMPALA

In Kenya and Uganda tens of thousands of asylum seekers flock to urban centers like Nairobi and Kampala when fleeing persecution or conflict in neighboring countries. Magnets of relative stability in a sub-region that is rife with conflict, repression, and insecurity, Kenya and Uganda host refugees who have fled from Burundi, the Democratic Republic of Congo (DRC), Eritrea, Ethiopia, Rwanda, Somalia, and Sudan. Many of these people have been living in Kenya or Uganda as refugees for over a decade. In 2001 the Ugandan government estimated that as many as 50,000[4] of the 184,000 refugees[5] hosted by Uganda were living in Kampala. UNHCR, the main U.N. agency charged with providing protection and assistance to refugees, reported that there were 218,500 refugees living in Kenya during 2001,[6] of whom as many as 60,000 were estimated to be in Nairobi.[7]

Although their numbers are significant, refugees in the two capital cities are largely unseen and forgotten by governments and UN policy-makers alike. Because of the policies of host governments and UNHCR, these refugees live a precarious existence, frequently subject to the abuse of their most basic rights.

Due to capacity and security concerns, as well as growing xenophobia, countries like Kenya and Uganda are requiring the majority of refugees arriving in their territories to live confined in camps located in remote areas. The presence of combatants or criminal elements among refugee populations has become a legitimate security concern for governments. However, refugees are an easy scapegoat, and around the world they are often indiscriminately accused of being major causes of unemployment, insecurity, and a source of crime and even terrorism. In addition, as a result of the preference in some countries for confining refugees to camps, those who find themselves in urban areas of those countries are being denied access to the protection and assistance for which they are eligible, and are easy targets for police harassment and extortion.

Government officials even go so far as to deny the very existence of refugees in urban centers. For example, when a Human Rights Watch

---

[4] Human Rights Watch interview with UNHCR official (quoting Ugandan government), Kampala, April 8, 2002.
[5] *See* UNHCR, *Uganda Annual Statistical Report*, February 2002. Of the 184,000 refugees living in Uganda, 158,000 were Sudanese, 17,000 were Rwandan, and close to 8,000 were Congolese. The remainder came from other countries in Africa.
[6] *See* UNHCR, *Kenya Annual Statistical Report*, Table III, February 2002. Of the refugees living in Kenya, 137,000 were Somali and 55,000 were Sudanese, and the remainder came from elsewhere in Africa.
[7] Human Rights Watch interview with UNHCR Official, Nairobi, April 3, 2002.

researcher spoke with a senior official of the Kenyan Office of Home Affairs in an attempt to get an interview regarding human rights abuses of urban refugees in Nairobi, she was told "there are no refugees in Nairobi."[8]

Asylum seekers come to Nairobi and Kampala in a variety of ways. They generally cannot plan their travel in advance, so they cobble together whatever means of transport they can secure—often walking long distances and getting rides where they can. They beg and bargain for transport with commercial truck drivers who have the city markets as their destination. Those with money purchase tickets on public buses (or even airplanes). They are rarely able to dictate their itineraries or routes by which they hope to flee to safety, and can spend days or weeks on the road. Frequently, they are dependent on the goodwill—and sometimes the courage and compassion—of those they meet en route who choose to help them cross borders. For example, Abdu T. was eighteen years old in 1995 when he was captured by the Sudan People's Liberation Army (SPLA) and forced to work as a laborer in southern Sudan. For Abdu, the moment he found a ride to Kampala was the moment he was able to escape from the SPLA. Needless to say, he never thought about asking to go to a refugee camp; he went wherever his driver was headed.

> [The SPLA] made me work with the relief trucks, to unload supplies…. I saw I had a chance to get away when the soldiers were busy with their new supplies. I spoke quietly with the driver [of one of the relief trucks] and he pulled me into his cab and covered me with the plastic seat. He drove with me like that all night. Eventually we reached Kampala.[9]

Other refugees are drawn to Nairobi or Kampala after experiencing the hardships of refugee camps. One of the major reasons why refugees in Kenya and Uganda make their way to the capital cities is that refugee camps are for the most part located in desolate and unsafe areas without adequate security or assistance. Life in a refugee camp in Kenya or Uganda is grueling. Refugees often face armed attacks or are subject to inter-ethnic tensions or discrimination, not to mention inadequate humanitarian assistance, medical care and educational opportunities. Only a very few are given permission to leave by UNHCR or the camp authorities. As a result, refugees simply slip out of the camps and make their way to the city.

---

[8] Human Rights Watch interview with Kenyan government official in the Ministry of Home Affairs, Nairobi, April 22, 2002.
[9] Human Rights Watch interview with refugee, Kampala, Uganda, April 13, 2002.

When asylum seekers or refugees first arrive in Nairobi or Kampala, finding a safe place to sleep is one of the first priorities. Almost everyone manages to learn which neighborhood is inhabited by refugees from their home country, and this is where they head—usually on foot. Sometimes individuals or families are lucky to find other refugees willing to take them in. Or, those with money may spend the first days in an informal rooms-only hotel. However, most come with very little money and they may have to spend their first nights sleeping on the streets or outside police stations or the offices of UNHCR, NGOs, or faith-based groups.

While no government is obligated to allow every refugee in its territory to live wherever she chooses, many refugees in Nairobi and Kampala have compelling reasons for remaining in urban centers, notwithstanding the tough conditions they encounter there. Often refugees with medical problems never consider going to a camp, as they want to live close to hospitals and to have access to medicines only available in the city. For those with security concerns, the city is a better place to remain anonymous than the controlled environment of a camp. Other refugees are fearful of the dismal conditions in the camps and generalized insecurity in the areas where the camps are located. Still others have individual reasons for fearing the camps because their ethnicity or previous political or religious activities, or those of family members, make them possible targets for ongoing persecution.

During the course of visits throughout the poorer neighborhoods of Kampala and Nairobi, Human Rights Watch witnessed the adversity asylum seekers and refugees confront in the urban environment. They face daily hardships that are easy to identify, but are routinely ignored by the authorities concerned. In essence, they are being punished by the national government and UNHCR for their decision to remain in an urban setting. Little effort is being made to improve their conditions or address their plight, perhaps as a "push" factor to force them back to the confines of a refugee camp.

UNHCR cooperates with the camp confinement policies of governments. For political and practical reasons, the agency is fearful of offending the governments concerned and wishes to minimize urban programs, which are assumed to be more complex and costly to run than camp-based assistance. Although it offers some help, in general urban refugees in need of protection are let down by what should be their main advocate and defender.

UNHCR's 1997 Policy on Refugees in Urban Areas is in desperate need of revision. The policy does not start from the simple premise that urban refugees are refugees living in any one of the world's cities, then go on to consider what specific protection and assistance measures they should be afforded. Instead, the policy casts urban refugees in a skeptical and wholly unwelcoming light:

They are viewed as people who overburden UNHCR's assistance programs, who move "irregularly," and who can be unreasonably demanding and even violent. The policy message is clear – many urban refugees are people who should not be in the city and whom UNHCR should not help. By delegitimizing their presence in urban centers, UNHCR itself is pushing these people back to camps where their lives are endlessly on hold and often at risk. Such policies appear particularly misguided in the face of the large numbers of urban refugees worldwide and the serious problems affecting them.

This report will examine abuses of the rights of refugees living in urban areas, measured against the obligations and policies of the key actors responsible. For refugees living in Nairobi and Kampala, the most important actors are the host governments of Kenya and Uganda, donor governments, governments with resettlement programs, and UNHCR. Specific responsibilities and policies will be addressed when individual cases of human rights abuse are examined later in this report. However, the general responsibilities of these key actors can be described in the following manner:

Host governments, such as Kenya and Uganda, are responsible[10] for preventing and punishing human rights abuses committed against all people within their territory – including asylum seekers and refugees.[11] Host governments have the following general responsibilities towards refugees:

- All parties to the 1951 Geneva Convention Relating to the Status of Refugees and the 1967 Protocol Relating to the Status of Refugees (the Refugee Convention),[12] such as Kenya and Uganda, are obligated to recognize refugees[13] under the Convention's definition,[14] and to ensure a series of rights for refugees meeting that definition.

---

[10] State responsibility under international law is linked to each state's sovereign right to exercise its jurisdiction. *See* e.g. *The Case of the S.S. Lotus*, P.C.I.J. Ser. A. No. 10, 1927.

[11] *See* e.g. *Mavrommatis Palestine Concessions*, P.C.I.J. Ser. A. No. 2, 1924.

[12] *Convention Relating to the Status of Refugees*, 189 UNTS 150, 1951, entered into force April 22, 1954. In 1967 a Protocol was adopted to extend the Convention temporally and geographically. *Protocol Relating to the Status of Refugees*, 19 UST 6223, 606 UNTS 267, 1967, entered into force October 4, 1967.

[13] *See* e.g. ExCom General Conclusion on International Protection No. 85, 1998, para (d). *See* note 23, below, for a description of ExCom.

[14] Article 1(A) of the Refugee Convention defines a refugee as a person who, "owing to a well-founded fear of being persecuted for reasons of race, religion, nationality, or membership of a particular social group or political opinion, is outside the country of his nationality and is unable or, owing to such fear, is unwilling to avail himself of the protection of that country."

- Their most important obligation is not to return refugees to a place where their lives or freedom are under threat. Article 33 of the Refugee Convention states this obligation, which is the most fundamental principle of international refugee law and is now an accepted principle of customary international law.[15]

- Under Article 35 of the Refugee Convention, governments are required to cooperate with UNHCR, particularly in its supervisory function.

- Kenya and Uganda are both parties to the 1969 OAU Convention Governing the Specific Aspects of Refugee Protection in Africa (the OAU Refugee Convention),[16] which enlarges the refugee definition to include people compelled to seek refuge "owing to external aggression, occupation, foreign domination or events seriously disturbing public order in either part or the whole of [the] country of origin."[17] Both Kenya and Uganda have implemented their obligations under the OAU Refugee Convention by affording *prima facie*[18] status to all refugees

---

[15] The customary international law norm of non-refoulement protects refugees from being returned to a place where their lives or freedom are under threat. International customary law is defined as the general and consistent practice of states followed by them out of a sense of legal obligation. That non-refoulement is a norm of international customary law is well-established. *See* e.g. "Problems of Extradition Affecting Refugees," ExCom Conclusion No. 17, 1980; ExCom General Conclusion on International Protection, 1982; Encyclopedia of Public International Law, Vol. 8, p. 456. UNHCR's ExCom stated that non-refoulement was acquiring the character of a peremptory norm of international law, that is, a legal standard from which states are not permitted to derogate and which can only be modified by a subsequent norm of general international law having the same character. *See* ExCom General Conclusion on International Protection No. 25, 1982. *See* note 23, below, for a description of ExCom.

[16] *OAU Convention Governing the Specific Aspects of Refugee Problems in Africa*, 1001 U.N.T.S. 14691, 1969, entered into force June 20, 1974.

[17] OAU Refugee Convention, Article I.

[18] Throughout the world, there are many situations in which refugees have fled conditions of generalized insecurity and conflict. When refugees flee in large numbers to neighboring countries, particularly in less developed regions of the world, it is not usually possible to ascertain whether every person involved in the influx actually meets the criteria for refugee status. Low-income countries frequently do not have the logistical, administrative, or financial capacity to undertake individual status determinations. Instead, there is a general assumption that when conditions are objectively dangerous in a country of origin, refugees are recognized on a *prima facie* basis (i.e. without the need for further proof), and are afforded protection accordingly. *See* e.g. "Protection of Asylum-Seekers in Situations of Large-Scale Influx," ExCom Conclusion No. 22, 1981 (noting that persons who "owing to external aggression, occupation, foreign domination or events seriously disturbing public order in either part of, or the whole of their country of origin or nationality are compelled to seek refuge outside that country" are asylum-seekers who must be "fully protected," and "the fundamental principle of non-refoulement including non-rejection at the frontier—must be scrupulously observed.").

fleeing Sudan and Somalia, as well as to some fleeing Ethiopia and the
DRC.

- In addition, Kenya and Uganda are obligated to prevent and punish
  abuses of the human rights provided for in (among other treaties): the
  International Covenant on Civil and Political Rights (ICCPR),[19] the
  Convention Against Torture (CAT),[20] the Convention on the Rights of
  the Child (CRC),[21] and the Convention on the Elimination of all Forms
  of Discrimination Against Women (CEDAW).[22]

Donor and resettlement governments also have responsibilities to protect
and assist refugees located in developing countries such as Kenya and Uganda:

- When donor governments adequately fund the refugee programs of host
  governments such as Kenya or Uganda, or agencies such as UNHCR or
  NGOs, they are fulfilling their international cooperation obligation. The
  Preamble to the Refugee Convention underlines the "unduly heavy
  burdens" that sheltering refugees may place on certain countries, and
  states "that a satisfactory solution of a problem of which the United
  Nations has recognized the international scope and nature cannot
  therefore be achieved without international cooperation."
- Numerous Conclusions of UNHCR's Executive Committee (ExCom)[23]
  also reiterate the need for international protection responsibility

---

[19] *International Covenant on Civil and Political Rights*, GA Res. 2200 A(XXI), U.N.
GAOR, 21st Sess., Supp. No. 16, p. 52, U.N. Doc. A/6316, 999 U.N.T.S. 171, 1966,
entered into force March 23, 1976.
[20] *Convention Against Torture and Other Cruel, Inhuman or Degrading Treatment or
Punishment*, U.N. G.A. Res. 39/46, 39 U.N. GAOR Supp. No. 51, p. 197, U.N. Doc.
E/CN.4/1984/72, Annex, 1984, entered into force June 26, 1987.
[21] *Convention on the Rights of the Child*, G.A. Res. 44/25, 44 UN GAOR, Supp. No. 49,
U.N. Doc. A/44/49, 1989, entered into force September 2, 1990.
[22] *Convention on the Elimination of All Forms of Discrimination Against Women*, G.A.
Res. 34/180, U.N. Doc. A/34/46, 1979.
[23] The Executive Committee of the High Commissioner's Program ("ExCom") is
UNHCR's governing body. Since 1975, ExCom has passed a series of Conclusions at its
annual meetings. The Conclusions are intended to guide states in their treatment of
refugees and asylum seekers and in their interpretation of existing international refugee
law. While the Conclusions are not legally binding, they do constitute a body of soft
international refugee law and ExCom member states are obliged to abide by them. They
are adopted by consensus by the ExCom member states, are broadly representative of the
views of the international community, and carry persuasive authority.

sharing,[24] particularly to assist host countries in coping with large refugee influxes.[25]

- Governments are also playing a critical protection and responsibility function when they agree to take in, or "resettle" refugees. On several occasions UNHCR's ExCom has emphasized that "[a]ctions with a view to burden-sharing should be directed towards facilitating. . . resettlement possibilities in third countries."[26]

UNHCR: Although primary responsibility resides with governments, when they fail to protect refugees, the U.N. General Assembly has entrusted UNHCR with "providing international protection. . . to refugees," and with "seek[ing] permanent solutions for the problem of refugees by assisting governments."[27] UNHCR has promulgated several important policies and guidelines that give detailed guidance on how the agency should perform these functions. While not legally binding, states are also required to follow these guidelines as part of their commitment to cooperate with UNHCR in the exercise of its functions under Article 35 of the Refugee Convention and as member states of UNHCR's ExCom. The policies most relevant to this situation include the following:

- UNHCR's *Policy on Refugees in Urban Areas*[28] (Urban Refugee Policy) provides insight into the agency's own perception of its responsibilities for urban refugees. This policy is critiqued in this report.
- UNHCR's involvement in status determinations for asylum seekers is governed by the standards it sets in the *Handbook on Procedures and*

---

[24] *See* e.g. ExCom Conclusion No. 67 (1991), No. 80 (1996), No. 85 (1998).
[25] *See* e.g. ExCom Conclusion No. 15 (1979), No. 22 (1981), No. 61 (1990), No. 85 (1998), No. 89 (2000).
[26] *See* "Protection of Asylum-Seekers in Situations of Large Scale Influx," ExCom Conclusion No. 22, 1981, para. 3. *See* also ExCom General Conclusion on International Protection No. 79 (1996), ExCom General Conclusion on International Protection No. 85 (1998). In addition, as one authoritative commentary on the Travaux Préparatoires to the Refugee Convention has noted, "the Preamble, by referring to the international nature of the refugee problems which has, inter alia, been affirmed in General Assembly Resolution 6(I) of February 12, 1946, and the need of international cooperation, proclaims the principle of burden-sharing.... It is clear from the debate that not only international cooperation in the field of protection but also in the field of assistance was meant." *See The Travaux Préparatoires Analysed with a Commentary by Dr. Paul Weis*, Cambridge International Documents Series, Vol. 7, The Refugee Convention, 1995.
[27] *Statute of the Office of the United Nations High Commissioner for Refugees*, GA Res. 428(V), December 14, 1950.
[28] *See* UNHCR, *Policy on Refugees in Urban Areas*, December 12, 1997.

Criteria for Determining Refugee Status,[29] which is founded in international law since it is based on the conclusions of UNHCR's ExCom.

- The agency's role in camp settings is governed by its *Handbook for Emergencies,*[30] which gives detailed guidelines for setting up and administering assistance and protection in refugee camps.

- The agency's obligations toward refugee women and children are detailed in its *Guidelines on Protection and Care of Refugee Children* (Guidelines on Refugee Children),[31] *Guidelines on the Protection of Refugee Women,*[32] *Guidelines on Policies and Procedures in Dealing with Unaccompanied Children Seeking Asylum* (Guidelines on Unaccompanied Children),[33] and *Guidelines on Prevention and Response to Sexual Violence Against Refugees* (Guidelines on Sexual Violence).[34]

- UNHCR's primary role with regard to refugee resettlement is to identify refugees in need of resettlement according to detailed procedures and criteria established in its *Resettlement Handbook.*[35]

Finally, much of this report refers to the responsibilities and sometimes failures of governments and UNHCR to "protect" refugees. Host governments' responsibilities for functional aspects of refugee protection include *inter alia*:

---

[29] UNHCR, *Handbook On Procedures And Criteria For Determining Refugee Status*, UN Doc. HCR/1P/4/Eng/REV.2, 1979, (edited 1992). The Handbook on Procedures and Criteria for Determining Refugee Status was prepared at the request of states members of UNHCR's ExCom for the guidance of governments. *See* Guy Goodwin-Gill, *The Refugee in International Law*, 1996, p. 34. The Handbook is an authoritative interpretative guide and is treated as such by governments. For example, the U.S. Supreme Court has found the Handbook's guidance "significant." *See INS v. Cardoza-Fonseca*, 480 U.S. 421, 439 n.22 (1987) (stating that the Handbook "provides significant guidance in construing the Protocol, to which Congress sought to conform.... and has been widely considered useful in giving content to the obligations that the Protocol establishes.").

[30] *See UNHCR, Handbook for Emergencies*, January 2000.

[31] *See* UNHCR *Guidelines on Refugee Children*, 2001.

[32] *See* UNHCR, *Guidelines on the Protection of Refugee Women*, July 1991.

[33] *See* UNHCR, *Guidelines on Policies and Procedures in Dealing with Unaccompanied Children Seeking Asylum*, February 1997.

[34] *See* UNHCR, *Guidelines on Prevention and Response to Sexual Violence Against Refugees,*1995.

[35] *See* UNHCR, *Resettlement Handbook*, Chapter 4, revised 1998. Since October 1995, UNHCR, resettlement governments and NGOs have gathered for annual consultations on resettlement at the Annual Tripartite Consultations on Resettlement (ATC). Under the auspices of the ATC, UNHCR developed its Resettlement Handbook in July 1997, which is used by UNHCR field offices and governments involved in the resettlement process.

establishing fair and efficient status determinations to ensure refugees are identified and granted protection,[36] incorporating refugee rights and protections into national legislation,[37] issuing identity documents,[38] "abid[ing] by [governments'] international obligations to protect the physical security of refugees and asylum-seekers and. . . tak[ing] measures to ensure that [sexual and other attacks on refugees] cease immediately,"[39] and by being "able to deter, detect, and redress instances of physical and sexual abuse as well as other protection concerns at the earliest possible moment."[40] Kenya and Uganda are sometimes failing to perform these necessary protection functions.

It is impossible to describe all of the daily activities that comprise UNHCR's performance of its protection function. Generally, "protection activity revolves around ensuring that refugees and others in need of international protection are recognized and granted asylum, and that their basic human rights are respected in accordance with international standards."[41] In Kenya and Uganda this implies a wide range of functions that UNHCR is performing, such as intervening with governments or police to stop violating the rights of refugees and asylum seekers, lobbying the host government to provide adequate documentation to refugees, housing refugees in UNHCR-run secure accommodation, or referring some individual refugees with security risks to one

---

[36] *See* e.g. ExCom General Conclusion on International Protection No. 71, 1993, para. (i).
[37] *See* e.g. ExCom General Conclusion on International Protection No. 81, 1997, para. (e).
[38] *See* e.g. "Identity Documents for Refugees" ExCom Conclusion No. 35, 1984.
[39] *See* ExCom General Conclusion on International Protection No. 79, 1996, para. (k).
[40] *See* "Refugee Women and International Protection," ExCom Conclusion No. 64, 1990, para. (a)v.
[41] *See* "UNHCR's Protection Mandate," *UNHCR 2002 Global Appeal*, p. 21.

of several governments who will consider them for resettlement. It also encompasses some functions that UNHCR, because of insufficient resources and ineffective program planning, is under-performing or not performing at all.

PART I: REFUGEES LIVING IN NAIROBI

Although the Kenyan government largely denies the presence of tens of thousands of refugees in Nairobi—stating that the only refugees in Kenya are those housed in the refugee camps—UNHCR reports that it assessed the status of 20,671 refugees in Nairobi at the end of 2001.[42] This figure errs on the conservative side, and UNHCR acknowledges that the actual number could be as high as 60,000.[43]

Largely unacknowledged by the government, and under-assisted by UNHCR,[44] urban refugees in Nairobi live in squalid housing conditions, often without access to food, clean water, medical care, jobs, or education. Many flee persecution only to wind up as targets of the same agents that harmed them or their families in their countries of origin. Women and children are subjected to sexual abuse at the hands of their fellow refugees. If asylum seekers can afford the time or money it takes to travel to UNHCR's offices to have their status as refugees assessed, they are caught up in a time-consuming and uncertain process that affords them pieces of paper that are then ignored and even destroyed by the Kenyan police. Almost all refugees, just like ordinary Kenyans, must pay bribes to escape spending time in Nairobi's crowded and filthy jails. Still others may find themselves summarily returned to the countries from which they fled.

SUB-STANDARD LIVING CONDITIONS FOR REFUGEES IN NAIROBI

Introduction: Why Refugees Come to Nairobi

As mentioned above, many refugees arrive in Nairobi directly from the countries where they have been subjected to persecution. Although analysis of the root causes of refugee flight to Kenya is beyond the scope of this report, Human Rights Watch and other organizations have documented the problems of political repression, armed conflict, and other human rights abuses in Burundi,[45]

---

[42] See UNHCR *"Kenya Annual Statistical Report,"* Table III, February 2002.

[43] Human Rights Watch interview with UNHCR official, Nairobi, Kenya, April 3, 2002.

[44] See notes 461-462, below, discussing UNHCR's funding shortfalls in Kenya and Uganda.

[45] See, e.g. "Burundi: Government Forcibly Displaces Civilians," Human Rights Watch/Africa Press Release, June 4, 2002; Human Rights Watch/Africa, *To Protect the People: Government Sponsored Self-Defense Program in Burundi,* December 14, 2001; "Burundi: Paramilitaries Commit Killings, Rapes," Human Rights Watch/Africa Press Release, December 14, 2001.

the Democratic Republic of Congo (DRC),[46] Ethiopia,[47] Rwanda,[48] Somalia,[49] and Sudan.[50]

However, many other refugees choose to leave refugee camps within Kenya to come to Nairobi. Although this subject is discussed in more detail in Part III, refugees leave camps for one or a combination of several reasons including: inadequate humanitarian assistance, general insecurity and attacks, insecurity for particular individuals, or insufficient educational opportunities or medical care. To flee camps for Nairobi is often a very serious, even life-or-death decision made by refugees who believe they have no other choice.

Once they arrive in Nairobi, asylum seekers and refugees have few places to turn to meet their basic needs. UNHCR is the main organization responsible, and the primary service the agency provides in Nairobi is to assess and regularize the legal status of refugees. Goal, an Irish relief organization, is UNHCR's main implementing partner in Nairobi providing psychotherapeutic counseling and medical care. It also runs a large secure accommodation center. A few international NGOs and faith-based organizations provide some limited housing and food assistance to refugees, described in more detail below.

Squalid Housing Conditions

Most refugees in Nairobi live in appalling and overcrowded conditions. Apart from a single secure accommodation center that houses 190 high-risk

---

[46] *See* e.g. Human Rights Watch/Africa, *The War Within the War: Sexual Violence Against Women and Girls in Eastern Congo*, June 20, 2002; "Congo: Kisangani Residents Again Under Fire, Rwanda's Congolese Proxy Force Killing Civilians, Closing Civil Society Groups," Human Rights Watch/Africa Press Release, May 24, 2002; "Congo: Ituri Civilians Need U.N. Protection," Human Rights Watch/Africa Press Release, May 19, 2002; Human Rights Watch/Africa, *War Crimes in Kisangani: The Response of the Rwandan-backed Rebels to the May 2002 Mutiny*, Vol. 14, No. 6(A), August 2002..

[47] *See* e.g. "Police Firing on Unarmed Protesters," Human Rights Watch/Africa Press Release, June 11, 2002; "Ethiopia: Halt Crackdown on Oromo Students," Human Rights Watch/Africa Press Release, May 22, 2002; "Ethiopia: Targeting Human Rights Defenders," Human Rights Watch/Africa Press Release, May 8, 2001.

[48] *See*, e.g., "Rwanda: Activists in Detention," Human Rights Watch/Africa Press Release, January 31, 2002; "Rwanda: Opposition Politician Shot, Others Detained," Human Rights Watch/Africa Press Release, January 9, 2002; Human Rights Watch/Africa, *Rwanda: Observing the Rules of War?*, December 20, 2001.

[49] *See* e.g. "Somalia: Child Soldiers Global Report 2001," the Coalition to Stop the Use of Child Soldiers (including Human Rights Watch), June 12, 2001; *Somalia: Landmine Monitor Report 2000*, International Campaign to Ban Landmines, August 1, 2000.

[50] *See* e.g. "Sudan: Backgrounder on Danforth Report," Human Rights Watch/Africa Backgrounder, May 16, 2002; "Sudan: Year-Long Detention of Turabi," Human Rights Watch/Africa Letter to President El Bashir, March 15, 2002; "Slavery and Slave Redemption in Sudan," Human Rights Watch/Africa Backgrounder, March 15, 2002.

security cases and a few ad hoc protected houses, UNHCR does not provide housing assistance, and only a few lucky refugees receive some housing assistance from nongovernmental or faith-based organizations.[51] Refugees live in some of the worst housing in Nairobi. The rooms are almost always located in the poorest and least safe neighborhoods: as one social worker working with refugees in Nairobi explained, "the refugees live in the places that no one else wants."[52]

Many live in rectangular sheds constructed out of corrugated tin sheets, divided into a single row of five to seven rooms, each with a door to the outside and either tin, wood, or cement walls dividing the rooms. Entire refugee families occupy single rooms as small as fifteen by fifteen feet. Often, there is only a communal pit latrine and limited piped water and electricity. Many have difficulty finding money to pay rent and cope by relying on the generosity of others for housing. Human Rights Watch visited many small houses in which a family was housing others. Other refugee families combine their meager resources and crowd into a single small house. However, most asylum seekers cannot rent an entire house and therefore they resort to renting a single room in a shelter that costs anywhere from Ksh.300 to 800 (U.S.$4 to 10)[53] per month in Nairobi. The following examples indicate the difficulties that refugees in Nairobi encounter in obtaining adequate housing:

- Mani W., a Congolese refugee, slept in a Baptist Church for the first two months after he arrived in Nairobi. When it was discovered that he was Catholic, he was asked to move out. When Human Rights Watch visited him in the Dagoretti neighborhood of Nairobi he was renting a room for Ksh.600 (U.S.$8) per month. He was lucky to have cement walls.[54]

- Human Rights Watch visited a Rwandan family of asylum seekers with two children who were living in a corrugated tin shelter with wooden slat walls. One child was sleeping on a piece of cardboard in the corner, and was covered in a tattered

---

[51] For example, one international NGO (name withheld at NGO's request) in Nairobi provides material assistance (such as food and blankets) to more than 2,000 asylum seekers and needy refugees, but only particularly vulnerable individuals receive rent assistance. No other organization systematically assists refugees in large numbers with housing, although some church groups and individuals offer ad hoc housing assistance.
[52] Human Rights Watch interview with social worker, Nairobi, Kenya, April 17, 2002.
[53] Throughout this report, the exchange rate used was 78 Kenyan shillings to the dollar.
[54] Human Rights Watch interview with refugee, Nairobi, Kenya, April 17, 2002.

blanket. She was obviously feverish and very sick. They had arrived a few months before from Rwanda.

- In the Dagoretti neighborhood, a Human Rights Watch researcher also visited an apartment building that was still under construction, just an empty cement shell without windows, toilets, water or electricity. The landlord was allowing newly-arrived asylum seekers to sleep in the unfinished rooms until the building was completed (whereupon they would be rendered homeless). When the researcher visited, two Congolese men and a single Congolese woman—all unrelated to each other—had been there since their arrival in late March 2002. [55] They were sleeping on flattened cardboard boxes. One man had three children staying with him and was desperately in need. He had a liver problem and had to use a catheter and bag for his urine. The woman had a blanket as well as a cardboard box for sleeping. She had no family with her. She could not afford kerosene or candles; instead she had a single eight-inch wick (but no oil) that she kept near her bed for emergencies.[56]

- Pauline S., a fifteen-year-old Rwandan girl living in the Riruta neighborhood and seeking asylum from UNHCR explained, "I went to UNHCR for an interview on March 21, 2002 and they gave me an interview date of July 22, 2002. My friends give me accommodation and they give me some food, but I do not know what will happen at the end of the month. My friends are saying I have to move out at the end of the month and that I should get my own place."[57]

As a result of not paying their rent, refugees are often in conflict with their Kenyan landlords. Fidèle G., a Rwandan boy said, "I couldn't contact UNHCR to tell them my problems, and now my aunt can no longer pay rent for me or herself. Our landlady took some of our property because we continued to live there without paying. I cannot pay the money to get my property back."[58] One Congolese man named Din M. found the struggles of life as an urban refugee in

[55] Human Rights Watch interview with refugee, Nairobi, Kenya, April 17, 2002.
[56] Human Rights Watch interview with refugee, Nairobi, Kenya, April 17, 2002.
[57] Human Rights Watch interview with refugee, Nairobi, Kenya, April 3, 2002.
[58] Human Rights Watch interview with refugee, Nairobi, Kenya, April 3, 2002.

Nairobi so difficult that "it might have been better if I died in the DRC." He explained, "Since my arrival in Nairobi I am living in the fifth house. Each time we must move before the rent is due because I cannot pay the landlord."[59]

The Struggle for Food and other Material Assistance

Apart from securing shelter, asylum seekers spend most of the remainder of their time trying to obtain food and other material assistance. For many it is a daily struggle. UNHCR does not provide food and material assistance to asylum seekers, only to a small portion of recognized refugees who are awaiting resettlement placement. Since the status determination process takes several months or even years in Nairobi, individuals spend a great deal of time waiting to be recognized and without access to the few resources that UNHCR does offer. Assistance from NGOs is limited, and reserved for the most needy. For example, one international NGO[60] provides food, blankets, and medical assistance to some 2,000 asylum seekers and refugees.

Consequently, in Nairobi, individuals live as asylum seekers in dire poverty for a long time—months, or even years. One middle-aged Congolese refugee explained to Human Rights Watch that, "My main problem is that I cannot feed my family.... Even since yesterday I have not eaten anything. I just survive day by day."[61] Jean F., another female refugee living in the Dagoretti neighborhood told a Human Rights Watch researcher that she was pregnant and she had another child who was about eight years old. She was separated from her husband during the chaos of their flight from the DRC. They were sleeping in a room made out of corrugated tin, and had few blankets or cooking utensils. During the course of her interview, it became obvious that her primary concern was food. She desperately explained how they had nothing to eat that day at all, and repeatedly asked for food while her son stood silently next to her.[62]

Children in particular have a difficult time finding food, especially when they have many younger siblings who are dependent on them. John D., a sixteen-year-old Rwandan who had recently arrived in Nairobi said, "I am here now with my three young brothers. They are ages five, eight, and thirteen. My biggest worry each day is where to get food for them. There is nowhere to find food for them."[63] Although John was receiving some assistance from an NGO

---

[59] Human Rights Watch interview with refugee, Nairobi, Kenya, April 4, 2002.
[60] The names of some of the NGOs working with urban refugees in Kenya and Uganda are being kept confidential at their request.
[61] Human Rights Watch interview with refugee, Nairobi, Kenya, April 4, 2002.
[62] Human Rights Watch interview with refugee, Nairobi, Kenya, April 17, 2002.
[63] Human Rights Watch interview with refugee, Riruta neighborhood, Nairobi, Kenya, April 3, 2002.

he insisted, like many other beneficiaries of the same program, that the once-a-week distributions did not fulfill his family's needs.

Lack of Medical Care: Torture and Sexual Violence Victims

In Nairobi, both asylum seekers and refugees are eligible to receive medical treatment from UNHCR and its implementing partner, the Irish nongovernmental organization called Goal.[64] However, in practice most never obtain treatment from UNHCR referrals for one of four reasons: (1) They cannot afford to pay for travel to the UNHCR office to obtain the referral; (2) many are misinformed that they are not allowed to go to UNHCR to ask for medical care until they have been recognized as refugees; (3) those refugees who have been referred to the camps are required to travel to the camps for treatment, unless their condition is extremely serious; or (4) if they do travel to UNHCR, they find that the procedure to receive a referral is particularly cumbersome and is exacerbated by long waiting times. An international NGO working in Nairobi further explained that in practice refugees are helped only in emergency cases and that in fact only the very sickest asylum seekers are ever assisted.[65]

Those refugees and asylum seekers able to reach UNHCR's offices must line up at about 7:30 a.m. in order to be considered for medical treatment. At approximately 8:30 a.m., the medical officer collects the papers of all the asylum seekers who have appointment slips[66] or are recognized refugees. The medical officer does not do an assessment of their medical problems, and instead they are referred to UNHCR's implementing partner, Goal, to do another assessment. If Goal cannot treat an individual at its clinic, he or she is sent to a hospital to get treatment. It is rare that a refugee can receive a referral from UNHCR and be seen by Goal within one day. At a minimum, the process takes two to three days. If an illness occurs over or approaching a weekend, it can take much longer. As one former employee of UNHCR explained, after all of these delays and referrals, "by the time you reach the hospital, your illness will have surely become more acute."[67]   Goal estimates that 15,000 refugees pass through its offices in Nairobi each year.[68]

However, as explained above, many refugees and asylum seekers forgo this entire process. Some are assisted by an NGO that provides medical vouchers that needy refugees can use at clinics located directly in their

---

[64] Human Rights Watch interview with UNHCR staff member, April 22, 2002.

[65] Human Rights Watch correspondence with international NGO, July 26, 2002.

[66] *See* discussion of appointment slips in text accompanying note 162, below.

[67] Human Rights Watch interview with refugee, Nairobi, Kenya, April 4, 2002.

[68] *See* Goal Kenya internet publication, available at www.Goal.ie (last visited on August 16, 2002).

neighborhoods. But this program does not reach every refugee or every neighborhood and eventually the supply of vouchers runs out. As one refugee living in Eastleigh explained, "When we need medical care we can come to [the NGO distribution center] to ask for a medical voucher. But these [medical vouchers] don't come very often because the number of refugees is very large."[69]

Torture victims and victims of sexual violence are in acute need of psychotherapeutic counseling and medical care. Many of these victims are not getting the treatment they need. Several torture victims in Nairobi have received counseling from Goal, which has several well-trained counselors and interpreters waiting to assist refugees, but refugees are only referred to Goal after a very long wait. Given the slow status determination process, and the large crowds of refugees showing up at UNHCR's offices every day, they are never interviewed in enough detail to reveal their need for treatment. In every case, an asylum seeker is only referred after he or she is able to sit down in a private setting with a protection officer to discuss his or her case. Such a lengthy private interview is only available when the asylum seeker is seen for the status determination interview. Often, the status interviews are conducted three to six months after an individual arrived in Nairobi. These delays are harmful to torture victims who are very much in need of immediate psychological support, and they contravene UNHCR's own recognition that "the personal, social and economic costs of failing to identify and intervene with [victims of extreme violence] are devastating."[70]

For example, a thirty-nine-year-old Ethiopian woman who had been a supporter of the Oromo Liberation Front (OLF)[71] was detained and tortured in Ethiopia several times before she fled to Kenya. She told Human Rights Watch that the last time she had been tortured began with her arrest, "by the Moyale police on April 3, 1999." She continued:

> They transferred me to Negele Civil Prison on May 7, 1999. I was released on March 3, 2000. During my time in prison I was raped by the guards repeatedly. I was also severely beaten. They would torture me by tying my breasts with strings. I had so many medical problems there and there was

---

[69] Human Rights Watch interview with refugee, Nairobi, Kenya, April 18, 2002.
[70] See UNHCR, *Training Module: Interviewing Applicants for Refugee Status,* 1995, p. 89.
[71] The OLF, an armed opposition group, has been involved in ongoing clashes with the ruling party EPRDF forces in Oromo-populated areas following a bid for Oromo independence. Government forces have been responsible for abuses against OLF members and Oromo civilians, including widespread torture.

no treatment for me. I was coughing and spitting up blood
every day. I had irregular menstruation and abdominal
pains.[72]

She went to UNHCR on June 9, 2000 and was referred for psychotherapeutic
counseling five months later, on October 12, 2000.

Jiksa B., a twenty-five-year-old Ethiopian man from Arsi Province in
Ethiopia was arrested several times for being an OLF supporter. Jiksa arrived in
Nairobi in June 2000 and had his status assessed by UNHCR and was referred to
Kakuma camp on November 14, 2001. In a state of clear distress, he explained
what had happened to him:

> I was first arrested for ten months in 1992. Then I was
> arrested in Goba Civil Prison from February 9, 1997 until
> September 9, 1997. Then I was arrested in September 1998
> and held until January 2000. During that time I had my feet
> and hands bound behind my back. I was also beaten with a
> board with nails in it and beaten on the soles of my feet. I was
> made to dig a pit and was told I would be buried alive there.
> They also boiled water and poured it on my groin and near my
> testicles.... Since that time I have lost my sexuality [become
> impotent].[73]

As of April 6, 2002 (when he was interviewed by a Human Rights Watch
researcher) Jiksa had received no counseling or medical treatment.

Of close to twenty refugees interviewed by Human Rights Watch in
Nairobi who were victims of sexual violence or other forms of torture in their
countries of origin, only one female Ethiopian refugee who had been raped
repeatedly in prison in Ethiopia had been referred for counseling in a timely
manner soon after her first visit to UNHCR.[74]

Failures to Assist Refugees in Nairobi
Refugees living in Nairobi are partly suffering from the poverty and
violence that is afflicting many Kenyans. However, the government of Kenya,
the international community, and UNHCR also bear responsibility for the living
conditions of refugees in cities like Nairobi, particularly when those conditions
put refugees' lives at risk. The government of Kenya denies any responsibility

---

[72] Human Rights Watch interview with refugee, Nairobi, Kenya, April 6, 2002.
[73] Human Rights Watch interview with refugee, Nairobi, Kenya, April 6, 2002.
[74] Human Rights Watch interview with refugee, Nairobi, Kenya, April 22, 2002.

for refugees' living conditions in Nairobi – often citing the position that refugees in Kenya should be in camps. UNHCR's acquiescence in the government's camp confinement policy means that it offers only minimal assistance to a small portion of the total refugees living in Nairobi. Nevertheless, UNHCR has a heightened obligation to address the assistance needs of at-risk refugees living in Nairobi such as women, unaccompanied and separated children, and torture victims, including victims of sexual violence.[75]

While UNHCR's mandate is to protect refugees, the agency often argues that it is through the provision of assistance that it gets access to and is best able to perform its protection function for refugees.[76] Moreover, UNHCR's statute requires it to facilitate the coordination of relief efforts for refugees.[77]

---

[75] UNHCR recognizes this responsibility when it recommends that "particular attention must… be paid to identifying the[] needs [of women, adolescents, and children]." *See* also UNHCR, *Guidelines on Prevention and Response to Sexual Violence Against Refugees*, 1995, p. 50 (noting that "it is essential that the victim receive counseling as early as possible.").

[76] *See* Executive Committee of the High Commissioner's Programme Forty Fifth Session *Note on International Protection* A/AC.96/830, September 7, 1994, paragraphs 14-18.

[77] *See Statute of the Office of the United Nations High Commissioner for Refugees*, General Assembly Resolution 428(V), December 14, 1950.

PROTECTION PROBLEMS FOR REFUGEES IN NAIROBI

Unsafe Housing or Lack of Housing: Fear, Attacks, Robberies, and Rapes
The first weeks in Nairobi are the most risky for asylum seekers, as they find shelter and situate themselves. Some of the refugees interviewed by Human Rights Watch became targets of violence while sleeping outside UNHCR's offices in Westlands, near a major thoroughfare. Amina P., a girl who had fled the fighting in Somalia in 1994 when she was twelve years old, had been raped repeatedly in the refugee camps[78] and was transferred to Nairobi by UNHCR when she contracted tuberculosis:

> [In 2001], I started sleeping outside UNHCR because I really needed more help from them. They kept telling me that now I was better I had to go back to the camp. But I could not go back to either camp—those places were not good for me. I slept in front of UNHCR for one month and seventeen days. One night, I had to cross the street to the shops to get some charcoal so I could cook some small food. I left from the last gate of UNHCR and went to the place to buy the charcoal—it was maybe ten yards away.

> There were four men standing there and one of them held a knife up to my throat. I tried to fight him off with my hands. He was "hanging" [choking] me. He pushed me down and pulled up my dress. They were all going to rape me—but I refused to open my legs, I kept them together. So, then he took his knife and sliced my thigh, from my thigh to above my knee [a Human Rights Watch researcher viewed the wound, which ran from her left labia down to above the knee on the inside of her left thigh]. They started raping me. I passed out eventually. They left me in the roundabout in the center of the road in front of UNHCR. Some other refugees found me some hours later, but I could not walk. They had to bring a blanket and make a cradle for me and carry me back to UNHCR like that. The next morning they took me to the hospital. They ran tests for HIV and for everything else. I

---

[78] *See* "Seeking Refuge, Finding Terror: The Widespread Rape of Somali Women Refugees in North Eastern Kenya," Africa Watch (now Human Rights Watch/Africa), October 1993, vol. 5, no. 13.

stayed there for sixteen days, just waiting for my wound to heal.[79]

Other refugees live in fear and at constant risk because of inadequate shelter, and because they have fled without other family members. The failure to identify and better protect these refugees is in direct contravention of UNHCR's own policies and procedures.[80] Pauline F. is a sixteen-year-old Rwandan refugee whose mother was killed in 1994 and whose father was abducted. She fled with her sister, who is five years old. Her housing situation in Nairobi made her feel terribly unsafe:

> I took a truck to Kenya with my little sister [in February 2002]. I slept outside at the UNHCR compound for one night, then a good samaritan kept me for one week in her house. Then, she told me I had to look for a place to stay. I found a small shelter, where we pay Ksh. 500 per month [U.S.$6], but I cannot pay this yet.

> ....There are some thieves who terrorize the neighbors, and I am very scared when they come. They have come four times, and I am in my little shelter with a very small child. The last time the thieves came was last Thursday. They cut someone very badly in the head with a panga [machete]. They took that person's television, and made demands for other things. So, they have stolen things from my neighbors but not yet from me, maybe they know I have nothing to give them?

> The main thing I am worried about is not those thieves, but the men who live around me, they keep on coming back to me, because anyone can break into our little house and they come and beat on the door and tell me to let them in. They come at night like that—I am very scared. I am afraid of that day and night.[81]

---

[79] Human Rights Watch interview with refugee, Nairobi, Kenya, April 5, 2002.
[80] See UNHCR, *Guidelines on the Protection of Refugee Women*, 1991, p. 29 (noting that "unaccompanied women and girls are particularly at risk of sexual and physical abuse.").
[81] Human Rights Watch interview with refugee, Nairobi, Kenya, April 3, 2002.

The insecurity suffered by unaccompanied children and women could be alleviated if UNHCR followed its own suggestion to "ensure, where practical, that women and girls are able to lock their sleeping and washing facilities."[82]

Finally, even those women and children who are lucky enough to find housing at the UNHCR "secure" accommodation center were fearful about sexual harassment[83] and their overall security, especially after the murder of two Rwandan children who had been living there in April 2002, discussed in the summary of this report. Protection problems in the accommodation center for women and children who are without accompanying adult male relatives could be alleviated if UNHCR had the resources to house them separately from men. A young Congolese woman who had found the corpses of the two slain Rwandan children said to a Human Rights Watch researcher,

> Since that incident... we are so scared. In that compound they don't let anyone in or out. Someone who can kill kids like that can kill even adults. I am scared.... They should not keep all the people in that same place, they should move people around from place to place. And, they should put women in a separate place.[84]

Political Targeting by Other Refugees

Complicated ethnic and military alliances that cross borders characterize the conflicts around the Great Lakes region (Rwanda, Burundi and the Democratic Republic of Congo). As a result, refugees in Nairobi often report being threatened, abused, or harassed by other refugees from their own country. For example, Lumumba S., a Banyamulenge refugee who had been very active in negotiating for the rights of his people with the Congolese government felt that several groups of refugees in Nairobi were openly hostile to him. He said:

> We have everyone against us. The [ethnic] Hutu are saying we are after them. The *genocidaires* [Rwandan Hutu

---

[82] See UNHCR, *Guidelines on Prevention and Response to Sexual Violence Against Refugees*, 1995, p. 13.

[83] One Ethiopian refugee woman told a Human Rights Watch researcher, "at the accommodation center I have also had problems. One man asked me for sex. I refused him and he said I wasn't a woman because I refused him. I was very upset at him at that time." Human Rights Watch interview with refugee, Nairobi, Kenya, April 22, 2002.

[84] Human Rights Watch interview, Nairobi, Kenya, April 22, 2002. This refugee woman's suggestion is completely in line with UNHCR's own policies. *See* UNHCR, *Guidelines on the Protection of Refugee Women*, 1991, p. 33 (noting that "unaccompanied women may want to establish a separate living area for themselves.").

extremists responsible for the 1994 Rwandan genocide] are here in Kenya and we are afraid of them. Also, those who are working with [current Rwandan President Paul] Kagame are against us. We have a problem with the Rwandese embassy here in Nairobi. They told me to be careful because [the Rwandans] want to kill the Banyamulenge. There is also graffiti in town against the Banyamulenge, near Kikomba market there is something written on the side of the houses against the Banyamulenge.[85]

Dawit S., an Ethiopian refugee who had been a student leader in Addis Ababa described the ethnic tensions that had developed in exile between him and Oromo refugees. He said, "in [the place I was living] there were already other Oromo students and they said I bought my status and started harassing me, saying I was against their tribe. They beat me once while accusing me of these things…. That was on August 19, 2001."[86]

Country of Origin "Security" Agents[87]

Refugees living in Nairobi report they were targeted by alleged security agents, and occasionally by the Kenyan police, for their activities in their countries of origin. While these accounts are sometimes fabricated or exaggerated by refugees, since it is widely believed that the incidents will help to secure resettlement places abroad, Human Rights Watch found some of these stories very credible, particularly those of Ethiopian refugees. The fact that Ethiopian agents operate in Nairobi is widely known.[88] A staff member with an organization working with the refugee community in Nairobi told Human Rights Watch that the "Ethiopian government is active in Nairobi. [Kenyan] police agents are bribed."[89] International NGO staff members have been able to trace to the Ethiopian Embassy license plate numbers taken down by refugees who

[85] Human Rights Watch interview with refugee, Nairobi, Kenya, April 21, 2002.
[86] Human Rights Watch interview with refugee, Nairobi, Kenya, April 4, 2002.
[87] The terms "country of origin agents" or "security agents" are used in this report to designate individuals from refugees' countries of origin who are alleged to trail, harass, beat, detain, and otherwise intimidate refugees. By using these terms, Human Rights Watch is not indicating that these individuals are in fact employed by the official security agencies of refugees' countries of origin, although some evidence supports that conclusion.
[88] UNHCR reported to Human Rights Watch that the agency was aware of six abductions of refugees from Nairobi in 2001, two of whom were Oromo refugees. Human Rights Watch interview with UNHCR official, Nairobi, Kenya, April 2, 2002.
[89] Human Rights Watch interview with NGO staff member, Nairobi, Kenya, April 2, 2002.

allege that they have been trailed.[90] In addition, the actions of such agents have even been publicly linked to murder: one politically motivated killing by Ethiopian security agents in Nairobi received international press attention in 1992.[91]

Berhanu C.'s story of security agent harassment is indicative of the problems experienced by refugees in Nairobi. Human Rights Watch documented ten other credible accounts of targeting by such agents during the course of our research in Nairobi. Berhanu is an Ethiopian man in his thirties who was involved in the EPRP[92] in the 1970s and because of this was arrested and detained in Ethiopia from 1980 to 1984. Upon his release he gave up his political activities and became a teacher, but he found himself suspected of continued work with the EPRP and was again detained for six months and tortured. His chest was severely burned with molten plastic and he was repeatedly beaten. He has large scars on his chest, viewed by a Human Rights Watch researcher, and broken cartilage in his knees resulting from the torture. Seeking to flee the country, Berhanu was arrested at the Kenya/Ethiopia border at Moyale on November 24, 1999 and was en route to Central Government Investigations in Addis Ababa when he managed to escape from the Ethiopian police. Two months later, in early February 2000, he crossed the border into Kenya. He told a Human Rights Watch researcher about the security problems he has experienced since that time:

> On June 20, 2000 at night Ethiopian security officers came to my room in Nairobi, on Tenth Street in Eastleigh when I was drinking tea. One of the security officers was one of the ones who held me at Moyale and they were with three Ethiopians. They told me that I should not try to live in Kenya any more. I wrote a letter about this to UNHCR. I was so afraid after this happened that I decided I would sleep during the day and stay awake all night. On September 5, 2000, three other Ethiopian security workers came to my place to attack me. Again, I wrote a letter to UNHCR.[93]

---

[90] Human Rights Watch interview with representative of international NGO, Nairobi, Kenya, April 4, 2002.
[91] See "Obituary for Colonel Jatani Ali," *The Daily Nation*, July 3, 2001. Jatani Ali was an Oromo liberation leader who was killed by TPLF/EPRDF agents in Nairobi on July 2, 1992.
[92] The Ethiopian People's Revolutionary Party is an urban-based movement that was formed in April 1972 to oppose the Derg and their repressive rule. Since the fall of the Derg members of the EPRP have continued to be persecuted by the ruling authorities.
[93] Human Rights Watch interview with refugee, Nairobi, Kenya, April 5, 2002.

Berhanu was harassed again on October 30, 2000 when he was visited unexpectedly by three Ethiopian security agents. Berhanu's roommate asked them to leave the room, but before they did, they said, "we are your shadow, you cannot hide from us. One day we will take you to Ethiopia dead or alive." Berhanu also wrote to UNHCR about this incident and a later one on December 15, 2000 when the same agent came to give him "a last warning." He told Human Rights Watch what happened next:

> Then, on Sunday January 28, 2001, I went out to walk on Eighth Street [in Eastleigh]. Three Ethiopian security forces came up to me and started shouting at me about who I was and what I was doing there. They put me in the middle of them and started hitting me on many sides. I received a very hard hit on my left eye and ear. Other people were watching what was happening, and they intervened to let me "pull away" [escape] from them, and I was trying to run but the road was muddy and I kept falling down. I fell at least four times. A man pulled up alongside the fighting in a car and shouted out my name, and they wanted to push me into that car, but I got away from that place. My Ethiopian friends advised me not to travel alone, and they took me to Goal where I received medical treatment. I went to UNHCR to tell them my problems, and the security guards at the gate and the reception workers would not let me in. My only solution was to write a letter again in which I said, "save my life from this danger and allow me to enter to your office to tell you my problem. I am waiting your decision outside the fence of UNHCR." I was seen that day for the first time by someone at UNHCR who paid attention, and I was referred to Goal accommodation center on February 1, 2001.
>
> But, even in Goal accommodation center I have been followed. Three times unknown Ethiopians have come to the fence at Goal to give me warnings. This happened on May 30, 2001; June 19, 2001; and July 2, 2001. Each time two men came and told me they were "following me like a shadow." I

reported these incidents to Goal. I remain without status or any
decision on my case until now.[94]

In Kakuma camp, which is in the north of Kenya, approximately 700
kilometers from Nairobi, a Human Rights Watch researcher met an Ethiopian
refugee who was one of the few who had hoped a camp would be safer for him
than Nairobi. He was wrong. He had been subject to several attacks in Kakuma
and was now being housed in the UNHCR protection area, behind barbed wire.
He originally thought the camp would be safer because his family had already
been harassed by Ethiopian agents operating in Nairobi. He told a Human
Rights Watch researcher that he had been held in Kenyan police custody, at the
behest of Ethiopian agents, from June 23, 1999 until February 1, 2000. He said,
"I was held in police custody in Muthangari [police station]. During that time
they kidnapped my elder son from Nairobi. It happened in August 2000. People
told me later it was Ethiopian spies that took him."[95]

Kenyan Police Harassment, Violence, and Extortion, and Refusal to Respect UNHCR Documents

In an interview with UNHCR, A Human Rights Watch researcher was told,
"The police are predatory. But this is a problem for everyone in Nairobi."[96]

Police in Nairobi routinely stop refugees and asylum seekers to ask for
their national identity cards. Since they do not have these cards, asylum seekers
only have their UNHCR-issued appointment slips to show, and recognized
refugees can show their UNHCR-issued protection letters[97] (also referred to by
refugees as their "mandates"[98]), some of which refer them to camps. Upon
inspection of these documents, the police routinely ignore or destroy the
documents and either threaten the individual with arrest and detention unless a
bribe is paid or bring the individual to the local police station.[99] If the first
practice is followed, the refugee will often try to pay the bribe to avoid arrest. If

[94] Human Rights Watch interview with refugee, Nairobi, Kenya, April 5, 2002.
[95] Human Rights Watch interview with refugee, Kakuma Refuge Camp, Kenya, April 23, 2002. As of April 23, this refugee's son was still missing.
[96] Human Rights Watch interview with UNHCR official, Kampala, Uganda, April 18, 2002.
[97] See description of the UNHCR protection letters in text accompanying note 172, below.
[98] See description of "mandate letters," at note 172, below.
[99] As of September 2002, UNHCR and the government of Kenya had agreed in principle to issue joint documents to refugees. However, when a Human Rights Watch researcher asked officials from the government of Kenya when these documents would be issued, she was told "in due course." Human Rights Watch interview with representatives of the government of Kenya, Geneva, Switzerland, September 27, 2002.

the second practice is followed, friends or family must locate the jailed refugee in one of Nairobi's many police stations and attempt to bribe the police to set him or her free.[100] Often, refugees described beatings by the police during the arrests.

In slum areas, refugees and Kenyans alike are targeted by the police for harassment and arrest. During a series of interviews with refugees in the Riruta neighborhood of Nairobi, a Human Rights Watch researcher came across a row of corrugated tin rooms populated by Congolese refugees. One door was locked shut. The neighbors explained that one day prior to Human Rights Watch's visit, the Congolese boy who lived in the locked shelter had been arrested by the police. His Kenyan neighbor had also been arrested.[101] Refugees told a Human Rights Watch researcher of their attempts to avoid police harassment by limiting their movements, dressing well when they go out, or in one case, carrying their child with them in the hopes that the police would not put a child in the police cells.

Young boys have particular concerns that they will be arrested for being "street boys," who are reviled and abused on a daily basis by Kenyan police. Peter L. told a Human Rights Watch researcher about his strategy for avoiding the police: Peter said, "another thing that worries me is that when I am dirty and my clothes are not clean, the police will see me and think that I am a street boy. I have no soap to wash my clothes and I have to buy water, it costs three shillings (U.S.$0.04) for each twenty liter jerry can." [102]

The Kenyan police are notorious not just among asylum seekers or refugees. Transparency International (TI), an NGO dedicated to curbing both international and national corruption, conducted a study of the incidence of bribery in urban Kenya which found that six out of ten urban residents pay bribes to the Kenyan police or are "mistreated or denied service if they do not."[103] The Prisons Department was cited as being the most rigidly corrupt institution to deal with in Kenya—in close to seven out of ten interactions with prisons, a refusal to bribe would result in no service.[104] Poor people (which

---

[100] As of September 2002, UNHCR informed Human Rights Watch that "important monitoring measures have been taken at police station levels to clarify the situation of potential refugees being arrested and ensure their early release." Written comments from UNHCR Branch Office Nairobi, October 8, 2002.

[101] Human Rights Watch interview with refugee, Nairobi, Kenya, April 17, 2002.

[102] Human Rights Watch interview with refugee, Nairobi, Kenya, April 3, 2002.

[103] See Transparency International, *Corruption in Kenya: Findings of an Urban Bribery Survey*, 2001, p. 10.

[104] Ibid.

would include both Kenyans and refugees) were found to be "significantly more vulnerable" to corruption than others.[105]

The TI Study also found that, on average, urban residents in Kenya paid Ksh.2,670 (U.S.$34) each month in their interactions with the Kenyan police. This amount may be slightly less than what urban refugees have to pay.[106] Refugees interviewed by a Human Rights Watch researcher cited interactions with the police occurring at least on a monthly and sometimes on a weekly basis. In each interaction, Human Rights Watch documented cases in which refugees paid between Ksh.400 (U.S.$5) and Ksh.4,000 (U.S.$51) to the police. UNHCR had documented cases of refugees in Kileleshwa police station who had to pay Ksh.20,000 (U.S.$256) to be released.[107]

Fikru C., a journalist who fled from Ethiopia to seek asylum in February 2002, told a Human Rights Watch researcher about an interaction he had with the Kenyan police in the Eastleigh neighborhood of Nairobi:

> Here in Nairobi, I first stayed with other Ethiopians in Eastleigh. There is terrible and unreported harassment for refugees there, especially from the police. They ask for so many shillings. One day in March they caught me and they tied my hands together. They asked me to pay them Ksh.5,000 [U.S.$64], but I really do not have that kind of money. I was so afraid that if they brought me to court I might be deported to Ethiopia. I showed him my appointment slip, but [the officer] told me, "you can put that in your pocket." I knew he only wanted money. I had no choice, they took me to Pangani Police Station and I had to pay KSh.2,000 [U.S.$26] for my freedom.
>
> I witnessed another incident in which the police arrested four women, one of whom was pregnant, again in March 2002. The police asked each woman for Ksh.5,000 [U.S.$64], but they didn't have that money. They were held while their families tried to raise money for them. The families and

---

[105] Ibid, p. 5.

[106] The authors of the TI Study were careful to point out that their respondents were better off and better educated than the urban population as a whole. Therefore, they note, "inference from this sample would understate bribery incidences in the general population." Ibid., p. 2.

[107] Human Rights Watch interview with UNHCR official, Nairobi, Kenya, April 18, 2002.

friends eventually paid the police Ksh.8,000 [U.S.$102] to
free the four women.[108]

Since bribery is a major revenue producer for police, and refugees are
prime targets for arbitrary arrest, NGO staff working in Nairobi commented
acerbically about the "competition" amongst officers to be stationed in the slum
neighborhoods where refugees live.[109] Police are also familiar with the offices
that refugees frequent, and stop and arrest refugees on their way to and from
UNHCR and NGO offices.

For example, a refugee who had been a university student in Addis Ababa
received his appointment slip from UNHCR on January 17, 2002. He told a
Human Rights Watch researcher what happened the very same day as he was
leaving UNHCR's offices: "The day I received this [UNHCR] letter I was
arrested on the road and some Ethiopians gave some money so the police would
release me. I had a letter from RCK [the Refugee Consortium of Kenya], but
the police do not pay attention to that."[110]

Yerodin A. is a seventeen-year-old refugee from the DRC. He fled from
Beni[111] because he feared being forcibly conscripted. He said, "When [the Mai
Mai[112]] come to the village and find young men, the entire family will be

---

[108] Human Rights Watch interview with refugee, Nairobi, Kenya, April 5, 2002.
[109] Human Rights Watch interview with international NGO staff member, Nairobi,
Kenya, April 6, 2002.
[110] Human Rights Watch interview with refugee, Nairobi, Kenya, April 4, 2002.
[111] Beni is located in the northeast of the DRC, in a Ugandan-backed rebel-controlled part
of the country about seventy kilometers from the border with Uganda. Mai-Mai and
Ugandan People's Defense Force (UPDF) forces have been fighting in this region. On
August 31, 2001, Congolese civilians in Beni began attacking the UPDF forces stationed
there in an apparent attempt to drive them from the country. A Human Rights Watch
report also describes an attack carried out by the Mai-Mai in Beni on November 14,
1999, resulting in the murder of a UPDF colonel and his bodyguards. See "*Uganda in
Eastern DRC: Fueling Political and Ethnic Strife*," Human Rights Watch/ Africa, Vol.
12, No. 2(A), March 2001.
[112] One of the main armed groups operating mostly in North and South Kivu in the DRC
is the Mai-Mai. This generic name applies to any one of a multitude of irregular forces
fighting against what they perceive to be foreign occupiers of their traditional domain and
their national territory. Many of the groups follow certain rituals thought to protect them
in battle. They typically enter into or repudiate alliances with outside actors according to
the priorities of their local agenda. Mai-Mai are generally thought to cooperate with local
people, although they can also prey upon them if they fail to support the ends of the Mai-
Mai. See *Uganda in Eastern DRC: Fueling Political and Ethnic Strife*, Human Rights
Watch/Africa, Vol. 12, No. 2(A), March 2001; Human Rights Watch/Africa, *The War
Within the War: Sexual Violence Against Women and Girls in Eastern Congo*, June 20,
2002.

victimized and the house will be torched." Yerodin A. fled on January 24 and crossed into Uganda, ultimately reaching Nairobi on January 27, 2002,

> On January 29 when we went to UNHCR to register, the police found us on our way back home at about four o'clock pm. They tied our [Yerodin and a young male friend's] shirts together, and wanted to tear up our appointment slips. First, they asked us for a Kenyan I.D., in the absence of this they said they would "tear up our papers and take us to jail at the police station." Each of us had to pay Ksh.1,000 [U.S.$13] to be set free. This took almost all of our money.[113]

In June 2002, Human Rights Watch was also informed that the police were arresting refugees as they went to and from their initial screening interviews with the Joint Voluntary Agency (JVA), the NGO responsible for initial screening of refugees for the U.S. resettlement program.[114] This allegation is especially worrisome, since refugees identified for resettlement are some of the most vulnerable, and are often high-risk security cases.

Those refugees who cannot pay the requisite bribe or who are brought directly to the police station by the police will likely spend some time in jail. UNHCR estimated that there were 2,300 detentions last year, although the senior protection officer admitted that "often UNHCR is not informed when refugees are held in detention."[115] During random visits by Human Rights Watch to police stations in Riruta, Eastleigh, Langata, and Industrial Area, police admitted to holding "foreigners" in their jails on a daily basis, and most had several "foreigners" detained on the day of our visit. The detention of asylum seekers and refugees without charge is very common. During the course of our research, Human Rights Watch documented cases in which refugees spent between one night and several weeks in detention without charge.

For example, Caleb M., a refugee who had spent several years in prison in Ethiopia had been arrested multiple times by the Kenyan police. He said:

> I cannot even count the number of times I have been arrested. It is probably less than one hundred, but it could be more than fifty. In just one day I was arrested five times. The police give me so many problems. One day I slept in jail at KICC

---

[113] Human Rights Watch interview with refugee, Nairobi, Kenya, April 3, 2002.
[114] Human Rights Watch interview with international NGO staff member, New York, June 3, 2002.
[115] Human Rights Watch interview with UNHCR Officer, Nairobi, Kenya, April 2, 2002.

[Kenyatta International Conference Center – a neighborhood] at night. The Kenyan police would not listen to me that I was a refugee, and they saw my mandate was for Kakuma.... He wanted money from me, and he checked my pockets and choked me with his hands around my neck. I slept on the cold floor that night. All the other prisoners forced me to sit in the place where someone had urinated and it smelled terrible in there.

Last February [2001], the police broke my door to get inside my room. They started shouting at me "who are you? Where do you come from?" I said that I am a UNHCR mandate refugee. The officer said, "What is that?" and he started beating me with a stick. My wife started crying when she saw that and he became angry with her for crying and beat her too. He took me into the station after beating us like that, again to KICC jail, which has underground cells. I could not bear to spend another night in a place like that so I paid Ksh.4,000 [U.S.$51] to be set free.[116]

Kalisa R., a forty-year-old Rwandan refugee, was subjected to a very common form of police mistreatment: the police order the refugee to walk around with them for a while until the refugee becomes either so publicly embarrassed or frustrated that he pays a bribe to be set free. He told a Human Rights Watch researcher what happened:

Last year [2001] in August, in the afternoon, I was on the street coming home. I came across the police and they asked me for my national I.D. card, so I showed them the HCR appointment slip paper. Immediately after... [they] saw the HCR papers, they handcuffed me and asked for Ksh.5,000 [U.S.$64], then it came down to Ksh.3,000 [U.S.$38]. The policeman was walking with me towards the police station, as soon as we were nearing the station, the policeman asked for 500 [U.S.$6]. I said I had absolutely nothing to give him. The policeman said he would tear up my appointment slip. He said, "this paper is not an I.D." When we got to the police station, they put me in jail. They said they would hold me

---

[116] Human Rights Watch interview with refugee, Nairobi, Kenya, April 4, 2002.

because I did not have a valid I.D. or protection from the HCR, they refused to recognize the HCR appointment slip.

When we arrived at the station, they put my name in the appointment book [most jails at stations have ledger books indicating who is in custody]. They put me in a cell that was approximately four by five feet. There were nine people in the cell with me. All we had for a toilet was a bucket in the corner. It smelled horribly in the cell. They gave us no food or water. The place was so small, the only way to sleep is if people line up sitting with their legs outstretched and their backs against the wall, then maybe one or two can stretch their legs over the others. But the smell was so terrible you could not sleep.

I stayed there overnight, and my wife came in the morning with Ksh.200 [U.S.$3], which she gave to a junior officer and she pled for my release. But the junior officer said he could do nothing without the approval of the senior officer. When she went to him, he demanded Ksh.2,000 [U.S.$26] for my release. My wife paid the Ksh.2,000 [U.S.$26] and they let me go.[117]

Sylvie O., a woman refugee[118] from Burundi who was living in the Eastleigh neighborhood, was traveling on the street with her two children, a boy aged three and a girl aged two. The presence of her children offered no protection from what happened next:

On April 8, 2002 I was arrested by the police during the day. I showed the police my paper and I was with my two children. The police ripped up my paper and they put me in Langata Police Station in Industrial Area. I spent two weeks there and I had to sleep with my children on the floor. They raped me in that prison and beat me over and over.[119]

---

[117] Human Rights Watch interview with refugee, Nairobi, Kenya, April 3, 2002.
[118] UNHCR is well aware of the problems that refugee women can face when they are stopped by police. See UNHCR, *Guidelines on the Protection of Refugee Women*, 1991, p. 31.
[119] Human Rights Watch interview with refugee, Nairobi, Kenya, April 18, 2002. Selam D., another Ethiopian woman refugee living in the Eastleigh neighborhood told Human Rights Watch, "Every time we go out of the house they arrest us. They take us to prison,

The number of refugees and asylum seekers detained in Nairobi is exponentially increased when police conduct "swoops" (a term regularly used in Kenya) of "foreigners" in Nairobi's slums. In a four-hour period in the early morning of May 30, 2002 approximately eight hundred foreigners were arrested amid widespread allegations of police brutality, rape, extortion, and theft.[120] The foreigners were held for several days in dismal conditions in an outdoor pen surrounded by barbed wire next to the Kasarani Police Station in Nairobi. The Kenyan government threatened to repatriate some of those caught in the swoop.[121]

As a result of the May 2002 swoop, the Kenyan government also detained one hundred and forty-five documented refugees, the majority of whom were from the Ethiopian Oromo ethnic group and one-third of whom were children, at the Gigiri Police Station near Nairobi. The refugees were charged with failing to register with the government of Kenya, a statutory violation that was enforced for the first time during the May swoop. The refugees were not able to comply with the statute because there has been no governmental registration service for the refugees since 1991.

The swoops against foreigners in Nairobi are a part of an ongoing public campaign in Kenya to criminalize allegedly unlawfully present non-citizens, including refugees. At the time of the May swoops, a police officer told a U.N. reporter, "refugees are not supposed to be in Nairobi. They should be in the camp; they are not authorized to be on the streets. The law is very clear. Who will take care of their needs if they are not in the refugee camps? That means they will be forced to steal for their survival. I don't like that."[122]

---

or they might find us at home. They will ask us for money, maybe between Ksh.400 [U.S.$5] and Ksh.1,000 [U.S.$13]. If we do not pay with money they will rape us either at home, or they take us to the station and rape us. We are always at risk of being arrested or raped. The police do not consider our mandate letters. Anyway, mine is for the camp. There is nothing in the camp. There is no food or water and it is very hot. With children it is very difficult to live there. We have decided to stay here." Human Rights Watch interview, Nairobi, Kenya, April 18, 2002. Incidents of sexual violence against refugee women committed by the Kenyan police or by fellow prisoners when the women were in police custody are serious violations of these women's human rights and are contrary to Kenya's obligation as a member of UNHCR's ExCom to adopt concrete measures to prevent sexual violence by developing and implementing "programmes aimed at promoting respect by law enforcement officers... of the right of every individual... to protection from sexual violence." UNHCR, "Refugee Protection and Sexual Violence," ExCom Conclusion No. 73, 1994.
[120] See "Eight Hundred Foreigners Held In Swoop," Daily Nation, (Nairobi, Kenya) May 31, 2002.
[121] Ibid.
[122] See "Police Say Crackdown on Illegal Aliens to Continue," IRIN Reports, June 4, 2002.

Similar round-ups occurred in September 1998, when refugees had to surrender their protection letters from UNHCR to police without being given replacement identity documents. More recently, group arrests of thirty to one hundred foreigners occurred in October 2001 and twice during February 2002.

Deportation and the Problem of Refoulement Following Charges Against Refugees

Whether singled out individually or caught up in an immigration swoop, refugees or asylum seekers should be brought before a court twenty-four hours after their arrest, according to Kenyan law. As a result, most are released or bribe their way to freedom in the first days after their detention. Eventually, however, some may find themselves charged with an immigration violation and brought before a magistrate. Asylum seekers and refugees are most often charged with illegal entry under Kenya's Immigration Act. In the course of several interviews with police officers throughout Nairobi, Human Rights Watch learned that this is the most common charge proffered against refugees.[123] Police readily admit to charging refugees with this statutory violation, and are even forthcoming about the fact that many have been sent back to their countries of origin without an assessment of whether they would face persecution upon return—a violation of Kenya's non-refoulement obligation under Article 33 of the Refugee Convention, which is the most fundamental principle of international refugee law and is now an accepted principle of customary international law.[124] For example, a police officer at Langata Police Station in Nairobi told a Human Rights Watch researcher, "In the past month [May 2002] we have charged five individuals with illegal entry and we have deported them. These individuals came from the Democratic Republic of Congo and Rwanda."[125]

Without an adequate assessment by the magistrate they appear before, refugees and asylum seekers who are charged with illegal entry are very much at risk of being returned to a place where they will face persecution.[126] An

---

[123] Human Rights Watch interviews with three Kenyan police officers, Nairobi, Kenya, April 18, 2002.
[124] See note 15 above for a description of the customary law norm of non-refoulement.
[125] Human Rights Watch interview with Kenyan police officer, Nairobi, Kenya, April 18, 2002.
[126] Representatives of the government of Kenya told a Human Rights Watch researcher that individuals have seven days to declare their interest in seeking asylum to "any administrative unit or to the Office of Home Affairs," and that it is those who do not so declare who can be charged with illegal entry. However, when the researcher explained that none of the refugees interviewed were aware of this reporting mechanism, and that they reported to UNHCR instead, Kenyan government representatives agreed that they have asked UNHCR to perform the status determination function and that asylum seekers

illustration of this problem arose during an interview a Human Rights Watch researcher conducted with a detained refugee at Langata Police Station. Abdikarim H., a twenty-three-year-old Somali national, was charged with illegal entry and served six months imprisonment at Industrial Area Prison. He was transferred to Langata Police Station pending his repatriation. During a visit to Langata, Human Rights Watch requested an interview with Abdikarim.[127] Abdikarim said, "I arrived in 1991. I came originally from Karisa. I was living in Dadaab before I came to Nairobi." At this point, a police officer interjected, "but he was not in the Dadaab [refugee camp] in Kenya. You know that there is a Dadaab in Somalia too and we plan to repatriate him to that Dadaab." A Human Rights Watch researcher asked Abdikarim, "Where did you get food in the Dadaab you were living in and what were your houses like?"Abdikarim responded, "We lived in houses that were organized into blocks and our food came from UNHCR." He continued:

> I don't want to go back to Somalia. I don't have any family
> left there, and I'm afraid. I came here to Nairobi to look for a
> job to pay for my mother's medicine. She is still in Dadaab
> and we cannot afford her medicine. She is very sick. But they
> found me and arrested me for having no documents. I don't
> have any documents right now and I am just waiting here for
> repatriation. It is good for me here [in Langata], they give me
> food and a place to sleep and medicine and they took me to the
> hospital when I got sick.[128]

One week later, purely by chance, a Human Rights Watch researcher met a police officer and Abdikarim H. in the waiting area of UNHCR's Nairobi office. The officer explained that he had been waiting four hours to turn Abdikarim over to UNHCR's custody, as he now realized that he was a refugee, and that he had taken time off of work to bring Abdikarim in to UNHCR.[129]

---

may also report to UNHCR. Human Rights Watch interview with representatives of the government of Kenya, Geneva, Switzerland, September 27, 2002.
[127] Human Rights Watch interview with officers at Langata Police Station, Nairobi, Kenya, April 18, 2002. This interview was conducted in the presence of two police officers. When a confidential room was requested, Human Rights Watch was informed that confidential interviews can only be requested when there is a complaint of police misconduct, which has been examined and endorsed by a magistrate.
[128] Human Rights Watch interview with refugee, Nairobi, Kenya, April 18, 2002.
[129] Human Rights Watch interview with Kenyan police officer, Nairobi, Kenya, April 24, 2002.

Abdikarim's case shows that refugees and asylum seekers are constantly at risk of being returned to their countries of origin if they fall into the hands of the police. The magistrate before whom Abdikarim had appeared simply charged him with illegal entry, gave him six months imprisonment, and ordered him repatriated without ever considering whether he was a genuine refugee. At the same time, his case also shows that it is not necessarily in the interests of the police to arrange for the return of all of these individuals, and that if the proper inquiries into their status are made, refoulement can be avoided.

Another officer in charge of arranging the repatriation of foreigners put the issue into stark economic relief, revealing that in fact refoulement may be more expensive for the Kenyan government. In other words, detaining and repatriating refugees costs money, but the police are compelled to do so by order of the magistrate. An officer at Industrial Area Police Depot explained the bind they are in to a Human Rights Watch researcher,

> The Industrial Area Police Depot houses foreigners who are charged in Kibera, KICC or Makedera Law Courts. When the magistrate directs a foreigner to us, we act in accordance with the order. Usually we have a specific amount of time to repatriate them. Our biggest problem is lack of funds for repatriation escorts. Some we can drive to the border, but some must be taken by plane. We lack funds for fuel even to drive them to the border. Sometimes we end up keeping them longer than the order because of lack of funds. But for us that is a big problem because then we can be held in contempt of court.[130]

In official 2001 statistics obtained from the provincial police of the Nairobi area, the Kenyan government charged 136 individuals with illegal entry during the year. Of those, seventy-five had been properly turned over to UNHCR, and eight were fined and presumably allowed to remain in Kenya. However, thirty-nine individuals were returned to their countries of origin. Thirty-five persons out of this group were fined between Ksh.100 and Ksh.10,000 [U.S.$1.28 – $128] in addition to being sent home. The great majority of those repatriated were Somali nationals—perhaps reflecting the Kenyan government's desire to "see the Somalis repatriate"[131]—although Rwandans and Congolese were also sent home. Police responsible for the housing and repatriation of these

---

[130] Human Rights Watch interview with Kenyan police officer, Nairobi, Kenya, April 18, 2002.
[131] Human Rights Watch interview with UNHCR officer, Nairobi, Kenya, April 2, 2002.

individuals cautioned Human Rights Watch that the centralized collection of statistics was not systematic, implying that many individuals charged, fined and/or repatriated were not counted.[132]   In addition to the provincial police statistics, UNHCR had official numbers indicating that 164 individuals were repatriated through the Moyale border crossing point with Ethiopia.[133] Therefore, the Kenyan government possibly refouled at least 203 refugees in 2001.

Based on Human Rights Watch's interviews with police in Nairobi, officers do not respect UNHCR documents because of the widespread (and misinformed) belief that all of these documents are forged. In addition, there is no mandatory procedure by which police ask non-citizens whether they will face persecution or civil war[134] if returned to their home countries. Refugees who appear before magistrates are also not asked this question as a part of standard procedures. Given the countries of origin of the 203 persons Kenya officially admitted to returning during 2001 – Somalia, Ethiopia, Tanzania, Congo, Uganda, and Rwanda – the Kenyan government has likely violated the norm of non-refoulement in these and (given the problem of under-counting) possibly hundreds of other cases.[135]

Failures to Protect Refugees in Nairobi

The Kenyan government is failing to guarantee to refugees in Nairobi, regardless of their legal status, their most basic human rights. These include: the right to liberty and not to be arbitrarily detained, the right to security of person including protection from torture and other mistreatment, and the right to freedom of movement.[136] It is also failing to take adequate action to bring to justice the perpetrators of human rights abuses against refugees, even when these individuals are the agents of another government.[137] In addition, Kenya

---

[132] Human Rights Watch interview with Kenyan police officer, Nairobi, Kenya, April 18, 2002.
[133] Human Rights Watch interview with UNHCR officers, Nairobi, Kenya, April 18, 2002.
[134] *See* notes 16 and 18, above, explaining Kenya's obligations under the OAU Convention and *prima facie* refugee status.
[135] In addition, Kenya reportedly refouled 3,000 Somali refugees after Kenyan police, "beat up the refugees and then forced them to return to Somalia." *See* "Refugees Forcibly Returned," *IRIN News*, July 18, 2002.
[136] *See* ICCPR Articles 7, 9, and 12, respectively. *See* also "Personal Security of Refugees," ExCom Conclusion No. 72, 1993.
[137] The requirement to "ensure" human rights, set forth in Article 2 of the ICCPR, means that governments cannot turn a blind eye to human rights abuses committed in their territory by other actors. *See* e.g. Human Rights Committee, General Comment No. 2(13) and 3(13), UN Doc. A/36/40 (1981). In addition, government law enforcement officials may not acquiesce in serious abuses committed by other actors. For example,

must allow refugees who have had their rights abused the same access as nationals to the police or to seek redress in the courts.[138]   While the police and security personnel are clearly preoccupied with Kenya's other serious law and order problems, they are nevertheless failing to respond adequately or appropriately to the security problems of refugees.

For its part, UNHCR is failing to identify refugees who are at risk when they first register at the office, in direct contravention of its own policies on refugee women and children, which require immediate identification[139] and attention to such individuals' needs.   For example, UNHCR should "promote safe living arrangements for refugee children and their families,"[140] and "where necessary, organize special accommodation for individuals at particular risk, such as unaccompanied young women, families headed by women, or abused children."[141]   In addition, refugees who have experienced violence and insecurity are unable to access UNHCR to report on their abuse, and when they do UNHCR often does not adequately track complaints or intervene with local police.   Even local human rights groups experience problems reaching UNHCR when they try to draw the agency's attention to these problems.

The failure to identify at-risk groups or individuals or to respond to security cases could be improved if UNHCR had the resources or the assistance of an implementing partner to screen individuals in the registration sheds and to receive and process reports about security incidents.   In addition, the agency could periodically deploy staff out to the areas where refugees live to learn about security incidents and at-risk refugees and to monitor their situation.[142]

---

the Convention Against Torture applies to torture inflicted by or *"with the consent or acquiescence of* a public official or other person acting in an official capacity." *See* CAT, Article 1(1) December 10, 1984 (emphasis added).
[138] *See* Refugee Convention, Article 16 (stating that "a refugee shall enjoy... the same treatment as a national in matters pertaining to access to the courts.").
[139] *See* e.g. UNHCR, *Guidelines on Prevention and Response to Sexual Violence Against Refugees*, 1995 p. 15 (requiring that UNHCR should "identify individuals or groups who may be particularly vulnerable to violence, e.g. lone female heads of household with disabled family members, or women who are economically successful, and develop appropriate strategies to address their particular protection and assistance problems."); UNHCR, *Guidelines on Policies and Procedures in Dealing with Unaccompanied Children Seeking Asylum*, 1997, p. 3 (requiring that "identification of a child as being unaccompanied should be done immediately upon the arrival of the child at ports of entry."); UNHCR, *Guidelines on the Protection of Refugee Women*, 1991, p. 15 ("early assessment of protection issues affecting refugee women is crucial....").
[140] *See* UNHCR, *Guidelines on Refugee Children*, 1994, at 83.
[141] Ibid.
[142] In fact, this is required by UNHCR's own policies. The agency's *Guidelines on Refugee Children* insist that the office "must act" to "strengthen UNHCR's presence in locations where the physical safety and liberty of refugee children is at risk." *See* UNHCR, *Guidelines on Refugee Children*, 1994 p. 81.

REFUGEE STATUS DETERMINATION IN KENYA

Background

Kenya, like every state Party to the Refugee Convention and the OAU Refugee Convention, is bound to uphold both treaties. Governments usually accomplish this task by setting up a domestic legal framework—such as domestic legislation—that implements their treaty obligations. Kenya has some law that is applicable to asylum seekers and refugees, but nothing that fully implements its treaty obligations. And, since 1991 Kenya has failed to fully implement the domestic laws that do exist—except for their most restrictive aspects.

Kenya's Immigration Act applies to all non-citizens, including refugees. The Act provides that all non-citizens who enter Kenya without a valid entry permit or pass are unlawfully present and subject to arrest and detention by immigration officers.[143] The Act describes a class of entry permit for individuals generally fulfilling the Refugee Convention definition (though not the OAU Refugee Convention definition)[144] of a refugee:

> CLASS M
>
> A person who is a refugee, that is to say, is, owing to well-founded fear of being persecuted for reasons of race, religion, nationality, membership of a particular social group or political opinion, unwilling to avail himself of the protection of the country of his nationality or who, not having a nationality and being outside the country of his former habitual residence for any particular reason, is unable or, owing to such fear, is unwilling to return to such country, and any wife or child over the age of thirteen years of such a refugee.

This provision, if administrative procedures were in place to implement it, would allow asylum seekers to apply for Class M entry permits from Kenyan immigration officers at entry points. However, there are no Kenyan immigration officers available to hear such applications either at the border or after an individual enters the country, even if she enters lawfully, for example with a tourist visa. As a result, regardless of what the law says, there is no way for a genuine refugee to ask for legal permission to enter or remain in Kenya as

---

[143] *See* Immigration Act, Para. 8, Para. 12.
[144] *See* notes 16 and 18 above, discussing the OAU Refugee Convention and the *prima facie* status of refugees.

a refugee through the use of an entry permit. And, practically speaking, asylum seekers report to UNHCR in order to receive refugee status. Consequently, asylum seekers simply enter the country—at which point they are "unlawfully present" under the Immigration Act, and subject to arrest and detention.

As aliens, asylum seekers and refugees are also subject to the provisions of the Aliens Restriction Act (ARA). The ARA sets out to accomplish what its title implies—to restrict the presence and rights of aliens in Kenya. The Act gives "the Minister," during "times of war or imminent danger" the power to impose several types of restrictions on aliens.[145] These include prohibitions on the entry of aliens to Kenya and requirements that aliens reside in designated areas.[146] Aliens who violate such orders are subject to a fine of Ksh.3,000 [U.S.$38] and imprisonment not exceeding six months.[147] Although the ARA was passed after Kenya became party to the Refugee Convention, there are no specific provisions for the status and rights of asylum seekers and refugees.[148]

Kenya's parliament has been debating a draft Refugee Bill since 1990. The latest version of the Bill obtained by Human Rights Watch is from 1994. The draft Bill falls short of international standards since it affords unfettered discretion to a single "Minister" in charge of refugee matters to receive recommendations for refugee status from an eligibility committee, to make the final decision on refugee status, and to hear appeals. The Bill requires asylum seekers to apply for status within seven days of their arrival, a limitation that is unreasonable. UNHCR has stated that "failure to submit an asylum request within a specified period should not lead to the exclusion of the request from consideration."[149] The draft Bill also requires refugees to live in refugee camps, without enacting exceptions to that policy in law. Other provisions of the draft Bill, such as the definitional sections, are unobjectionable and would implement Kenya's obligations under international law. Finally, the draft Bill does envisage establishing "transit centers" for asylum seekers while their applications are being considered. This provision, if implemented in accordance with human rights standards, might help to alleviate the incidents of rape and

---

[145] See *Aliens Restriction Act*, Article 3, para. 1.
[146] See *Aliens Restriction Act*, Article 3, para.1 (a), (c), (d).
[147] See *Aliens Restriction Act*, Article 3, para. 3.
[148] Some of Kenya's obligations under the Refugee Convention have been enacted into Kenya's extradition law. According to this law, if requests for extradition are made by the requesting country in order to prosecute or punish an individual on grounds other than his alleged criminal offense, the request can be rejected after an assessment of the case by an adjudicator. See *The Extradition (Commonwealth Countries) Act*, 1968, Article 6.
[149] See UNHCR, Sub-Committee on International Protection, *Note on Asylum*, August 30, 1979, para. 16.

other abuses that have been shown here to occur during the first weeks an asylum seeker is in Kenya.

Pre-1991 Refugee Status Determination in Kenya

Before 1991, the Kenyan government used an ad hoc administrative refugee status determination (RSD) system to recognize refugees, despite the fact that it lacked domestic laws providing for their rights and status. Asylum seekers were interviewed by an Eligibility Committee, made up of representatives from the Ministry of Home Affairs, the Immigration Department, and UNHCR observers. The Committee usually heard individual cases and applied the Refugee Convention definition, as provided for in the Class M Entry Permit category, but the Committee did not apply the OAU definition. Most newly arriving refugees were processed through a reception center established in October 1981 at Thika,[150] a town near Nairobi.[151]

Conflict in Uganda, Somalia and Sudan brought large numbers of refugees to Kenya in the early 1990s. Kenya hosted 14,400 refugees in 1990, but as a result of the increase in regional conflicts, the number had risen to 120,000 by 1991.[152] Just one year later, in 1992, 401,000 refugees were living in Kenya.[153] The large numbers overburdened the Eligibility Committee, causing Kenya to ask UNHCR to set up refugee camps. UNHCR and international NGOs were needed at the time since the large numbers of arrivals far outstripped the government's ability to ensure their well being. While there was an obvious need for an emergency response from the international community, the agencies involved usurped Kenya's refugee administration almost completely. This all-or-nothing approach scrapped the positive aspects of Kenya's pre-1991 refugee policy, including, for example, the laissez-faire approach by which refugees were allowed to locally integrate, and enjoy rights to work, education and freedom of movement.[154] Most fundamentally, the Kenyan government's pre-1991 role in refugee status determination was surrendered to UNHCR and quickly forgotten.

---

[150] The reception center was used by the Kenya government from 1981 until April 1995. Afterwards in 1996, it was briefly re-opened to screen refugees and asylum seekers arrested during an immigration swoop in Nairobi.

[151] See *Report of the United Nations High Commissioner for Refugees*, General Assembly Official Records: Thirty-seventh Session Supplement No. 12 (A/37/12), United Nations, New York, 1982, para. 114.

[152] See UNHCR, *The State of the World's Refugees 2000: Fifty Years of Humanitarian Action*, Oxford University Press, 2000, p. 311-313

[153] Ibid.

[154] See Guglielmo Verdirame, "Human Rights and Refugees: The Case of Kenya," *Journal of Refugee Studies*, Vol. 12, No. 1, 1999, p. 57.

Post-1991 Refugee Status Determination in Kenya

Once UNHCR took over status determinations in Kenya in 1991, the entire system changed. UNHCR contracted with its then implementing partner, Jesuit Refugee Service (JRS), to create a status determination center at Wood Avenue in Nairobi. After the status determination interview, each asylum seeker would either receive refugee status and be directed to a camp, or in exceptional cases receive permission to remain in Nairobi. Alternatively, the asylum seeker would be rejected and instructed to depart from the country.

The status determinations run by JRS were a problematic delegation of the responsibilities of Kenya and UNHCR to an NGO. The process was also criticized by refugees.[155] However, the most problematic aspect of the system was that the government of Kenya ceased to be actively involved in recognizing and protecting refugees in its own territory. The government's acknowledgement of its duties towards refugees was eroded to the point that in 1998 it refused to recognize the UNHCR protection letters issued by JRS.[156] Thereafter, the government has engaged in an alternating policy of benign neglect and open hostility towards refugees and the documents recognizing their status, granted under the authority of UNHCR.

In December 1998, JRS determined that it was unable to follow its mission statement while running status determinations. The NGO also decided that it would no longer perform a function that was, in fact, the responsibility of the Kenyan government and of UNHCR. In the absence of governmental willingness to take over, UNHCR began running the determinations in January 1999.

UNHCR-run Status Determinations
First Contact with UNHCR's Offices

Since 1999, refugee status determinations in Nairobi have been conducted entirely out of UNHCR's Westlands offices in Nairobi. Unfortunately, UNHCR's attempt to fill the gap created by the Kenyan government has fallen short of its own standards applicable to status determinations. These can be

---

[155] For example, one refugee interviewed by Human Rights Watch had been in Nairobi since 1997. Although he was not Rwandan, he had spent some time in Rwanda before reaching Kenya, and perhaps because of this (men from Rwanda were under extreme suspicion of being *genocidaires*), he was told that his status could not be assessed. In fact, this same refugee alleged that JRS was refusing to interview most male asylum seekers at the time. Human Rights Watch interview with refugee, Nairobi, Kenya, April 4, 2002.

[156] *See* Guglielmo Verdirame, "Human Rights and Refugees: The Case of Kenya," *Journal of Refugee Studies*, Vol. 12, No. 1, 1999, p. 58 (citing *The East African*, September 7, 1998).

found in *UNHCR's Handbook on Procedures and Criteria for Determining Refugee Status* (Refugee Status Determination Handbook), which is founded upon international law since it is based upon the conclusions of UNHCR's Executive Committee.[157]

According to the Refugee Status Determination Handbook, applicants for refugee status should "receive the necessary guidance as to the procedure to be followed."[158] In Nairobi, the only guidance asylum seekers receive about where to seek asylum and what procedures to follow comes from other asylum seekers. UNHCR does not provide applicants with guidance about the process they are about to undergo even after they reach UNHCR's office.

The first step in seeking asylum in Nairobi is to go to the Westlands UNHCR office. Located in a suburban business district, the office is not easily accessed from most of the neighborhoods in which refugees are living. Refugees with some money use matatu buses[159] to reach the office. A round-trip fare can cost as much as Ksh.100 (U.S.$1.28). Most do not have money, and so they must make the journey on foot, sometimes walking for several hours before reaching the office.

Refugees soon learn that they must arrive very early in the morning in order to be seen by UNHCR. On April 25, 2002—described to us as an average Thursday[160]—a Human Rights Watch researcher arrived at the offices by 7:45 a.m. and counted approximately 200 individuals waiting to be seen by UNHCR, who were transferred through a series of holding areas and lined up in various locations by UNHCR security staff.[161] Some elderly men who were unable to stand for a long period of time were abruptly and aggressively ordered to stand in line like everyone else. Aside from these altercations, the process of lining up and transferring refugees from place to place was handled by the UNHCR security staff without incident.

At approximately 9:00 a.m., the refugees were brought into two larger, covered sheds where seating consisted of a haphazard array of unfastened boards lying on top of metal supports. Public toilets for men and women were within easy reach of the sheds. The refugees sat and waited until staff from

---

[157] For an explanation of UNHCR's ExCom, *see* note 23, above.

[158] *See* UNHCR, *Refugee Status Determination Handbook* para. 192(i).

[159] "Matatus" are mini-van buses run by private individuals in Nairobi. They are the only means of inexpensive public transport in Nairobi.

[160] Thursday is one of two days designated for reception of Great Lakes refugees.

[161] A Human Rights Watch researcher waited with the group of refugees, who were first ushered into a shed with a row of benches, surrounded by high walls and gates, on the outside perimeter of UNHCR's offices. The space was just large enough to hold the group. At approximately 8:30 a.m., the refugees were taken out of this holding area and asked to line up in the mud road outside the next set of gates.

community services and the eligibility center arrived to process their requests, at approximately 10:30 a.m.

On their first visit to UNHCR, most asylum seekers are given an "appointment slip."[162] The slip is approximately six-by-eight inches, and is made out of ordinary copy paper. Each asylum seeker's photograph is dry-sealed to the slip, and the stamp of UNHCR is affixed over one corner of the photograph and the slip itself. The slip indicates the individual's name, number of dependents, gender, nationality, and date the slip was generated. It also provides a space for the date and time of the appointment and the category of UNHCR officer to be seen.

The appointment slip becomes the asylum seekers' only piece of identification for subsequent visits, and for life in Nairobi. Some of the people waiting to see UNHCR already had their slips; some were coming to UNHCR for the first time and had no documentation.

As of the time that Human Rights Watch departed the sheds, approximately 1:00 p.m., only the asylum seekers without appointment slips had been called into the eligibility center, presumably to have the slips prepared for them. Those asylum seekers who had slips, many of whom had appointments scheduled for that day, could wait until as late as 4:00 or 5:00 p.m. before being seen. Many would be told that their appointments would have to be rescheduled.

Waiting Time Between Procurement of Appointment Slips and First Interview Date

New asylum seekers come to UNHCR in order to be granted an appointment date for their status interview. The appointment slip is the only piece of identification that asylum seekers have to show to police or other authorities. Since asylum seekers must hold on to the slip for such a long time, the papers become very tattered and dirty. This is despite the fact that each refugee interviewed by Human Rights Watch tried to preserve the slips by keeping them in a special place, such as a plastic bag or a paper folder.

Most first-time visitors to UNHCR's offices leave on the same day with an appointment slip, although some refugees interviewed by Human Rights Watch had to return repeatedly before they were given the slip. Once assigned a slip, asylum seekers must wait for their interview date. Most often, that date is three to four months away. Given the extremely difficult conditions of life for asylum seekers in Nairobi, waiting three to four months for any detailed attention from UNHCR is risky and even life threatening.

---

[162] See Annex B, below for an example of a UNHCR appointment slip.

Pierre K., a seventeen-year-old boy from the DRC arrived in Nairobi on January 27, 2002. He spent two days looking for shelter and learning about UNHCR's procedures from his fellow refugees. He showed a Human Rights Watch researcher his appointment slip that indicated that he went to UNHCR on January 29, 2002 and received an appointment slip for an interview on May 30, 2002.[163]

A man with six children showed a Human Rights Watch researcher his slip and said, "When I first came to Nairobi I went to UNHCR. I arrived there on February 21, 2002. I was given an appointment for June 2, 2002. What will I do until then?"[164] Another Ethiopian asylum seeker had to wait for four months—he showed his slip to Human Rights Watch and explained, "I went to UNHCR on October 29, 2001 and was granted an appointment for February 28, 2002."[165]

Status Determination Interviews

During the status determination interviews, asylum seekers are interviewed by a member of UNHCR's eligibility center staff. The officer who conducts the interview reviews the facts after the interview, sometimes doing additional research or cross-checking information, and either recommends that UNHCR grant or deny refugee status. Next, the recommendation is received by senior protection staff who review the file and make the final decision on an individual's status. In 2001, UNHCR in Nairobi considered the eligibility of 400 to 500 cases each month.[166] In the beginning of 2001, there was a 50 percent rejection rate. By year's end, the rejection rate was 40 percent.[167] UNHCR told a Human Rights Watch researcher, "the eligibility process has still been slower than what we desire. Our aim was to process claims within two to three months. However, claims are taking up to six months to process."[168]

Asylum seekers are not given information about the standards against which their cases will be measured, nor are they given a sense of how long the process will take, including how much time it should take to assess their file if they have to appeal or if they are in need of resettlement. As noted above, this

---

[163] Human Rights Watch interview with refugee, Nairobi, Kenya, April 3, 2002.
[164] Human Rights Watch interview with refugee, Nairobi, Kenya, April 4, 2002.
[165] Human Rights Watch interview with refugee, Nairobi, Kenya, April 6, 2002.
[166] Human Rights Watch interview with UNHCR official, Nairobi, Kenya, April 2, 2002.
[167] Human Rights Watch interview with UNHCR official, Nairobi, Kenya, April 2, 2002.
[168] Human Rights Watch interview with UNHCR official, Nairobi, Kenya, April 18, 2002. UNHCR informed Human Rights Watch that as of September 2002, asylum claims were being processed "in about three months after registration." Written comments from UNHCR Branch office, October 8, 2002.

lack of information is contrary to UNHCR's own Refugee Status Determination Handbook.

Staffing limitations are clearly a major part of the problem. With only fourteen eligibility officers and one refugee status determination specialist on staff, the four to five hundred cases received each month cannot be adequately dealt with. The UNHCR Nairobi eligibility officers who interview asylum seekers are a team of mostly Kenyan attorneys, who have been trained in refugee law. Each attorney can see about four cases each day.[169] The attorneys do not receive the files of the asylum seekers they are interviewing until the morning of the appointment.[170] As a result, each officer only has a few hours to prepare for the interview, at most.[171]

Asylum-seekers who are recognized as refugees receive a letter from UNHCR. The letter is often referred to as the "protection letter" or the "mandate letter"[172] by refugees. The A4-size letter on standard-weight copy paper recognizes the status of its holder as a refugee, and is affixed with the refugee's photograph and the seal of UNHCR. Many of the letters require the holder of the letter to travel to one of Kenya's refugee camps. A few allow the individual to remain in Nairobi for one of the exceptional reasons (discussed in Part III, below).

Appeals

Ten to fifteen percent of the persons rejected by UNHCR appeal their cases. However, rejected asylum seekers do not receive written information about the reasons for their rejection, apart from *pro forma* letters indicating that their case has been rejected for failure to fulfill eligibility criteria. Human Rights Watch met several refugees who had been rejected, but had managed to

---

[169] Human Rights Watch interview with individual wishing to remain anonymous, Nairobi, Kenya, April 22, 2002.
[170] Human Rights Watch interview with individual wishing to remain anonymous, Nairobi, Kenya, April 22, 2002.
[171] Human Rights Watch interview with individual wishing to remain anonymous, Nairobi, Kenya, April 22, 2002.
[172] This colloquial use of the term "mandate letter" by refugees is often inaccurate. In any refugee situation, including in Kenya and Uganda, UNHCR has the power to recognize refugees under the agency's "mandate" to protect refugees. In Kenya, the UNHCR protection letters (erroneously referred to as "mandates") are not issued by the agency under its "mandate," but are instead documents recognizing the individuals as refugees in accordance with Kenya's obligations under the Refugee Convention and the OAU Refugee Convention. In Uganda, refugees also use the terms interchangeably, which is more confusing since in Uganda there are government-issued documents recognizing refugees and a completely separate process for some who are in fact recognized under UNHCR's "mandate," sometimes after the refugees have been rejected by the Ugandan government.

learn what procedures to follow to launch an appeal and had successfully done so. Again, information about appeals procedures was gleaned from other refugees and from the only local refugee rights NGO in Nairobi, the Refugee Consortium of Kenya (RCK). Several others had decided not to appeal their case, and still others had no idea that an appeal was possible.

Appeals are heard by a different protection officer in the UNHCR eligibility center, not by the officer who made the original decision. Current UNHCR staff told a Human Rights Watch researcher that appointments for appeals are often rescheduled and delayed because preparing and reviewing the files takes a great deal of time.[173]

Resettlement Referrals

Once their status has been recognized, refugees living in Nairobi may raise their need for resettlement with UNHCR. Only those cases warranting additional review will be examined for possible referral according to criteria established in UNHCR's *Resettlement Handbook*. A threshold inquiry is whether the refugee is vulnerable in the country of first asylum. If he or she is found to be vulnerable, then refugees fulfilling one of eight criteria may be referred. These are refugees with: legal and physical protection needs, survivors of violence and torture, medical needs, women at risk, family reunification, children and adolescents, elderly refugees, and refugees without local integration prospects.[174]

UNHCR then refers the potential case for resettlement to one of several governments. The governments accepting the highest numbers of refugees from East Africa are the United States, Canada, Australia, and Norway.

---

[173] Human Rights Watch interview with UNHCR staff member, Nairobi, Kenya, April 22, 2002.
[174] *See* UNHCR, *Resettlement Handbook*, Chapter 4.

PROTECTION FAILURES IN THE STATUS DETERMINATION PROCESS

Responsibility for Status Determinations

It is the responsibility of the government of Kenya to assess the status of refugees in its territory, but UNHCR recognizes that where governments fail to do so, in some cases it must "directly undertak[e] individual status determination."[175] UNHCR recognizes that one of its most "crucial" protection activities is to "ensure that asylum-seekers are given access to status determination procedures."[176]

Although UNHCR considers that running status determinations, as it does in Nairobi, is "neither necessary nor in line with the traditional functions of [its] office,"[177] where it is responsible for status determinations, UNHCR must set an example by adhering to the guidelines and procedures to which it holds governments accountable. These include the Refugee Status Determination Handbook and its *Training Module on Interviewing Applicants for Refugee Status* (Status Interviews Training Module).[178]

UNHCR in Kenya lacks the capacity to meet guarantees and principles stated in its own guidelines on status determination. Insufficient funding, while certainly a limitation on the resources available, is often presented as the justification for lack of efficiency and fairness in the status determination process.[179]

Failures of Accessibility and Registration

The only way asylum seekers can receive status and protection from UNHCR or the Kenyan government is if they are recognized as refugees by

---

[175] *See* UNHCR, *2002 Global Appeal*, "UNHCR's Protection Mandate," p. 21.
[176] *See* UNHCR, *2002 Global Appeal*, "UNHCR's Protection Mandate," p. 21.
[177] *See* "Follow-up on Earlier Conclusions of the Sub-Committee on the Determination of Refugee Status, inter alia, with Reference to the Role of UNHCR in National Refugee Status Determination Procedure," UN Doc. EC/SCP/22, August 23, 1982.
[178] The *Training Module* states that it is to be used by "UNHCR and government personnel involved in refugee status determination procedures in the field." In addition, the module advises decision makers that they "should never forget that being recognized – or not – as a refugee will have direct implications on the life and well-being of the applicant and his or her family. This places a heavy burden of responsibility on the person conducting the interview whether or not this person is the final decision maker." *See* UNHCR, *Training Module on Interviewing Applicants for Refugee Status*, 1995, p. iii.
[179] The importance of guaranteeing the efficiency and fairness of these procedures has been reiterated by UNHCR's ExCom on several occasions. *See*, e.g. ExCom General Conclusions on International Protection No. 71 (1993) and 82 (1997).

UNHCR, but, as already noted, since the status determination process is rife with delays, refugees in Nairobi are vulnerable for months at a time before the process is complete.

Of course, UNHCR cannot be held responsible for asylum seekers who do not come forward to present their claims, but at the same time, misinformation in the refugee communities about prejudice against certain groups of refugees is not being countered by UNHCR. Jacques P., a young Rwandan Tutsi refugee, explained his decision not to present his claim to UNHCR:

> In 1994 my father was killed. In 1996 I went to Tanzania, but then everyone had to go back to Rwanda.[180] In Rwanda, they said I had to go into the military but I refused, so they put me in prison. When I was in prison they beat me and I had to go to the hospital for treatment. My mother told me I had to flee from Rwanda. On August 5, 2001 I fled to the DRC and from there I went to Uganda. But in Uganda, I found the same soldiers that I was running from in Rwanda, the same ones who had tortured me there and I was afraid to stay in Uganda. So, on December 19, 2001 I fled to Nairobi. Even here the Hutu are against me. A group of them came to my small room in Riruta in the night... [they attacked me] and they cut me. I have security problems all the time walking around, going out. It is as if I cannot move. I am afraid to go to UNHCR because so many Rwandese have been rejected. I am not accepted here by UNHCR, and I am not accepted by the Hutu. I am not accepted at home in Rwanda either. I have nothing left.[181]

Moreover, contrary to the "widely recognized principle that children must be among the first to receive protection and assistance,"[182] unaccompanied and separated children and women at risk are not being identified by UNHCR when they first appear in the registration sheds. As a result, women and children are waiting for several months to be interviewed by UNHCR, and must fend for themselves before and often after they are seen by the agency. By conducting

---

[180] On December 5, 1996, the Tanzanian government and UNHCR issued a joint declaration setting a deadline of December 31, 1996 for the return of all Rwandan refugees living in Tanzania. Two weeks later, a stand-off developed between camp leaders who were resisting return and the Tanzanian army. Ultimately close to 500,000 Rwandan refugees were sent home, many "under military escort." *See* UNHCR, *The State of the World's Refugees*, 1997, p. 22.
[181] Human Rights Watch interview with refugee, Nairobi, Kenya, April 4, 2002.
[182] *See* "Refugee Children," ExCom Conclusion No. 47, 1987, para. (c).

interviews at random in the slum neighborhoods where refugees and asylum seekers live, Human Rights Watch identified the following individuals who were in need of special attention but did not receive it even after registering for an appointment with UNHCR:[183]

- Beatrice G., fourteen-year-old Rwandan girl living with an elderly priest.[184]
- Pauline F., a sixteen-year-old Rwandan girl living with her five-year-old sister.[185]
- Gaetan B., a fourteen-year-old boy from Baraka in South Kivu, DRC,[186] who was visibly frightened and trembled during his interview with Human Rights Watch. He slept in front of UNHCR's office from May 31, 2002 until April 2, 2002, but was told to move by UNHCR security staff. He was given an appointment on April 2, 2002 for August 14, 2002.
- Amina F., introduced above, who had been sleeping outside UNHCR's offices and was only transferred to safe housing after she had been gang-raped by four men, one of whom sliced her thigh open with a knife.[187] Her case shows how in some cases UNHCR takes action only after a separate serious incident proves that a particular unaccompanied child or young woman is at risk.

Finally, since accessing UNHCR is so difficult, it is particularly problematic for recognized refugees to add new family members to their files. This violates UNHCR's own recognition that birth registration is "essential"[188] for "activating certain rights"[189] and that "refugee women... have access to whatever registration process is used."[190] For example, a Congolese refugee had

---

[183] For its part, UNHCR responded to this criticism by stating that "we identify women and children and refer them to camps immediately" after registration. Human Rights Watch interview with UNHCR official, Nairobi, Kenya, April 18, 2002.
[184] Human Rights Watch interview with refugee, Nairobi, Kenya, April 3, 2002.
[185] Human Rights Watch interview with refugee, Nairobi, Kenya, April 3, 2002.
[186] South Kivu has also been the scene of fierce fighting between the Mai-Mai, RCD-Goma (Rwandan-backed) and various other armed groups. In October 2001, thousands of Congolese fled South Kivu province to escape the clashes. See "Refugees Flee Fighting," Monitor (Kampala, Uganda), October 27, 2001. More recently, fighting over the town of Walungu in South Kivu has been reported by Western media. See Agence France-Presse, "Rebels Retake Congo Town from Mai-Mai Traditional Warriors," February 11, 2002.
[187] Human Rights Watch interview with refugee, Nairobi, Kenya, April 5, 2002.
[188] UNHCR, Guidelines on Refugee Children, 1994, p. 103.
[189] Ibid.
[190] UNHCR, Guidelines on the Protection of Refugee Women, 1991, p. 33.

been repeatedly visiting UNHCR's offices for eight months to add his eight-month-old daughter to his file. Another female refugee had experienced difficulties adding her husband and three-year-old son, who had arrived after her, to her file. She said, "I have been explaining to UNHCR for so many years, and now I want my husband and son on my papers. But they listen to men, not women. Because I am a refugee woman they are not treating me as they treat others. When I go to HCR I have to wait a whole day."[191]

The Problem of Delays

A foremost concern stemming from the lengthy status determination processes in Nairobi is that asylum seekers waiting for interviews lack the protection and assistance guaranteed them by international law and UNHCR policy.[192] This is in direct contradiction to UNHCR's mandate and leaves asylum seekers vulnerable to harassment and abuse.

The three to four month waiting time for an appointment is bad enough, but Human Rights Watch met very few refugees who had actually been seen by UNHCR on the date indicated on their appointment slips.[193] Sometimes asylum seekers fear being rejected by UNHCR and they forge the slips, crossing out the original date and writing in a later one themselves. However, this kind of fraud can be detected – genuinely rescheduled appointments are usually written next to, and then when necessary, above the original date – whereas forged ones are often written below or off to the side. In addition, some genuinely re-scheduled appointments are highlighted. Other obvious signs such as signatures supposedly indicating that the same UNHCR officer had signed the slip, but with a different hand, were easy to recognize.

Human Rights Watch examined several credible slips that indicated that appointments had been re-scheduled numerous times. For example, Bernard P., a Rwandan refugee whose slip credibly corroborated his story explained,

---

[191] Human Rights Watch interview with refugee, Nairobi, Kenya, April 24, 2002. The allegedly discriminatory treatment that this woman encountered is contrary to many ExCom conclusions, including No. 73 (1993), which calls upon States and UNHCR "to ensure the equal access of women and men to refugee status determination procedures and to all forms of personal documentation relevant to refugees' freedom of movement, welfare and civil status."
[192] UNHCR informed Human Rights Watch that as of September 2002, asylum claims were being processed "in about three months after registration." Written comments from UNHCR Branch Office Nairobi, October 8, 2002.
[193] See Annex B for an example of a UNHCR appointment slip.

When I first went to HCR, it was a Monday. They don't see
people on a Monday – only Thursday for Rwandans.[194] They
took a photo and issued me an appointment slip.... I had my
first appointment on May 11, 2001. I went there and they
didn't let me see them, I was there at 8:00 a.m., and they took
my paper and other people's papers and then they came back
at 3:00 p.m., and they said they couldn't see me and then I was
re-scheduled for July 30, 2001. I came back again, and again
they couldn't see me, so I was rescheduled for December 6,
2001. I came back then and they rescheduled me for April 17,
2002.[195]

Delay sometimes arises for reasons other than appointment re-scheduling.
An Ethiopian refugee called Abebe S. had been asked to pay a bribe to a
UNHCR-employed interpreter[196] and was suffering from long processing delays
as a result. Abebe S. has been trailed and beaten by security agents from
Ethiopia on at least eight occasions and has written to UNHCR to alert them to
the problem repeatedly. He explained how the request to pay a bribe has added
to the delays plaguing his case:

I arrived in Nairobi on February 10, 2000. On February 16,
2000 I went to UNHCR to seek an appointment.
Unfortunately, my appointments were rescheduled for two
months later. I became frustrated with this and asked a
translator who worked with UNHCR to shorten my
appointment [to give Abebe S. an appointment sooner].
Instead, he took me aside and said I could "get resettlement" if
I paid [U.S.]$3,000. But, I am a simple refugee with no
money. I could not pay such a high price!

On September 18, 2000 I was finally called by the same
translator for my appointment. He only talked with me for
thirty minutes. Now, this translator, the same one who asked
for money has been resettled to the United States in June or
July 2001. On October 2, 2000 I received a letter indicating I

---

[194] UNHCR has instituted a policy of only seeing refugees from particular countries of
origin on particular days.
[195] Human Rights Watch interview with refugee, Nairobi, Kenya, April 3, 2002.
[196] For further discussion of the problem of corruption, see section entitled "Problems
Plaguing Resettlement in East Africa," in Part IV, below.

was rejected from refugee status. I knew this was because I
had refused to give the [U.S.]$3,000. I wrote a letter of appeal.
I received an appointment slip for my appeal interview to
happen on November 22, 2000. I went to UNHCR for my
appointment on November 22, 2000. They rescheduled me for
January 15, 2001...

I went for my interview on January 15, 2001 and again they
rescheduled me for January 23, 2001. I went again to
UNHCR on January 23, 2001. The man I met asked me "are
you coming on hand?" [meaning – do you have money?] I
challenged him that the question was not a correct one for him
to ask me. He kept joking with me, and I started crying
because I was so frustrated. He didn't talk to me about my
problems, he just sent me away. But before I left he told me,
"I hate poor people." I asked for another appointment since
that man didn't talk to me about my case. He wrote a date on
my slip, but only later I realized it was for February 3, 2001—
which is a Saturday and not a work day! I was so frustrated
.... On April 26, 2001 I received a call to go to an interview
with UNHCR on my appeal. I went for that interview, but I
still have had no decision... I remain without status or any
decision on my case until now.[197]

Rescheduled appointments, just like the original delays, are a terrible
source of stress in the refugee community. Moreover, because these practices
leave asylum seekers and refugees vulnerable to human rights abuse, they
constitute a dismal failure by UNHCR to fulfill its protection obligations. Olana
T., an Ethiopian refugee who had been tortured in Ethiopia and with serious
security concerns in Nairobi went to UNHCR's office on December 5, 2001. He
was given an appointment slip for April 15, 2002. However, he became
increasingly afraid for his security and went to UNHCR repeatedly asking that
he be interviewed sooner. These interventions resulted in him being granted an
appointment for March 6, 2002. He explained,

I went there on March 6 and they said they couldn't see me so
they rescheduled for March 16, 2002. Again I went there and
they gave me another one for March 26, 2002. When I went

[197] Human Rights Watch interview with refugee, Nairobi, Kenya, April 5, 2002.

on March 26, 2002 they told me there was no one to interview me so come back on April 15, 2002. I was there on April 15, 2002 until 6:00 p.m. and the guards told me I had to get out. When I first arrived they had collected my papers in the morning. When the guards told me to leave they didn't give me my papers again. My paper went in in the morning and it never came out again. I said to them "I'm here now and I will stay the night here unless you give me the paper back." I said "I cannot go on the street without my paper." I spoke to the interpreter and said, "give me my paper back." He explained to me nicely that he would let me in first thing in the morning even though I had no slip. He told me to go home. I refused to leave their offices and they said they would call the police. So I told them I would sleep the night under the tree.

I went in the morning and the interpreter let me in as he promised. He saw me soaked from the night of rain but he couldn't trace my paper. He gave me a whole new paper, but this time I got an appointment for tomorrow [April 18, 2002]. I'm really scared even to go back. I am really scared whether the Ethiopian security has something to do with all these problems I am having. I am scared to go to UNHCR... I wish I had another place to run to, but this is the only place I could find.

After all the trouble of the past nine years it is this problem with UNHCR that causes problems with my mind and my body. Now more than ever I feel my body and my mind giving up on me. I have a severe headache problem and I just can't think anymore. It seems like my hope of life is getting dim. At times I cannot hear properly.[198]

On April 18, 2002 Olana waited at UNHCR for the whole day. However, UNHCR did not see him. In the morning they had collected the second appointment slip, but they refused to replace it when he was not seen that day. An altercation broke out when he again refused to leave without a new appointment slip. A UNHCR staff security officer took Olana out of the

---

[198] Human Rights Watch interview with refugee, Nairobi, Kenya, April 17, 2002.

compound. Olana told a Human Rights Watch researcher he was beaten on the back and on his hand and that other refugees witnessed the incident.[199]

Procedural Deficiencies in the Status Determination Process

It is undeniable that UNHCR officers conducting status determinations face heavy responsibilities. There is little time to do thorough investigations into the facts of a refugee's circumstances, and the opportunity for monitoring and evaluation of their work is rare. However, contrary to its own training manual, UNHCR staff members regularly fail to provide information about the status determination process or to review the asylum seeker's rights with them prior to the interview.[200] The interviews last, on average, for forty minutes.[201] In many cases of rejection, UNHCR is unable or unwilling to provide reasons to the asylum seekers

The caseload in Nairobi is enormously complex. Many of the asylum seekers have suffered years of torture or other personally traumatic events, such as rape. Interviewing these types of victims takes time and skill. The intensity of the issues can lead to burnout in protection staff responsible for doing the interviews, and can re-traumatize the asylum seeker. The result is that asylum seekers may be prevented from communicating all the necessary details in their cases, and some may be wrongfully rejected or will not be referred to services they need.

Some asylum seekers interviewed by Human Rights Watch believed that the UNHCR interviewer did not spend enough time to fully understand the facts of the case. Others explained that they were unable to communicate all the details of their stories because they were asked to stop or edit themselves by UNHCR protection officers or translation staff, a common avoidance reaction among overly stressed humanitarian workers.[202] However, such incidents are in violation of the standard established in the Refugee Status Determination Handbook that the examiner should "ensure that the applicant presents his case as fully as possible and with all available evidence."[203] UNHCR examiners who

---

[199] Human Rights Watch interview with refugee, Nairobi, Kenya, April 18, 2002.

[200] *See* UNHCR *Training Module, Interviewing Applicants for Refugee Status*, 1995, p. 14 (explaining that "before commencing the interview the applicant must be provided with certain information... [including] the applicable refugee definition; the procedures followed with respect to the determination of refugee status.").

[201] Human Rights Watch interview with a person wishing to remain anonymous, Nairobi, Kenya, April 22, 2002.

[202] *See* e.g. Danieli, Rodley, Weisaeth eds., *International Responses to Traumatic Stress*, 1996 at 410 ("when working with victims of disasters, helpers often experience an array of stress (countertransference) reactions [including] 1) avoidance reactions, characterized by distancing, denial, detachment, and withdrawal.").

[203] UNHCR, *Status Determination Handbook* at para 205 (i).

do not allow asylum seekers to fully explain themselves or refuse to examine whatever evidence is available, including physical evidence, are shirking their duties to fully consider the applicant's case.

For example, Ahmed S. from Bale province in Ethiopia was detained by the government of Ethiopia from August 1992 until October 1994. During this first period of detention, "I was tortured and beaten. I was beaten on the soles of my feet and with a plastic whip and they would take me out at night and threaten to shoot me." [204] At a government rally in February 1998 to garner support and recruit soldiers for the war with Eritrea,[205] Ahmed said he shouted from the crowd, "what benefit will that war have for the Oromo people?" He explained what happened next:

> They arrested me for asking a wrong question. I was held at Goba again, and this time they poured [hot] oil on my body. They also heated nails and pressed them into my skin [the scars resulting from both sets of injuries were viewed by a Human Rights Watch researcher]...
>
> I crossed the border on February 21, 1999 on foot. I came to UNHCR in February 1999. They gave me an appointment for one month later. But at the interview they didn't let me show them the tortured places – they told me they didn't want to see that. I wasn't allowed to explain my problems very well. They didn't allow me to.[206]

Bela K. is a young Congolese refugee who had been violently attacked and witnessed both of her parents killed by "militaires"(soldiers) in Congo in 1997 when she was twelve years old. She fled a few days later with her sister who

[204] Human Rights Watch interview with refugee, Nairobi, Kenya, April 6, 2002.
[205] On May 6, 1998 Eritrea launched what Ethiopia claimed was a "war of aggression" along the border region between the two countries. Eritrea, on the other hand, claimed that Ethiopia was encroaching on its territory and demanded the withdrawal of Ethiopian troops from the region. The disputed border region between the two countries had been a major source of contention for the past half decade since Eritrean independence. This war continued for two years causing tens of thousands of deaths until a peace accord was signed between the two countries in December 2001, although sporadic fighting continued until recently. See Agence France-Presse, "Ill-defined Border at Heart of Asmara, Addis Ababa Row," May 19, 1998; Agence France-Presse, "Eritrea Stands Firm in Border Dispute with Ethiopia," May 21, 1998; Hisham Aidi, "The End of a 1000-Day War: Ethiopia and Eritrea Sign Peace Accord," (available at http://www.africana.com /DailyArticles/index_20010102.htm.).
[206] Human Rights Watch interview with refugee, Nairobi, Kenya, April 6, 2002.

became ill and died during their flight. Bela became pregnant after a relationship she had with the man who ran an orphanage she was placed in after her sister's death. Now, at the age of seventeen, she had a young son to care for while living as a refugee in Nairobi. She explained what happened when she first arrived in Nairobi and was interviewed by UNHCR:

> On May 30, 2001 I had an interview with UNHCR. The translator kept telling me not to cry because the officials would think I was afraid of talking and not telling the truth. But I was crying because of what has passed in my life![207]

The doubts that these interviewees had are only exacerbated by the fact that there is often no way of determining the accuracy of the transcript as prepared by the protection officer. UNHCR's training manual recommends that the person conducting the interview read back notes to the asylum seeker in order to ensure accuracy.[208] However, few refugees interviewed by Human Rights Watch were provided with such an opportunity. Refugees might also gain confidence in UNHCR's procedures if they were allowed to bring legal representatives with them to their interviews. UNHCR's guidelines recognize the value of independent legal assistance for those applying for refugee status with governments, but these representatives are rarely allowed into UNHCR-run status determinations. Finally, an applicant's appeal is often reconsidered by the same UNHCR office. Thus, in countries like Kenya where the government does not conduct its own status determinations, UNHCR is both the judge of refugee status and the protector/provider for refugees at every stage of the process.[209]

Conclusion

As this section has demonstrated, the UNHCR-run status determinations in Nairobi are rife with problems. The UNHCR office is not physically accessible for many asylum seekers, and even for those who manage to have their status assessed, the office's lack of accessibility for updating files and registering births causes ongoing problems. Inaccessibility is also preventing at-risk asylum seekers from being identified and referred to needed services at an early stage. All asylum seekers are subject to extremely serious delays in the processing of

---

[207] Human Rights Watch interview with refugee, Nairobi, Kenya, April 22, 2002.
[208] See UNHCR, *Training Module: Interviewing Applicants for Refugee Status*, 1995, p. 55 (noting that "a useful technique is to read back or go over those parts of the claim which remain unclear.").
[209] See Verdirame, Guglielmo. "Human Rights and Refugees: The Case of Kenya," *Journal of Refugee Studies*, Vol. 12, No. 1, 1999.

their claims, which leaves them vulnerable to abuse. In the status determination interviews with UNHCR protection staff, the agency is falling short of its own standards on keeping applicants informed about their rights and the procedures to be followed, and on conducting interviews in a manner that allows all the evidence to be considered. Finally, the agency's conflicting roles as service provider and status adjudicator cause refugees to lack confidence in the system. It is this last problem that provides the strongest rationale for the Kenyan government to fulfill its responsibility to conduct status determinations.

There is no doubt that some of these serious deficiencies are due to UNHCR's resource limitations. For example, UNHCR has had to re-direct its protection staff to other tasks, most notably in Nairobi, to the processing of thousands of Somali Bantu resettlement files for the United States government in late 2001 (see below).[210]

---

[210] Human Rights Watch interview with UNHCR official, Nairobi, Kenya, April 18, 2002.

PART II: REFUGEES LIVING IN KAMPALA

The estimated 50,000 urban refugees and asylum seekers in Kampala also face a difficult situation. For example, urban asylum seekers are very much at risk immediately after their arrival in Kampala, and asylum seekers and refugees are trailed and harassed by security agents from their countries of origin. In contrast to Kenya where Ethiopian refugees are most often targeted, it is the Congolese and Rwandans who are most seriously persecuted by these security agents.

While low-level police harassment of refugees is nowhere near the epidemic proportions of such harassment in Kenya, refugees in Kampala sometimes suffer from more sophisticated individual targeting by the Ugandan military and police. In addition, given the geopolitical role of Uganda in countries such as Sudan, Rwanda and the DRC, refugees and asylum seekers are often deeply fearful of the refugee status determination process itself, which in contrast to Kenya, is mostly run by the Ugandan government.

SUBSTANDARD LIVING CONDITIONS FOR REFUGEES IN KAMPALA

Introduction: Why Refugees Come to Kampala

Many refugees arrive directly to Kampala after fleeing persecution in their countries of origin. Although analysis of the root causes of refugee flight to Uganda is beyond the scope of this report, Human Rights Watch and other organizations have documented the problems of political repression, armed conflict and other human rights abuses in Burundi,[211] the DRC,[212] Ethiopia,[213] Rwanda,[214] Somalia,[215] and Sudan[216] which often give rise to refugee flight.

Of the refugees in Kampala, many have come there directly, before they even learn about or consider going to one of the refugee camps located in the north of the country. The rationale is both a function of the forms of transport selected—truckers and buses are headed for Kampala and not for remote villages where camps are located; and of geography—especially for Great Lakes refugees, Kampala is the first city they reach. However, even Sudanese refugees sometimes come directly to Kampala without ever stopping in one of the camps closer to the Ugandan-Sudanese border. Although many refugees living in

---

[211] *See* note 45, above.
[212] *See* note 46, above.
[213] *See* note 47, above.
[214] *See* note 48, above.
[215] *See* note 49, above.
[216] *See* note 50, above.

Uganda's camps never consider moving on to Kampala, and many find the more rural nature of camps, and the possibility to grow food, both preferable and more familiar, others do go to refugee camps first, and then subsequently leave. Refugees leave camps for one or a combination of several reasons (discussed in more detail in Part III), including: inadequate humanitarian assistance, general insecurity and attacks, or insecurity for particular individuals.

Once they arrive in Kampala, asylum seekers and refugees have few places to turn to meet their basic needs. UNHCR is, of course, the main organization responsible, but the agency only provided assistance to 274 refugees in 2001.[217] InterAid, a Ugandan organization that serves as UNHCR's main implementing partner, provides intake counseling for asylum seekers and refugees, some medical care, and income-generating initiatives for a small number of refugees. InterAid reported 10,315 "visits" by refugees and asylum seekers during 2001.[218] A few NGOs and faith-based organizations provide assistance only when asylum seekers are waiting for their status to be assessed. Once recognized as refugees, most must sign an agreement verifying that they will be "self-sufficient" in Kampala. Keeping this promise is very difficult for refugees, given that they are living in a city where Ugandan citizens themselves are suffering from unemployment and poverty.

Inadequate Food and Material Assistance
In Kampala, newly arrived asylum seekers sleep and spend their days near the Old Kampala Police Station. This is the police station where their first interviews occur, and it is located just around the corner from InterAid, the main implementing partner of UNHCR in Uganda. The newest arrivals are allowed to share the once-a-day food rations of the prisoners jailed at the police station. Each adult refugee gets one portion of the total amount intended for the prisoners, which is donated by charitable agencies in Kampala.[219] Mothers must share their portion with their children.

One international NGO in Kampala provides housing and food assistance to some asylum seekers. Although the Kampala program was closed for several months in late 2001 and early 2002, by April 2002 it was assisting over three hundred very needy asylum seekers. The assistance is cut off once an asylum seeker is recognized as a refugee, or after six months, whichever comes first.

---

[217] See UNHCR, *Uganda Community Services Report*, 2001 (on file with Human Rights Watch).
[218] See InterAid Uganda, "Data Showing Visits By Refugees and Asylum Seekers During the Period January to December 2001," (on file with Human Rights Watch).
[219] Human Rights Watch interview with Deputy Officer Thomas at Old Kampala Police Station, Kampala, Uganda, April 9, 2002.

This policy is strictly enforced by the NGO, although persons still in dire need may obtain ongoing assistance after a home assessment visit from the NGO's staff. Matthew K., a forty-one year old Sudanese man, although very grateful for this assistance since it had helped his six-year-old son, said, "My son became anemic in the camp. UNHCR would not respond to his needs. I brought him here to Kampala and the only rescue we received for food came from [the NGO]. My child got a bit better but now my child is remaining without support. There is no longer money from them to help us."[220]

Elizabeth N., a thirty-year-old woman from Lumule, Sudan, fled with her fourteen-year-old son to Kampala when her husband was killed during the war and all but one of her children died from hunger. They arrived in Kampala in February 2002 and were part of a group of new arrivals sleeping outside in the Old Kampala neighborhood. She said, "I am having so many stomach problems, and now I am also hungry. I have to eat the 'food to deceive the stomach' [a starchy, filling porridge] when I can find it. I have to sleep outside at InterAid and when it rains it comes on to me. I have nowhere to go.... Sometimes we get food from the police."[221]

Sara L., a Sudanese refugee living in the Kabowa neighborhood of Kampala said, "I can't steal or work to get food. I am looking for a way to go back to Sudan. My child is always hungry."[222] Another refugee woman living in the Wankulukuku neighborhood told a Human Rights Watch researcher that she had coped at first in Kampala by cooking and selling street food. Then she ran out of money for this business. She explained, "When I first came here I went looking for UNHCR, but I found no help from them.... [Now that she cannot sell food on the street anymore], our problems are food and where to sleep. We have no covers and no good place to sleep. My girl does not even go to school. I cannot even get her food to eat."[223]

Inadequate Housing

Since newly arriving asylum seekers often come without money or other support networks, their first concern is to find a safe place to sleep at night. Some are lucky and find shelter with friends or family, or with one of the two church leaders who give refugees shelter on church property. Others decide that since they need to be in Old Kampala to seek asylum or obtain services, they

---

[220] Human Rights Watch interview with refugee, Kampala, Uganda, April 15, 2002.
[221] Human Rights Watch interview with refugee, Old Kampala, Uganda, April 12, 2002.
[222] Human Rights Watch interview with refugee, Kampala, Uganda, April 15, 2002.
[223] Human Rights Watch interview with refugee, Kamapla, Uganda, April 15, 2002.

will sleep outside near the Old Kampala police station and InterAid.[224] Several refugees explained that prior to the time of Human Rights Watch's visit they had been allowed to sleep inside a broken-down school bus that had been parked near the Old Kampala police station. Several spoke longingly about the shelter and warmth the bus had provided. However, the bus had been allegedly towed away after journalists planned to write a story about it.[225]

Once an individual obtains refugee status in Kampala, UNHCR assists a very small portion of them with a subsistence allowance for accommodation. Many others must rely on charity to meet their needs. One female human rights activist interviewed by a Human Rights Watch researcher explained that she had a place to sleep when she first arrived because a Congolese family took her in. They had since left, but had paid the rent for her three months in advance so she would have time to find another place.[226]

Finding money to pay rent is a daily struggle for refugees in Kampala. Monthly rent for a room is commonly between Ush.9,000 – 30,000 (U.S.$5 – $17).[227] In Kampala, most refugees live in crowded rectangular rooms made out of cement blocks. One neighborhood a Human Rights Watch researcher visited was the Kisenyi-Mengo neighborhood, where many Somali refugees live. In one cement room that measured approximately thirty-by-thirty feet, there were

---

[224] In March 2002, several newly arrived asylum seekers had begun sleeping in the gated courtyard outside of InterAid. Pierre T., a Congolese refugee, explained that the large group was mostly made up of new arrivals, coming from the DRC and Burundi. He estimated there to have been at least forty people in the group, although UNHCR insisted that there were fewer people sleeping outside. Human Rights Watch obtained a copy of the correspondence sent by InterAid to the police, requesting that the asylum seekers be rounded up on the night of March 12, 2001. Addressed to the District Police Commander at Old Kampala Police Station, the request explained that "for about a month now many people claiming to be refugees and asylum seekers sleep at InterAid offices.... Even some of those who have been explained to what procedures to follow have insisted on staying around. To make matters worse, we get reports that some of them drink and fight here, not to mention the fact that they soil the whole compound which now is very dirty and smelly, something we fear may cause an epidemic here." Letter from Mr. David Obot, Executive Director of Interaid to the District Police Commander, Old Kampala Police Station, March 12, 2002 (on file with Human Rights Watch). The next morning, Pierre T. went to InterAid to find out what happened and found the refugees dispersed in different locations. The group then walked the long distance to UNHCR by foot to protest this treatment and demand a solution. A UNHCR staff member took the refugees back to InterAid and sent two families to UNHCR houses in Kampala. The others were taken to the police. Some left from the police station for the camps and others continue to stay at InterAid, or right next to InterAid. Human Rights Watch interview with refugee, Kampala, Uganda, April 16, 2002.
[225] Human Rights Watch interview with refugee, Kampala, Uganda, April 9, 2002.
[226] Human Rights Watch interview with refugee, Kampala, Uganda, April 10, 2002.
[227] Throughout this report, the exchange rate used was 1,795 Ugandan shillings to the dollar.

ten foam mattresses on the floor, and a few had been pulled into the street outside for airing. Each mattress belonged to one family. One man with ten children explained that they had to take turns sleeping on their one mattress.[228]

Elsewhere, Mulumba T., a Congolese refugee, explained his struggle to find rent, "I have to find rent money… but I have no options. Also, my wife is pregnant. She is just about to give birth, and I don't know what to do with her and the medical costs we will have. Our rent is Ush.35,000 [U.S.$19] and we cannot pay it. The landlord will send us out soon. I cannot sleep outside with my pregnant wife. There are so many other refugees with the same problems."[229]

Some refugees, usually women and girls, obtain shelter by working as domestics. Usually they work only for room and board, without a salary. They are vulnerable to sexual and other exploitation. Zola R., a twenty-year-old Congolese refugee woman explained,

> I found a job working as a domestic for an Algerian woman. She had four children and no husband. She gave me food and a place to sleep. I worked from five in the morning until midnight every day. I had to do a lot of work for her. I didn't receive any pay, but food and a sleeping place. But she had to switch her jobs and she left on April 5, 2002. Even though that was so difficult, I would like to find a new job like that. Right now I am sleeping with other Congolese. We only have one small room where five people have to sleep together.[230]

UNHCR is reluctant to continue assisting even the small number of refugees it helps in Kampala. Human Rights Watch attended a press conference in Kampala where UNHCR made its policy preferences quite clear. Mr. Saihou Saidy, the UNHCR Representative in Kampala told the press, "It is easier for HCR to deal with refugees in the camp setting. At some point we have to stop paying the rent of refugees. We recommend to refugees that they should go to the settlements."[231]

---

[228] Human Rights Watch interview with refugee, Kampala, Uganda, April 16, 2002.
[229] Human Rights Watch interview with refugee, Kampala, Uganda, April 10, 2002.
[230] Human Rights Watch interview with refugee, Kampala, Uganda, April 15, 2002.
[231] UNHCR Uganda Representative (speaking at a UNHCR/Human Rights Watch Press Conference), Kampala, Uganda, April 16, 2002.

Inadequate Medical Care

Asylum seekers in Kampala are not eligible for medical assistance from NGOs. Asylum seekers normally must go to Mulago Hospital, one of Kampala's public hospitals, to try to get treatment. Some asylum seekers go to independent clinics, where treatment is more immediately available and where medicines can be purchased. Others have to ask Ugandans to help. Doris K., a young woman who had been a student activist in the DRC fell sick with malaria immediately after arriving in Uganda. A Ugandan helped her and paid for the medical costs.[232] However, most forgo treatment because they simply cannot afford it.

Once a refugee's status has been recognized in Kampala, she can receive some triage care from InterAid's offices, which is officially tasked with providing medical care to refugees. InterAid has a small clinic, which was visited by Human Rights Watch, where sick refugees are seen on Tuesdays and Thursdays. Funding for drugs is provided by the German organization, Gesellschaft für Technische Zusammenarbeit (GTZ). Emergency or more complex care must be obtained at Mulago Hospital. If a refugee requires treatment that has to be paid for, a referral to Mulago must be made by InterAid, which is sometimes difficult to obtain.[233]

Each part of this system is fraught with problems. First, most refugees interviewed by Human Rights Watch explained that they did not receive care at InterAid's clinic either because no one on staff spoke their language, or because they were told that they should be self sufficient or that they should be in the camps. This latter reason was a common complaint amongst Sudanese. A twenty-eight-year-old Sudanese refugee woman, Inas M. said, "I have an internal bleeding problem with my menstruation cycle. I have gone to their offices at InterAid and they do not help me. They tell me, 'you go back to the border where you come from.' I am sick and I am losing weight."[234]

Others complained that the medical care offered at InterAid was inadequate. For example, Fidèle D., a Rwandan refugee had typhus and malaria just prior to Human Rights Watch's visit. When he had typhus he went to a medical center and was treated. When he had malaria he went to InterAid. He found them very badly equipped. He said:

> They did not do the malaria test. They gave me about five
> injections, during five days. I did not stay there, but came back

---

[232] Human Rights Watch interview with refugee, Kampala, Uganda, April 10, 2002.
[233] Human Rights Watch interview with NGO representative, Kampala, Uganda, April 9, 2002.
[234] Human Rights Watch interview with refugee, Old Kampala, Uganda, April 15, 2002.

every day. When it did not get any better, I went to Nsambya hospital. It was very serious. They admitted me immediately and gave me several infusions. The first night I was so sick I had no idea where I was, I was not clear in my head. They told me afterwards I had a very high fever.... Getting treated there [at InterAid] is really hopeless. ("Se faire soigner la-bas, c'est vraiment sans espoir").[235]

When Fidèle went to InterAid afterwards they refused to pay the bills, saying that he should not have gone to the hospital without their reference if he wanted reimbursement. He was unusually lucky because eventually he found an NGO that paid the bills for him.

Finally, since so many medical cases wind up in one of Kampala's hospitals, the government of Uganda would like to receive more help from UNHCR. One government official explained that he felt the agency was not doing its job for medical cases,

> Normally, UNHCR doesn't listen to our referrals on... medical grounds. For example, we recently referred a case that required urgent medical attention to UNHCR. They wrote a letter back to us stating that the individual concerned should seek care at Mulago hospital. The letter [seen by a Human Rights Watch researcher] stated that "the only referrals we will receive are those regarding individuals in need of resettlement."[236]

Lack of Medical Care: Victims of Sexual Violence and Other Forms of Torture

Torture victims are not receiving adequate care in Kampala, a particularly egregious fact, since it is in contradiction to UNHCR's own guidelines[237] and the agency's recognition that "the personal, social, and economic costs of failing to identify and intervene with [victims of extreme violence] are devastating."[238]

---

[235] Human Rights Watch interview with refugee, Kampala, Uganda, April 9, 2002.
[236] Human Rights Watch interview with senior Ugandan government official, Kampala, Uganda, April 8, 2002.
[237] See UNHCR, *Guidelines on the Protection of Refugee Women*, 1991, p. 54 (suggesting that UNHCR should "institute counseling and mental health services for refugee women, particularly for victims of torture, rape, and other physical and sexual abuse.").
[238] See UNHCR, *Training Module: Interviewing Applicants for Refugee Status*, 1995, p. 89.

When Human Rights Watch enquired about the counseling available at InterAid, we were told that UNHCR and InterAid give counseling to asylum seekers and refugees about the pros and cons of remaining in Kampala versus going to the refugee camps. Refugees are "counseled" about how difficult it is to be self-sufficient and about "the need for them to go to settlements, especially to receive education for their children."[239]

When Human Rights Watch enquired later about counseling for sexual violence or torture victims, UNHCR explained that they do have a system of referrals for refugees (not for asylum seekers) to an NGO called the Transcultural Psychosocial Organization (TPO).[240] However, in a telephone interview with Human Rights Watch, the Director of TPO explained that TPO does not provide any psychotherapeutic counseling for torture victims in Kampala, only in Uganda's refugee camps.[241]

Vincent A., a Congolese refugee living in Kampala showed a Human Rights Watch researcher deep scars ringing his shoulders, indicating that large cuts had been made all the way around the shoulder joints of both of his arms. He had been living in North Kivu and on July 9 and 10, 2000, his village had been attacked.[242] He said,

> They killed so many in that situation. They killed many of the displaced. They wanted to exterminate the civilian population. But we weren't the aggressors.... They... subjected me to the "vest system"—the objective was to cut

---

[239] Human Rights Watch interview with UNHCR Community Services staff member, Kampala, Uganda, April 8, 2002.

[240] TPO is an NGO founded in 1995 and based in Amsterdam, The Netherlands. TPO collaborates with the World Health Organization to assist refugees and others traumatized by war, human rights violations and other atrocities. Staff train local workers in affected locations as well as provide experts in the field when governments or aid agencies request their assistance. TPO is active in Algeria, Bosnia-Herzegovina, Cambodia, the DRC, Ethiopia, Gaza, India (among Tibetans), Mozambique, Namibia, Nepal, Sri Lanka and Uganda and is primarily financed by the Netherlands Ministry of Foreign Affairs. *See* TPO website, http://www.xs4all.nl/~tpo/.

[241] Human Rights Watch telephone interview with Director of TPO, New York, September 20, 2002.

[242] North Kivu has been the site of ongoing fighting, death, and displacement. According to UN estimates there were approximately 450,000 displaced people in the region during the period of this refugee's flight. *See* IRIN, "Tension in North Kivu," July 28, 2000. The fighting in the region between various militia groups and the Rwandan-backed rebels is the main reason for the continued displacement. On July 10, 2000 Sake village was attacked. Twenty-nine civilians were killed and several more wounded when unidentified attackers entered the village, burning huts and attacking occupants with knives and machetes. *See* Reuters, "Attackers Kill Twenty-nine Civilians in Rebel-held Congo," July 10, 2000; IRIN, "Feature on Tension in North Kivu," July 28, 2000.

> both of my arms off. They didn't manage to cut through the
> bones, but they made these two long cuts at my shoulders.[243]

Vincent had not received any medical or psychotherapeutic treatment for his
torture.

Raphael S., a Congolese refugee living in Kampala who had been a
pharmacist in Goma, eastern DRC, was tortured by security agents of the rebel
force controlling his area, the Congolese Rally for Democracy (RCD-Goma).[244]
He was accused of unfairly raising the price of products for an RCD soldier.[245]
He told a Human Rights Watch researcher about the torture he had suffered in a
Goma jail, and what medical care he had received since arriving in Uganda:

> I fell unconscious from the beatings and so they brought me to
> the hospital at about 11:00 p.m. I spent eleven days in the
> intensive care unit. The tests showed that [as a result of the
> torture] my kidneys had been crushed, and I also had a broken
> clavicle. [After becoming a refugee in Uganda], except for the
> first two months I was here I have received nothing. I have to
> find rent money and there is inappropriate medical care. I
> know that the care at InterAid is terrible. They give people
> inappropriate   medicine   without   doing   the   necessary
> examinations and checks.   Because of my injuries I need

---

[243] Human Rights Watch interview with refugee, Kampala, Uganda, April 10, 2002.

[244] The RCD launched a rebellion against the government headed by Laurent Kabila in
August 1998. They vowed to restore democracy and respect for human rights within the
DRC but the RCD-Goma and its Rwandan allies as well as the other parties to the
conflict in the Kivus have regularly slaughtered civilians in massacres and extrajudicial
executions. *See* "Eastern Congo Ravaged: Killing Civilians and Silencing Protest,"
Human Rights Watch/Africa, May 2000, Vol. 12, No. 3(A). *See* also Human Rights
Watch/Africa, *The War Within the War: Sexual Violence Against Women and Girls in
Eastern Congo*, June 20, 2002; ; Human Rights Watch/Africa, *War Crimes in Kisangani:
The Response of the Rwandan-backed Rebels to the May 2002 Mutiny*, Vol. 14, No. 6(A),
August 2002.

[245] In September 1999, the DRC government ordered all exchange bureau closed and
declared that it would be illegal for Congolese to hoard foreign exchange. This decree
caused a large fluctuation in the national currency, and the government blamed a number
of companies for attacking the Congolese franc and causing the depreciation. In response
to the plummeting value of the currency, the government put in place price controls on
many products. *See* Agence France-Presse, "DR Congo Forbids Foreign Cash Holdings,
Closes Money Change Bureaux," September 18, 1999; AP, "Congo Under Kabila Looks
a lot Like the Mobutu Era," March 6, 2000.

proper care, including urinary tract treatment, but I have no options.[246]

Aaron H., a Rwandan refugee who told a Human Rights Watch researcher that he had been detained and tortured in Kampala by agents of the Rwandan government, was too afraid to tell his story to InterAid in order to ask for counseling assistance. He was only receiving legal counseling because the NGO that offered it was the "only place I feel safe."[247] UNHCR recognizes that "it is essential that…victim[s] receive counseling as early as possible;"[248] and yet, of eight victims of sexual violence or other forms of torture, not a single victim interviewed by Human Rights Watch in Kampala received psychotherapeutic counseling, and only half received medical treatment from UNHCR or its implementing partner, InterAid.

Responsibility for Refugees' Living Conditions in Kampala

Refugees living in Kampala are partly suffering from the poverty and violence that is afflicting many Ugandan nationals.   While the Ugandan government does allow some refugees to work and provides them with access to its public hospital, the government could do more.   For example, the government's opposition to the presence of Sudanese refugees in the capital has meant that their access to assistance has been even more restricted than other refugees.

For its part, UNHCR has not challenged the government's strict policy requiring that refugees be "self-sufficient" if they live in the city. NGO and UNHCR assistance for recognized refugees is extremely limited.

---

[246] Human Rights Watch interview with refugee, Kampala, Uganda, April 10, 2002.
[247] Human Rights Watch interview with refugee, Kampala, Uganda, April 11, 2002.
[248] *See* UNHCR, *Guidelines on Prevention and Response to Sexual Violence Against Refugees*, 1995, p. 50.

PROTECTION PROBLEMS FOR REFUGEES IN KAMPALA

In Uganda, the several arms of the Ugandan government involved in refugee protection include the Office of the Prime Minister (OPM), the Special Branch (the security arm of the Ugandan police) and the Refugee Eligibility Committee (REC). Their functions will be discussed in the section entitled "Refugee Status Determinations." UNHCR performs its protection function through its involvement in Uganda's refugee status determination system, and through a range of protection-oriented activities, such as lobbying for improved refugee legislation in Uganda. UNHCR's main implementing partner in Kampala, InterAid, is not involved in assessing the status of refugees, but the agency does provide some services (such as running safe houses for "high profile"[249] refugees and asylum seekers) that can help to protect refugees. In April 2002 there were two houses in operation in Kampala where fifteen refugees were living.[250]

Physical Protection Problems for Newly-Arriving Asylum Seekers

Asylum seekers may spend several weeks or months sleeping outside in Old Kampala. Women and men and people from different nationalities are mixed together, creating risky situations. In addition, several refugees told a Human Rights Watch researcher that alleged security agents from countries of origin are aware that asylum seekers sleep outside in Old Kampala, and they will comb the small gatherings of people to search for individuals they are tracing. The Old Kampala police[251] and other NGO staff are aware of how dangerous it is for people to sleep outside. For example, in an interview with a Human Rights Watch researcher, the Director of InterAid admitted "we do need a place here in Kampala for people to sleep safely when they first arrive."[252]

---

[249] The term "high profile" is used in this report to refer to cases of particularly well-known refugees and/or to cases that have received public attention.

[250] Human Rights Watch interview with InterAid, Kampala, Uganda, April 8, 2002.

[251] Acknowledging that sleeping outside is unsafe for refugees, one police officer told Human Rights Watch, "of course we would allow them to be locked inside the cells if they want for their protection." Human Rights Watch had the opportunity to examine the corridor in front of the cells, which was easily visible through a set of bars that in turn were open to an inner courtyard. Given the stench and crowding of prisoners even in that corridor, it is difficult to imagine any asylum seeker agreeing to be locked in with the criminal prisoners—no matter how frightened he or she was about sleeping outside. Human Rights Watch interview with police officer, Old Kampala Police Station, Uganda, April 9, 2002.

[252] Human Rights Watch interview with InterAid, Kampala, Uganda, April 8, 2002.

NGOs repeatedly receive complaints from women and children who are subjected to harassment and abuse while sleeping outside in Old Kampala.[253] Lishan W., a twenty-seven-year-old Eritrean woman, told a Human Rights Watch researcher,

> But what can I do for myself here in Kampala? There are very bad conditions for a lady alone here. At first InterAid let me sleep in their corridor. They let me sleep there for fifteen days. Now, I have to sleep outside and the police tell me, "you are a lady, it is not good to sleep outside." But what can I do? I have to wear two trousers to protect myself from someone who wants to rape me. Sometimes it is also too cold.[254]

Rebecca I., a twenty-five-year-old Sudanese woman from Loboni, Sudan, fled with her two small children, Amani, a five-year-old girl and Nada, an eight-month-old boy. The family had been sleeping outside in Old Kampala. She explained,

> Now we are sleeping outside of InterAid.... But in the place where I am sleeping outside, the Congolese men who are there are always causing problems for me. They are always pushing me but I refuse them. Every night they come and push at me, but I refuse. One man even beat me because I refused him, and he said, "you are not a woman!" After that man beat me I told the police and they came to warn him and that made that one man stop. But there still are others.... Even at night when I sleep I worry about those men. I cannot sleep with them, it is very dangerous for me.[255]

Tensions Within the Refugee Community

Refugees' countries of origin are often devastated by armed conflict, and often political or military leaders manipulate ethnic identities as a source of power. As a result, refugee groups sometimes experience internal conflicts. Some of these tensions reflect the divisions in the refugees' home countries, and some are new tensions that arise from different refugee communities living together. Human Rights Watch documented both types of conflict in

---

[253] Human Rights Watch interview with NGO, Kampala, Uganda, April 8, 2002.
[254] Human Rights Watch interview with refugee, Kampala, Uganda, April 12, 2002.
[255] Human Rights Watch interview with refugee, Kampala, Uganda, April 11, 2002.

Kampala—discrimination and violence between clans in the Somali community or between the Hutu and Tutsi in the Rwandan community, as well as tensions between, for example, Sudanese and Congolese, or Somali and Ethiopian refugees.

Refugees subject to discriminatory treatment are without protective networks within the refugee community to help them when problems arise. In the worst cases, physical violence and even death threats can occur. For example, a refugee in his late twenties called Mohammad has a mother who is Ethiopian and a Somali father. Mohammed has been living in Uganda without his parents since November 22, 1993, and has been discriminated against for his mixed background. He explained,

> I was sleeping in the street when I first arrived. I slept in the street for three months. I couldn't sleep early if I needed to, I would go to sleep at midnight and wake myself early in the morning. This was because I was caught between two communities in Kampala and each one hated me. The Somalis didn't like me for being from a Christian mother and the Ethiopians hated me for having a Somali father. The UNHCR helped me at first. They gave me a small allowance of accommodation assistance for the first five years.... The resettlement officer at that time was married to a Ugandan security [officer] who told me to be careful and that someone would kill me. I ran from her office because she scared me so much.[256]

Freedom of Expression and Assembly

The ICCPR provides that everyone, including refugees, possess the rights to freedom of expression and to peacefully assemble.[257] As a party to the ICCPR, Uganda may limit the right to freedom of expression, when necessary, to protect public order or the rights of others.[258] The right to assemble is contingent upon assemblies being "peaceful" (without violence or threats of violence), and Uganda may also limit this right to protect public order (among other reasons).[259]

In July 2001, Pierre T., the head of an organization of Great Lakes refugees, "Association des Refugies Francophones" (ASSOREF), wrote a letter

---

[256] Human Rights Watch interview with refugee, Kampala, Uganda, April 14, 2002.
[257] *See* ICCPR, Articles 19 and 21.
[258] *See* ICCPR, Article 19, para. 3(b).
[259] *See* ICCPR, Article 21.

to UNHCR sharply criticizing the role of InterAid. On the morning of August 21, 2001, Pierre met with the UNHCR Protection Officer to discuss the letter. According to Pierre, the Officer broadly rejected the claims.[260]   A group of refugees gathered outside InterAid in order to learn the results of the meeting.[261] According to Pierre, when he left the building he explained to the gathering that "nothing" had come of the meeting.[262] The refugees became agitated and started to sing angry songs. UNHCR called the police and they arrested four refugees. Pierre was "arrested" by police who pulled him aside and told him to sit quietly and wait. Three others were taken away.

At approximately 2:00 p.m., Pierre was taken to Old Kampala Police Station. He was held in an overcrowded cell for about three days. According to Pierre, he was threatened and beaten by detainees in the police station (he told Human Rights Watch that he believes the police use detainees deliberately to beat up other detainees). After three days of detention, Pierre was taken to City Hall Court, together with two other Congolese refugees who had also been arrested and beaten by co-detainees. After a few hours the three were taken to Luzira prison.

The three refugees were brought before a magistrate and, in a session that was not translated into French, charged with "being idle and disorderly" under Article 162 (I) (d) of the Ugandan Penal Code. Pierre was held for forty-four days in Luzira prison before being released. Pierre explained that another Congolese, Alain H. was beaten so badly in Old Kampala Police Station that he had to be held in the hospital of Luzira prison. Alain was released a few days before the others. He has since left Uganda.

Human Rights Watch also interviewed Claude M., a Congolese refugee who had been one of the leaders of the demonstration and was arrested by the Ugandan police. Claude told a Human Rights Watch researcher that the police had undressed him and beaten him with batons and rifle butts. Claude was then taken to Old Kampala Police Station and detained in a cell he described as "very overcrowded." The next morning he was beaten again. On the third day he was brought before a magistrate. During his hearing, he was represented by the Refugee Law Project. He was then taken to Luzira prison where he was held for forty-four days with Pierre T., and François C.

---

[260] Human Rights Watch interview with refugee, Kampala, Uganda, April 9, 2002.
[261] The intention of Congolese refugees in Kampala to hold a peaceful demonstration was reported in one of Uganda's daily newspapers. See "Congolese Refugees Plan Street Demo," *The Monitor*, August 21, 2001. More recently, on May 14, 2002, Ugandan police arrested four Congolese protesters and confiscated their placards as they were protesting outside the InterAid offices in Old Kampala against the poor living conditions in refugee camps. See "Refugees Protest Poor Conditions," *New Vision*, May 14, 2002.
[262] Human Rights Watch interview with refugee, Kampala, Uganda, April 9, 2002.

François C., a third Congolese refugee from Goma present at the demonstration told a Human Rights Watch researcher that he was beaten by other prisoners—those "who act on behalf of the police." As a result of these beatings in detention he has problems in the lower back, with walking, and with carrying things. He told a Human Rights Watch researcher that the incident had affected his concentration: "my intelligence does not function any more."[263]

When asked about this incident, the UNHCR Representative in Kampala told members of the press and a Human Rights Watch researcher, "refugees are not above the law. We called the police because there was a law and order problem with these individual refugees."[264] When asked, he gave no details as to what the "law and order problem" was.

As noted above, refugees have the right to peacefully assemble and to express their opinions, and the Ugandan government should have allowed them to exercise these rights as long as there was no threat of violence or threat to public order. Finally, if local press accurately reported UNHCR's statement at the time that "refugees have no right and authority to stage a demonstration of any kind,"[265] then UNHCR also disregarded these rights of refugees.

Country of Origin "Security" Agents[266]

UNHCR, InterAid, and refugees themselves all acknowledged the presence of alleged security agents in Kampala. All parties spoke openly about the latters' attempts to infiltrate the offices working with refugees. Several Sudanese and Rwandan refugees told Human Rights Watch researchers that they had met security agents from their countries of origin who were waiting with the refugees at InterAid or at OPM.[267] These allegations were later confirmed by an official in the Ugandan government, who said to a Human Rights Watch researcher, "In some cases security agents pose as refugees, and we must identify these individuals."[268] Officials at InterAid also confirmed that they had received visits from security agents on several occasions, during which the agents asked InterAid to turn over confidential files (something InterAid assured Human Rights Watch that it consistently refuses to do).[269]

---

[263] Human Rights Watch interview with refugee, Kampala, Uganda, April 11, 2002.
[264] Human Rights Watch interview with UNHCR Uganda Representative (speaking at joint UNHCR/HRW Press Conference), Kampala, Uganda, April 16, 2002.
[265] See "UNHCR Warns Refugees," Monitor, (Kampala, Uganda) August 23, 2001.
[266] See note 87 above, discussing the use of the term "security agent" and "country of origin agent" in this report.
[267] Human Rights Watch interview with refugee, Kampala, Uganda, April 11, 2002.
[268] Human Rights Watch interview with government official, Kampala, Uganda, April 8, 2002.
[269] Human Rights Watch interview with InterAid, Kampala, Uganda, April 8, 2002.

A staff member of a local human rights organization also confirmed these reports to Human Rights Watch: "The Ugandan government cannot protect people living in Kampala. Many SPLA officers live in Kampala. They commit abductions and take young people back to Sudan. Unfortunately, the police send people with complaints to Old Kampala and to OPM, but Sudanese often meet the same people persecuting them at InterAid and at OPM. Therefore, people are not able to express their problems and some don't come forward at all because of fear."[270]

But these agents are not merely a threatening presence: occasionally they actively hunt and harass individual refugees. While pursuing its military and political objectives abroad, Uganda appears unwilling or unable to control these agents who are operating in Kampala. In some cases, these agents are alleged to be working with the Ugandan police or military. Since so much of this is linked to Uganda's foreign policy, Uganda's relations with three key neighboring countries will be described briefly in the following paragraphs, followed by several refugees' own experiences of harassment by country of origin agents operating in Uganda.

Uganda's Relations with Refugees' Countries of Origin
Rwanda

Relations between the Rwandan and Ugandan governments were close for several years after the Rwandan Patriotic Front (RPF) took power in Rwanda in 1994 and ended the genocide in which about 800,000 people died. The RPF had very close ties with the Ugandan government as many of its leaders came from the exiled Tutsi community in Uganda and had become an important force within Museveni's[271] rebel force, the National Resistance Movement, when it was still fighting against the previous government. As a result, many members of the elite in Rwanda look back on a period of military training in Uganda, and retain close links with the Ugandan military. Rwanda and Uganda joined forces in the DRC (then Zaire) in 1996 to help Laurent Kabila unseat Zairean leader Mobutu Sese Seko, but then jointly invaded the DRC two years later to fight on the side of anti-government rebels.

Over the past few years, tensions between the two governments have risen, however. Increasingly, Rwanda and Uganda are competing, as both governments attempt to maximize their regional influence, military control and economic gains from resource exploitation in the region, in particular in the DRC. Since 1999, Uganda and Rwanda have been supporting different armed opposition groups in the eastern DRC. Uganda sided with the Movement for the

[270] Human Rights Watch interview with NGO, Kampala, Uganda, April 11, 2002.
[271] Yoweri Museveni is the president of Uganda.

Liberation of Congo (MLC) and the smaller Congolese Rally for Democracy-Liberation Movement (RCD ML), while Rwanda continued to support the RCD's main arm, RCD-Goma.[272] The Rwandan-Ugandan conflict broke out most violently in military confrontations between the two armies in Kisangani in August 1999 and in May and June 2000, in which hundreds of civilians were killed. Rwanda managed to keep control over Kisangani, said to be a matter of lingering Ugandan resentment.[273]

There also seems to be an alienation between the leaders – Museveni and Kagame – and some of their aides, as the Ugandans tended to see the Rwandans as their protégées, but the Rwandans aimed to take on a more independent role. Despite intermittent efforts at improving relations, each side accuses the other of subversion. Uganda charges Rwanda with harboring its opponents and recruiting forces for two exiled Ugandan People's Defense Force (UPDF) soldiers who have vowed to attack Uganda, and with moving its troops into the DRC territory vacated by UPDF forces.[274] Rwanda complained in September 2001 that Uganda massed troops along its border (the UN rejected this allegation), and accuses Uganda of harboring inside the Mgahinga Park area of southwestern Uganda Rwandan Hutu rebels who might have been involved in the 1994 genocide in Rwanda, and of allowing them to operate in the DRC.[275]

Sudan

Uganda has been involved in Sudan's civil war since 1986, when the current Ugandan government came to power and began its support of the rebel Sudan People's Liberation Movement/Army (SPLA), which has fought the Sudanese government in Khartoum since 1983; since 1989 that government has been controlled by the Islamist political party the National Islamic Front (now National Congress). The SPLA favors a united, secular Sudan, in contrast to the Arab Islamist state now existing. The SPLA is based largely in the southern third of the country but has operations and bases in the Nuba Mountains and in Blue Nile state and other eastern areas of the country.

Kampala insists that its support of the SPLA has been moral, not military. In public comments, President Museveni has said that Uganda "cannot accept

---

[272] *See* note 244, above, for a short description of the RCD. *See* also "Uganda in Eastern DRC: Fueling Political and Ethnic Strife," Human Rights Watch, March 2001, http://www.hrw.org/reports/2001/drc/drc0301-03.htm.

[273] *See* Inter Press Service, "Deep-seated Animosity between Rwanda and Uganda," November 15, 2001.

[274] Xinhua News Agency, "Uganda Confirms Deployment of Troops near Rwanda," September 8, 2001.

[275] *See* Africa News Service, "Interahamwe Reported Present in Kampala," May 22, 2002.

the suppression of the southern Sudanese people."[276] But Ugandan observers say Uganda provides a haven for SPLA soldiers and at times involves itself directly in offensive actions.[277] Financial and other assistance is implied from comments by Ugandan members of Parliament in late 1999 and 2000.[278]

Kampala severed diplomatic ties with Khartoum in 1995 when a dispute broke out over arms supposedly hidden for the Lord's Resistance Army (LRA, a Ugandan rebel group) inside a Sudanese embassy building in Kampala. Uganda has accused Sudan of backing the LRA in its war against the Museveni government, and of harboring the LRA in camps close to the Ugandan border.[279] The LRA is known to abduct children from northern Uganda and force them to fight for the LRA.[280] Bomb blasts in Kampala and the discovery of arms shipments from Sudan have also been blamed on Khartoum.[281]

Some Ugandan Parliament members, along with Sudan's president, have alleged that Uganda's support of the SPLA is directly to blame for Sudan's support of LRA activity.[282] The two governments agreed in Nairobi in December 1999 through mediation of the Carter Center to refrain from sponsoring each other's rebel movements, and to restore diplomatic relations.[283] Sudan cut some support to the LRA, and the events of September 11, 2001 and the U.S. listing of the LRA as a "terrorist organization" speeded up the process of Sudan's distancing from the LRA. Lack of food supplies began to be noticeable, as the LRA turned to looting food from the southern Sudanese civilian population, many of them Acholi. The governments of Sudan and

---

[276] *See* Agence France-Presse, "Museveni Hits out at Sudan's Support of LRA," May 24, 1998
[277] Uganda assisted in the SPLA capture of the towns of Yei, Yirol, Rumbek, Tonj and others in Western Equatoria and Bahr El Ghazal in 1997. *See* "Global Trade, Local Impact: Arms Transfers to all Sides in the Civil War in Sudan," Human Rights Watch/Africa, vol. 10, No. 4 (A), August 1998, p. 46.
[278] *See* BBC Monitoring Service: Middle East, "Sudanese Rebel Leader Garang Welcomes Uganda-Sudan Accord," December 14, 1999; BBC Monitoring Service: Africa, "Parliament Asks Government to Stop Supporting Sudanese Rebels," December 11, 2000.
[279] *See* Agence France-Presse, "Uganda, Sudan Make Fresh Pledges Towards Normalizing Relations," September 27, 2000.
[280] *See* Human Rights Watch/Africa, The Scars of Death Children Abducted by the Lord's Resistance Army in Uganda, September 1997.
[281] *See* "Sudan in Strife: a Catalyst for Conflict," *Jane's Intelligence Review*, December 1, 1999
[282] *See* BBC Monitoring Service: Africa, "Parliament Asks Government to Stop Supporting Sudanese Rebels," December 11, 2000; Agence France-Presse, "Sudan's Beshir says Khartoum No Longer Backs Ugandan Rebels," August 20, 2001.
[283] *See* e.g. Agence France Presse, "Sudanese, Ugandan Presidents Agree to Stop Backing Rebels," December 8, 1999.

Uganda then reached an agreement whereby Sudan would allow the UPDF to enter Sudanese territory for the purpose of eliminating the LRA.

These overtures by Sudan to cut support to the LRA and allow the UPDF into southern Sudan to track down LRA rebels have gone unmatched by Uganda. The Ugandan operation in southern Sudan called "Operation Iron Fist" did not locate the LRA in Sudan; they fled to the Imatong Mountains in southern Sudan and then, eluding the UPDF, most of the LRA crossed over into northern Uganda a few months after the operation started, in May-June 2002. Afterwards, their attacks in northern Uganda started up again.

In April 2002, Khartoum and Kampala agreed to renew diplomatic ties at the ambassador level, and Uganda is trying to keep SPLA fighters from taking advantage of Uganda's presence in southern Sudan to attack Sudanese government forces.

The Democratic Republic of Congo (the DRC)

Uganda has been involved in the DRC's civil wars since helping Laurent Kabila and his Alliance of Democratic Forces for the Liberation of Congo-Zaire (ADFL) overthrow Mobutu Sese Seko in 1997. In late 1998, when Kabila tried to expel from the DRC Rwandan forces that had also helped him seize power, Uganda switched sides, invading the DRC together with Rwandan forces. The Ugandan government has cited security concerns for its involvement in the DRC, fearing attack by Sudan-backed insurgents operating in the DRC's northeast. Uganda's army headquarters in the DRC are in the Bunia region, where it trains the military wing of the RCD-LM.[284] The UPDF has trained children, tortured political opponents and illegally detained political leaders.[285]

Ugandan military activity has gone further than helping the RCD-LM fight the government forces of current DRC President Joseph Kabila. The UPDF reportedly controls the country's northeast, even setting up a separate administrative province, Ituri, for which it has named local leaders. The UPDF has recruited fighters from the area's Hema and Lentu ethnic groups, reportedly siding with the Hema as they fight the Lentu over land issues, a conflict which has killed tens of thousands of people and displaced 200,000. Fighting between the Hema and Lentu and division among RCD-ML leaders have allowed Uganda to continue to exploit natural resources in the DRC. Ugandan military

---

[284] "Letter to Museveni," Human Rights Watch, August 23, 2000, www.hrw.org/press/2000/08/drc-tr0822.htm.
[285] See Human Rights Watch/Africa, *Uganda in Eastern DRC: Fueling Political and Ethnic Strife*, Vol. 13, No. 2(A), March 2001.

and political officials profit from the extraction and sale of timber, coffee, gold and coltan[286] from Ituri.[287]

On September 7, 2002, the governments of Uganda and Rwanda agreed to withdraw their troops from eastern DRC and to normalize relations. Under the agreement, Uganda was granted five days to withdraw its forces from the cities of Beni and Gbadolite, and one hundred days to withdraw from the city of Bunia. As of early October, Ugandan and Rwandan troop withdrawals proceeded according to schedule but concerns were raised about the vacuum they left behind, causing clashes between rebel groups in the region and tens of thousands of civilians to become internally displaced.[288]

Refugee Accounts of Harassment by Security Agents
Rwanda

Leonard N. is a twenty-year-old refugee from Kigali, Rwanda. His parents and brothers, except one who fled to South Africa, were killed during the 1994 genocide. Leonard explained to a Human Rights Watch researcher that his family had been very wealthy, with several cars and a large home. However, a Rwandan military major occupied his home and took his family's cars and other property. Since he was alone in Kigali and very young, Leonard did not challenge the officers. Instead, he continued his education at a boarding school where he had been enrolled prior to the genocide. Eventually, he ran out of money and was encouraged by his teachers to ask the major for rent. Leonard's attempts to recover rent from the major led to several altercations with the military. Eventually, his teachers advised him that his life was at risk and they purchased a bus ticket for him to flee to Uganda. He arrived in Kampala on September 17, 2001, registered at the police, went to InterAid for his interview, and was refused refugee status all within two weeks of his arrival. His story implies collaboration between the Rwandan and Ugandan military. He explained what happened:

---

[286] "Coltan" is the abbreviation for "columbite-tantalite," a heat-resistant metallic ore that can hold a high electrical charge. It is used in the manufacture of circuit boards for small electronics such as laptops, cell phones and pagers. *See* "What is Coltan?" ABC News on line, available at www.abcnews.go.com (last visited July 26, 2002).
[287]*See* Human Rights Watch/Africa, *Uganda in Eastern DRC: Fueling Political and Ethnic Strife*, Vol. 13, No. 2(A), March 2001.
[288] *See* e.g. "Kabila and Museveni Sign Troop Withdrawal Protocol," IRIN News, September 9, 2002; "Ugandan Troop Pullout Near Completion," IRIN News, September 25, 2002; "DRC: Shabunda Reported Calm Following Mayi-Mayi Takeover," IRIN News, October 4, 2002.

After only two weeks of me being here in Kampala, the major learned that I was here. He sent intelligence [agents] here to look for me. I was easy to find because I had to sleep out in the open outside of Old Kampala Police Station. Some people came to ask for me there. Some other Rwandans knew that the people asking for me were army officers. They warned me to leave that area and not sleep there any more. I snuck away very early on the morning of October 24, 2001. Before I left they gathered Ush.1,000 [U.S.$.55] for me so that I could transport myself to [another] neighborhood of Kampala. However, when I got there the same people picked me up off the street. They had vehicles behind them and pushed me into one of the vehicles. I was packed in the vehicle with many soldiers. They kept asking me questions and beat me up in the vehicle. One used barbed wire to beat me over and over on the legs. He cut me very badly on my leg. My teeth were also broken from that beating. [He showed a Human Rights Watch researcher his broken teeth and a scar on his leg]. They drove me to Kololo Army Base, where they have a military intelligence office, for eleven days. On the eleventh day they wrote a letter to the Central Police that I should be deported with immediate effect.

They picked me up in a tinted army vehicle [i.e. with tinted windows] and took me to Central Police, where I was detained for thirty-one days. At Central Police they beat me so hard and I even still have pains in my back from those beatings. During the time they held me they brought some Rwandan Embassy staff to Central Police, and those staff took pictures of me. That happened on about November 18, 2001.

I was so frightened in prison…. they eventually released me on April 12, 2001 but the police took the whole bag of my clothes and my glasses too. I still cannot see properly.

….I cannot go to Rwanda – they will kill me. The authorities here have completely rejected me, including UNHCR. Even the government of Uganda cannot offer me protection because they are the ones who are working with the Rwandans. I have

no place to go—I am just like the air blowing around, no place
to stay...[289]

Another Rwandan refugee, André G.,[290] was afraid for his safety in
Kampala because of his past criticism of the Rwandan government. André had
been employed by a government institution in Rwanda and had been a member
of the Rwandan Patriotic Front[291] (RPF, or FPR in French) since the early 1990s.
Because he criticized the human rights record of the RPF in an internal meeting,
he was abducted and beaten. At the internal meeting he had said that the RPF is
the brain ["cerveau"] of everything that happens in Rwanda, so it is also
responsible for some things going wrong, ["Ce qui ne va pas, cela tombe sur la
tete du FPR."]. André had suffered many problems in securing adequate refugee
protection from other governments before he finally reached Uganda.[292]   On
September 19, 2001, a former colleague from government service called André
on the telephone and told him that his situation was precarious. He told him to
come back to Rwanda, otherwise he would be returned by force. On September
21, 2001, the same former colleague and another agent of the Rwandan
government came to see him. André was very frightened about this and alerted
the Special Branch but they said they could not do anything.

After these incidents with his former colleague, André informed InterAid
about his security concerns but they said they could not protect him. They told
him, "that is the job of the Ugandan police." [293] An official at InterAid said, "it is
the government that currently looks after you." [294] But, even after subsequent
visits André could not find protection from the police. Two male agents came to
his home and asked for him by name on March 26, 2002. He told them his name
was not André, and they went away. Then again on March 27, 2002, one of the
men came back but André was out. Later that night, at approximately 4:00 a.m.,
the men came and knocked on the gate of the compound saying they were

---

[289] Human Rights Watch interview with refugee, Kampala, Uganda, April 11, 2002.
[290] Human Rights Watch interview with refugee, Kampala, Uganda, April 11, 2002.
[291] The Rwandan Patriotic Front defeated the civilian and military authorities responsible
for the 1994 genocide in Rwanda. In their drive for victory and to end the genocide, the
RPF killed thousands, including noncombatants as well as government troops and
members of militia. Today, the Rwandan Patriotic Front is the dominant party in the
government. See Human Rights Watch/Africa, Leave None to Tell the Story, March
1999; "No Contest in Rwandan Elections," Human Rights Watch Press Release, March 9,
2001.
[292] In order to protect his identity, Human Rights Watch has kept confidential the details
of André's experience abroad (in countries outside of Africa), which involved serious
violations of his rights as a refugee.
[293] Human Rights Watch interview with refugee, Kampala, Uganda, April 11, 2002.
[294] Human Rights Watch interview with refugee, Kampala, Uganda, April 11, 2002.

looking for the Rwandan who lived there. The people in André's house refused to open the door. The next morning he reported the incident at Old Kampala Police Station. The police said, "it is difficult to protect you." [295]

Olivier C. is a twenty-one-year-old Rwandan refugee whose father and sister were killed in the 1994 genocide. Some of his surviving family members had since been involved in high profile opposition activities. For very specific reasons, Olivier C. was afraid that his life was in danger in Rwanda and he traveled by bus from Kigali to Kampala. After two weeks of sleeping outside Old Kampala Police Station, Olivier was picked up off the street, detained in Kampala and repeatedly beaten by Rwandan agents over the course of eleven months. This happened after Uganda and Rwanda started supporting different rebel groups in the DRC. The high tensions between the two governments at this time suggest that Ugandan authorities were not complicit and were unaware of what was transpiring with Olivier C. He told a Human Rights Watch researcher what happened:

> I arrived in Uganda on April 13, 2000. When I arrived, the employees from the embassy of Rwanda found me near the Old Kampala Police station. They arrested me immediately and kept me from April 2000 until June 2001. They drove me to a big house that had a smaller shed in the back. They immediately put me in that small house and locked me in. The whole compound had a gate around it too and there were always guards there. They forced me to stay there because they had so many questions to ask me and because they wanted to deport me. They wouldn't let me wash, but they did give me food and drink. They also gave me times to go to the toilet and some times to walk in the yard. I slept on the floor with only one blanket on cartons. The area I was in was a place with many houses. The one house I was in back of was just a big house, but I cannot describe the front of it very well because I only saw it one or two times during that whole year.

> So many people came to ask questions during all those months about my [family] and about the government in Rwanda. They asked, "where is your [family member involved in political opposition]?" I said he is in the U.S., but they would never believe me, and they would say that he was here in Kampala.

---

[295] Human Rights Watch interview with refugee, Kampala, Uganda, April 11, 2002.

They wanted me to show them where [he] was. Every time they didn't like my answers they beat me on the feet to get me to say where my [family member] was—they beat me with a long stick. They also beat me with their hands. When I got sick they would take me to a doctor, but always with a guard.

One day they let me go with a guard to a tap to wash my clothes. When I had my clothes off except for some shorts and was washing them, the guard went to get beer and cigarettes at a shop. When I saw him start to walk into that shop I just dropped the clothes I was washing and ran from there and I left my clothes behind. The guard had a pistol, but he didn't see me run away. I ran all the way to InterAid. I slept for a weekend outside InterAid and then I went to the police on the Monday.[296]

The DRC

The RCD has an active presence in Kampala. Several refugees interviewed by Human Rights Watch mentioned spotting agents they were familiar with on the streets of Kampala. One agent in particular, Telexie Rubuye [his real name], an RCD security agent responsible for security in South Kivu province, had been spotted by several refugees and had stopped and questioned one refugee.[297]

A Congolese refugee, Angeline Y., had worked for a local human rights NGO in Goma. In November 2000, she was arrested when doing research in Masisi about illegal detention cases.[298] When she stayed overnight in the area, soldiers followed her and tried to arrest her. But local people protected her and told the soldiers to come back the next day. She then fled to Goma, where she was still pursued. Three days after the first attempt to arrest her, some soldiers were waiting at her home in Goma. Other soldiers went to her sister's home to look for her. Angeline fled for Kampala and arrived there in December 2000. Shortly after Angeline arrived in Kampala, she was told that a Rwandan soldier had come twice to UNHCR to ask for her. His name was Mundeki, one of the RCD soldiers from Masisi who had threatened her.

---

[296] Human Rights Watch interview with refugee, Kampala, Uganda, April 15, 2002.
[297] Human Rights Watch interview with refugee, Kampala, Uganda, April 12, 2002.
[298] Angeline had documented the use of open pit prisons where detainees were held in holes dug into the earth, in the town of Mweso in Masisi province. One of the open pit prisons was right next to a military base. She spoke to the father of a detainee who died in such a prison and to a friendly Hutu soldier who gave her names of people detained there. Human Rights watch interview with refugee, Kampala, Uganda, April 10, 2002.

The fact that the UPDF has been fighting in the DRC has created complicated security problems for some Congolese.   Kibunda H. came to Kampala in 1999.   Prior to his flight, Kibunda's wife had been abducted by a group of UPDF officers, a practice that was common in the war in the DRC.[299] On September 19, 2000 the UPDF officers came to Kampala with the women. An article later appearing in the Ugandan press explained that the women were brought to Kampala with their UPDF "husbands" who had been taking rest and recreation in Katakwi in eastern Uganda.[300] Purely by chance, Kibunda H. saw his wife one day on the street. The two were reunited and she went home with him that day.

> Since that time, the man who brought my wife here is after me. He came to my house to kill me once. I hid myself and the man spoke with my friends. Another time a man came to my house to ask questions about me but again I just hid myself and my wife—I never came out. At UNHCR they understand my problem. But I can only leave my house at night…. The security problem for me is eternal—it is ongoing. The man who took my wife accused me of being with the Mai-Mai[301] at the police in March 2001. Because of this I never can go to the police for help with my security problems.[302]

Refugees from the territories of the DRC controlled by Uganda until October 2002 are under the control of the same authorities responsible for their original persecution.   Human rights activists and other prominent community leaders are frequently followed by security services of the RCD-Goma, and sometimes threatened. The situation is so difficult for some refugees that they are terrified to leave their shelters. For example, Celestin R. was a human rights activist in Congo and fled after having several run-ins with security officers there. He fled to Uganda in early January 2001, and very soon afterwards gave an interview on French radio regarding the use of child soldiers in Congo. After the interview he received threatening phone calls at his home. Subsequently,

---

[299] The U.S. State Department reported that in 2000, RPA, Ugandan troops, and RCD rebels all abducted many young women from the villages that they raided, mainly in the Kivu Provinces. *See* U.S. Department of State, *Country Reports on Human Rights Practices – Rwanda 2000*, February 23, 2001 (available at http://www.state.gov/g/drl/rls/hrrpt/2000/af/720.htm.).
[300] *See* "UPDF Congo Wives Want Refugee Status," *Monitor*, (Kampala, Uganda) August 16, 2001.
[301] *See* note 112, above, for a short definition of the Mai-Mai.
[302] Human Rights Watch interview with refugee, Kampala, Uganda, April 8, 2002.

RCD agents inquired about him at one of the church shelters for refugees. On the night before Human Rights Watch's interview with Celestin, he had detected people outside his shelter and heard knocking at the door. He and others living with him made a great deal of noise to scare the prowlers away. He said he is so afraid of exposing himself to risk that he almost never leaves his home ("Je préfère rester a la maison que de m'exposer").[303]

Ugandan Military and Police Harassment

Given Uganda's role in the region, Ugandan authorities occasionally work in tandem with security agents to harass refugees. Or, in the case of Congolese suspected of opposition to the occupation of eastern DRC by Ugandan forces, the refugees may have continued to be targeted by the UPDF inside Uganda. In other cases, refugees are accused of being responsible (by virtue of being Congolese) for the deaths of Ugandan soldiers in the DRC.

For example, on March 17, 2002 a male local government leader (who was the chairman for the local district designated as "LC1") came to the home of Congolese human rights activist and refugee Angeline Y. (introduced previously) and asked for her papers, which she showed him. He accused her landlady, an elderly Ugandan woman, of housing refugees. He came back with another man who was armed, and asked the landlady to chase Angeline away. On March 19, 2002 the LC1 chairman again came to her house with six other men, his advisors. They said, "Ugandans die in your country."[304] They threatened to beat Angeline and asked for her papers again. They said, "She could kill someone—you cannot know." [305] A Human Rights Watch researcher later learned that Angeline escaped another attack on July 23, 2002.[306]

The Ugandan Military

The involvement of the Ugandan military in the war in the DRC has meant that once they are back in Uganda, soldiers have attempted to intimidate individual Congolese they assumed to be in opposition to their military presence (up to late September 2002) in the DRC. As a result, the Ugandan military has been implicated in several security incidents[307] with Congolese refugees.

---

[303] Human Rights Watch interview with refugee, Kampala, Uganda, April 10, 2002.
[304] Human Rights Watch interview with refugee, Kampala, Uganda, April 10, 2002.
[305] Human Rights Watch interview with refugee, Kampala, Uganda, April 10, 2002.
[306] Human Rights Watch telephone interview with colleagues of Angeline, London, U.K., July 25, 2002, and correspondence received from Angeline detailing the attack on August 8, 2002.
[307] Another case of military harassment involved Kamara S., a deacon in the Baptist Church in Kisangani who had worked for a human rights organization in that city. His human rights work had put his life and safety under threat, so he fled to Uganda. He told

On June 9, 2002, Celestin R. (introduced previously) and Anatole B.,[308] both from the DRC, were arrested by Ugandan army soldiers as they were walking down the street in Makindye, a neighborhood of Kampala. Celestin was on his way to church and Anatole was on his way home after visiting Celestin. When they passed the nearby military camp in Makindye, they were called in by several soldiers and ordered to sit in a small room, and verbally threatened. The soldiers accused the refugees of political activities, and of being agents who had "plans to destabilize Uganda."

The refugees were suspected of being RCD spies, an accusation that lacks any basis. The soldiers threatened to take the refugees to another place where they would force them to reveal their "real identities." They also confiscated Celestin's mobile phone, and as he tried to resist this, they threw him against a wall. After some disagreement among themselves, the soldiers released the refugees but kept their UNHCR protection letters, OPM protection letters, and other important documents such as an address book.

The Ugandan Police

The Ugandan police have also been accused of committing violence against refugees. At times refugees are not specifically targeted, and violence suffered in custody is no different to that experienced by Ugandan nationals. However, sometimes the police violence appears to be linked to government suspicions about certain nationalities of refugees. Asylum seekers and refugees may wind up in custody after being individually arrested, but most often they are detained after being caught up in one of Uganda's immigration "swoops" (a word commonly used in Uganda).

Uganda regularly uses swoops as a method of identifying, detaining and deporting illegal immigrants. In March 2002, when the Ugandan government arrested and detained illegal immigrants, a senior immigration officer said that they would be locked up in police cells pending disposal of their cases, which normally end in imprisonment, fines, and deportation.[309] In 1998 and 2000 the government engaged in similar actions to collect and deport illegal

---

Human Rights Watch that on February 1, 2001, four Ugandan soldiers arrested him in Kampala and took him to a private house. They asked for his papers. They told him that they were from security. He showed them all his papers and also the membership card of his association. There was a witness to his arrest, and so a Ugandan priest was alerted and came to negotiate his liberation. He was released at around 2:00 a.m. the next day. Human Rights Watch interview with refugee, Kampala, Uganda, April 10, 2002.
[308] Human Rights Watch correspondence and telephone conversations with Celestin R. and Anatole B., June 10-11, 2002.
[309] See Africa News Service, "City Swoop Nets Illegal Immigrants," March 21, 2002.

immigrants.[310] It is not clear whether any of the detainees in these operations were asylum seekers or recognized refugees, or whether the Ugandan government, in deporting any of the immigrants, was guilty of refoulement.

In a recent swoop conducted in August 2001, the Ugandan police were accused of brutality and sexual violence against a group of detainees, some of whom were asylum seekers and refugees. Béatrice K.[311] is a Rwandan refugee who fled from Kigali with her six children in 2000, and was part of a group of several Rwandan refugees who were arrested during the August 2001 swoop. In an interview with a Human Rights Watch researcher, she estimated that she was one of eighteen people arrested and detained at Kololo military base. She told Human Rights Watch that the Ugandan police came there with several vehicles. They beat her, and kicked her repeatedly in her middle torso, harming her bladder. After the beatings she had blood in her urine for three days. She also received kicks on her legs and feet and showed a Human Rights Watch researcher scars from these beatings.

Béatrice told a Human Rights Watch researcher that she and her fellow detainees were "thrown like manioc[312] sacks into the car."[313] They were brought to Kiira Road police station. Contemporary press reports confirm that seventeen "asylum seekers" were arrested and in police custody at Kiira Road at this time.[314] Béatrice was detained at that station from August 21 to 31, 2001. Béatrice told a Human Rights Watch researcher she was also beaten at the Kiira police station with planks ["planches"] of wood with nails. Children, women, and men were held together. Asked whether the men assaulted the women, she told a Human Rights Watch researcher "The policemen harassed us every day. A woman was taken and then raped."[315]

Paul M.[316] is a Burundian refugee who arrived in Kampala on March 6, 2001. He is from Muyinga, a northern province in Burundi. He was a brick

---

[310] See BBC Monitoring Service: Africa, "Immigration Department Swoop Nets Over 70 Illegal Immigrants," December 14, 2000; Agence France-Presse, "Ugandan Forces Make Kampala Arrests in Anti-Rebel Swoop," September 28, 1998.

[311] Prior to coming to Uganda, Béatrice was detained in Rwanda in April 1996 and in October 1999 because her husband was a member of the FAR (former Rwandan army) and has disappeared, apparently at the hands of the authorities—as has been the case with several other ex-FAR members from Rwanda.

[312] Manioc, otherwise known as cassava, is a carbohydrate-rich tuber, the pulp of which is removed, washed and roasted, creating a coarse meal or flour that is often stored in sacks.

[313] Human Rights Watch interview with refugee, Kampala, Uganda, April 11, 2002.

[314] See "Police Holds Seventeen Asylum Seekers," Monitor, (Kampala, Uganda) August 27, 2001.

[315] Human Rights Watch interview with refugee, Kampala, Uganda, April 11, 2002.

[316] Human Rights Watch interview with refugee, Kampala, Uganda, April 11, 2002.

maker but he was recruited by force into the army. He deserted after one month and fled Burundi for Uganda. On November 19, 2001, he was stopped at around 9:00 p.m. by Ugandans who asked for his name and said he must be Rwandan.[317] They searched him and beat him badly. He screamed during the beatings, and eventually he fell on the ground. The Ugandans took him to Old Kampala police station. Two policemen joined the group detaining him and they beat him as well. They kicked him with their boots and hit him with the handle of a gun.

Paul told a Human Rights Watch researcher that he believes that he was arrested and beaten because the Ugandans mistook him for a Rwandan. Paul was then put into a lockup and they took all his papers from him, including his UNHCR documents. He was released shortly afterwards. Paul sought help from the government-based Ugandan Human Rights Commission (UGHR), which agreed to take up his case. He was also referred by the UGHR to the African Centre for Torture Victims where he was treated and a complaint for the police was prepared. As of April 4, 2002 no action had been taken on his complaint and the UGHR sent a reminder to the police asking about his case.

Conclusion

While it is undoubtedly a major challenge for Uganda's police and security agencies to control the activities of country of origin agents in Kampala and for the government to find the necessary resources for the task, Uganda's involvement in conflicts in the region contributes to the problem. Most worrying is the fact that in some cases the government of Uganda is not even interested in stopping security agents—or even its own military and police—from trailing and harassing refugees. This is particularly true for Congolese refugees from the areas of the DRC that were until October 2002 under UPDF control who find themselves when they reach Uganda under the authority of the same power that had persecuted them at home.

Responsibility for Protection Problems

Asylum seekers, refugees recognized under the Refugee Convention, and *prima facie* refugees must be guaranteed certain basic human rights. The rights

---

[317] In November 2001, the Rwandan government accused Uganda of arbitrarily arresting about 100 Rwandans and Ugandans of Rwandan origin. The statement released by the Rwandan embassy in Kampala denounced "arbitrary arrests, detention in alarming conditions and in some cases torture of Rwandans living in Uganda." *See* "Kigali Condemns Arbitrary Arrest in Uganda," *Monitor*, (Kampala, Uganda) November 20, 2001. This statement was released at a time when relations between Uganda and Rwanda were at a low point, with each government accusing the other of supporting, training and arming dissidents planning to launch coups d'etat. *See* also text accompanying notes 271-275 above, describing the tensions between Uganda and Rwanda at this time

most relevant to the protection problems documented by Human Rights Watch in Uganda include: the right to freedom of speech, the right not to be tortured, the right to liberty and not to be arbitrarily detained, the right to security of person, and the right to freedom of movement.[318]

Article 19(3) of the ICCPR, to which Uganda is a party, provides aliens with the right to freely express opinions; and Article 21 provides for the right of peaceful assembly. The Human Rights Committee, which is charged with the responsibility to interpret and monitor the ICCPR, has explicitly stated that "[aliens] have the right to hold opinions and to express them. Aliens receive the benefit of the right of peaceful assembly and of freedom of association."[319] While Uganda and UNHCR are allowed to limit these rights of refugees when public order is under threat, or when a particular demonstration is likely to lead to violence, it is not apparent that the August 21, 2001 demonstration outside the offices of InterAid threatened public order or was likely to lead to violence.

The activities of country of origin security agents are also the concern of the government of Uganda. Under international law, Uganda cannot turn a blind eye to the activities of such agents.[320] The government of Uganda is also responsible when its own police or military agents conspire to commit, encourage or are significantly involved in human rights abuses themselves.[321] In addition, Uganda must allow refugees who have had their rights abused the same access as nationals to the police or to seek redress in the courts.[322] Uganda has begun to sensitize some police officers, particularly those working in Old Kampala, about refugee protection. However, as discussed more fully above, Uganda has strategic interests in the countries of origin of refugees that

---

[318] *See* ICCPR Articles 7, 9, and 12, respectively. *See* also "Personal Security of Refugees," ExCom Conclusion No. 72, 1993.

[319] U.N. Human Rights Committee, "The Rights of Aliens under the International Covenant on Civil and Political Rights," General Comment No. 15, 1986, para. 7.

[320] The requirement to "ensure" human rights, set forth in Article 2 of the ICCPR, means that governments cannot turn a blind eye to human rights abuses committed in their territory by other actors. *See*, e.g. Human Rights Committee, General Comment No. 2(13) and 3(13), UN Doc. A/36/40 (1981).

[321] For example, CAT applies to torture inflicted by or with the acquiescence of "a public official or other person acting in an official capacity." CAT, Article 1(1) December 10, 1984.

[322] Refugees recognized under the Refugee Convention or the OAU Convention enjoy the same rights as nationals in every respect with the exception of political participation. These rights include: equality before the courts, protection against discrimination, protection against arbitrary expulsion, the right to a fair trial, the rights to freedom of expression, association and peaceful assembly. Of course, these refugees must also receive the most fundamental protection they are entitled to as refugees – the right not to be returned to countries where their lives or freedom may be in danger (called non-refoulement).

sometimes prevent the police and security personnel from responding adequately or appropriately to such incidents. At other times, the police themselves are to blame, leaving refugees without a safe place to turn to.

Except for high-profile refugees, who are usually referred to UNHCR for resettlement,[323] the Ugandan government is reluctant to accept full responsibility for providing protection to refugees at risk in Kampala. Instead it chooses to blame UNHCR for not doing enough to protect high-risk security cases. The Office of the Prime Minister told a Human Rights Watch researcher, "When a refugee has serious security problems, we have to remind UNHCR that their core mandate is to protect refugees. We are unable to extend physical protection to all of them, and sometimes we refer them for resettlement. But, ultimately we rely on UNHCR to accomplish this. Normally, UNHCR doesn't listen to our referrals on security or medical grounds."[324] Another official in OPM put it this way, "A major question I would like to ask is: 'why doesn't UNHCR take medium term measures to take care of refugees with security problems?'"[325]

UNHCR is a convenient scapegoat when the presence of certain refugees compromises Uganda's military or political objectives in the region. Uganda cannot pick and choose which refugees it wants to protect – by doing so the government is failing to fulfill its obligations under the Refugee Convention and the OAU Refugee Convention, and is putting refugees' lives at risk.

At the same time, UNHCR asserts that the Ugandan government is not doing enough to protect refugees. In an interview with a Human Rights Watch researcher, UNHCR in Uganda noted that, "The security of refugees is the responsibility of governments, and the government of Uganda is equipped to deal with the security of refugees."[326] A UNHCR official in Uganda insisted that, "we need to make the government accountable for [the security of refugees].... they are overlooking the role of the police to protect [the refugees]."[327] An example of how the security concerns of refugees are shuttled between the government of Uganda and UNHCR is presented in Annex D, below.

---

[323] A Ugandan government official told a Human Rights Watch researcher that "high-profile asylum seekers are dealt with expeditiously." Human Rights Watch interview with Ugandan government official, Kampala, Uganda, April 8, 2002.
[324] Human Rights Watch interview with Ugandan government official, Kampala, Uganda, April 8, 2002.
[325] Human Rights Watch interview with Ugandan government official, Kampala, Uganda, April 13, 2002.
[326] Human Rights Watch interview with UNHCR official, Kampala, Uganda, April 8, 2002.
[327] Human Rights Watch interview with UNHCR official, Kampala, Uganda, April 8, 2002.

While the government does need to do more to guarantee the protection of refugees whose lives are in danger in Uganda, Human Rights Watch also found that UNHCR is failing in some of its protection functions. UNHCR is not actively tracking or responding to the individual incidents of insecurity experienced by refugees on a daily basis and documented in this report. Refugees are unable to access the office to report on beatings or other harassment. Even local human rights groups experience problems accessing UNHCR or convincing UNHCR to intervene with the Ugandan government on behalf of refugees. The agency lacks sufficient staff to be able to visit refugees in custody or intervene with authorities in cases that are not high profile.

In addition, Human Rights Watch interviewed several women refugees and their children who were vulnerable to abuse because UNHCR had not identified them as at-risk individuals and provided them with safe housing when they were interviewed at InterAid's offices.

The failure to identify any of these at-risk groups could be improved if InterAid were better resourced to provide adequate screening and service delivery functions. UNHCR could also periodically deploy staff out to the areas where refugees live to learn about at-risk refugees and monitor their situation.

Finally, the agency could take a more interventionist role in situations (as it has with high-profile cases) where refugees are detained by the government of Uganda, or are subject to abuse at the hands of security agents. One obvious function the agency could play would be to secure refugees' early release from detention and refer more of these cases for resettlement.

REFUGEE STATUS DETERMINATION IN UGANDA

Uganda, unlike Kenya, plays an active role in assessing the status of refugee applicants. Uganda's major piece of domestic legislation is the Control of Alien Refugees Act (CARA), which was enacted in 1960 before Uganda acceded to the Refugee Convention.[328] CARA grants the "Minister in charge" the power to create a definition of refugee by statutory instrument (or regulation).[329] Most of the remainder of CARA is focused upon what the title implies—controlling the presence of refugees in Uganda through limiting their freedom of movement. CARA also allows the minister in charge to appoint a director of refugees.

Uganda has developed a largely unregulated set of administrative practices for assessing the status of refugees. The Directorate of Refugees developed these between 1960 and the late 1980s. Prior to 1998, the Directorate of Refugees was located within the Ministry of Local Government. However, in 1998 the Ugandan government shifted responsibility for refugees from the Ministry of Local Government to the new Ministry of Disasters and Emergency Preparedness, which is located within the Office of the Prime Minister (OPM). This restructuring reflects a desire on the part of the Ugandan government to centralize the management of refugee affairs in Uganda.[330] Within the Office of the Prime Minister, the Minister of Disasters and Emergency Preparedness oversees the work of the Commissioner for Refugees and the Senior Settlement Officer in the Refugee Directorate.

Uganda's parliament has been considering draft refugee legislation for the past two years. The current Bill would greatly improve the legal protections afforded to refugees in Uganda. The Bill would institute regularized procedures for determining the status of refugees, and the definitions and procedures applied would largely fulfill Uganda's obligations under international law. The Bill would require that the reasons for refusing status be provided to applicants in writing, and that applicants or their advocates may appear before the Refugee Eligibility Committee during appeals. In addition, the Bill provides for all of the rights and obligations of refugees as set forth in international law. The Bill also guarantees the same rights to refugees regardless of whether they are recognized through individual procedures, or through *prima facie* recognition.

---

[328] Uganda acceded to the Refugee Convention and its Related Protocol on September 27, 1976.
[329] *See* CARA, Section 3(1).
[330] *See*, e.g. Tania Kaiser, *UNHCR's Withdrawal From Kiryandongo: Anatomy Of A Handover*, October 2000 (available at http://www.unhcr.ch./refworld/pubs/pubon.htm.).

Perhaps most interestingly, the Bill guarantees the freedom of movement rights of refugees, "especially for the purpose of study, professional training, gainful employment, voluntary repatriation and resettlement in another country." Although it is not clear how this provision would be interpreted, in order to avoid any doubt, it would greatly improve the Bill to include more "purposes" for which freedom of movement would be allowed (see recommendations in this report) and to clarify through what procedures refugees may seek to fulfill one of these "purposes." It is hoped that the Bill will be adopted in 2003.

Under the current process, there are at least four and up to six steps in the process of seeking asylum in Uganda, depending on the complexity of the case. Asylum seekers first register with the police, then they interview with counselors at InterAid, then they are interviewed by UNHCR and finally, they are interviewed by OPM. If the case cannot be decided at the level of OPM, the asylum seeker must interview with the Special Branch (the security arm of the Ugandan police), and have her case finally determined by the Refugee Eligibility Committee (REC, a panel of government officials). The following sections examine the role of each of these entities in more detail. While these descriptions may give the impression that the processing of asylum seekers is orderly and clearly understood by all participants, there are several problems that will be addressed below.

Registration

The Aliens Registration and Control Act [ARCA] requires that "every alien" register "within thirty days of his arrival in Uganda," and that the Minister in charge designate any immigration office or police station "to be registration centers."[331] Every asylum seeker arriving in Kampala soon learns that, in fact, she must register at Old Kampala Police Station. Most asylum seekers go there to register within the first month of their arrival. For example, Zola R., a twenty-year-old Congolese woman, explained what she did when she arrived, alone, from the DRC.

> When I arrived here I didn't know anybody so I just stayed at the bus station. I met a woman there who was Congolese. Her name was Binta. I talked with her a lot and she let me stay with her for two weeks. She gave me information on how to go to the police as a refugee. I got information together for two weeks. Then, the refugees showed me that police station and I went there to tell my story in late May or early June.[332]

---

[331] See ARCA, Article 1(1); and Article 4(1).
[332] Human Rights Watch interview with refugee, Kampala, Uganda, April 15, 2002.

Refugees who wait for several months before going to Old Kampala Police Station may face problems in their status interviews. UNHCR informed a Human Rights Watch researcher that "[w]e take the position that 'within a reasonable time' refugees should register themselves with the police. If you stay for such a long time without registering, it cuts down on your credibility."[333]

Although there is only one police officer doing registration interviews each day, and sometimes asylum seekers have to wait a few days to be registered, Human Rights Watch did not receive complaints about delays during this part of the process. The police officer in charge of refugee registration at Old Kampala told Human Rights Watch, "I usually take four or five stories each day, but some days I take as many as ten."[334]

The registration interviews are generally short, and focus mainly on biographical information about each individual asylum seeker, albeit two refugees interviewed by Human Rights Watch with particularly complicated cases had been interrogated by the police for several days.[335] The reasons for flight are discussed, but not in any detail.

David Obot, the Executive Director of InterAid, explained the rationale for involving the police in registration. He explained to a Human Rights Watch researcher that it was important to involve the police because: 1) some refugees are criminals; 2) some refugees who need protection need to be able to go to the police; and 3) involving the police demystifies the refugees' fear of the police and gets police involved in refugee protection. He said, "We try to inform them that interaction with the government is important. It is because of the need to involve the government that we developed the program in which refugees register with the police."[336] While Human Rights Watch questions the focus on the criminality of refugees, our research did reveal that many of the officers at Old Kampala are sensitive about the rights and problems of refugees. At the same time, however, this sensitivity has not permeated all of Uganda's police, since officers have also seriously abused the rights of refugees, including one violent incident that occurred at Old Kampala police station and was documented by Human Rights Watch.[337]

---

[333] Human Rights Watch interview with UNHCR protection officer, Kampala, Uganda, April 8, 2002.
[334] Human Rights Watch interview with deputy officer, Old Kampala Police Station, Kampala, Uganda, April 9, 2002.
[335] Human Rights Watch interviews with refugees, Kampala, Uganda, April 9, 2002.
[336] Human Rights Watch interview with InterAid, Kampala, Uganda, April 8, 2002.
[337] See text accompanying note 316, above.

Intake Interview with Social Workers at InterAid

In no more than a few days after registration with the police at Old Kampala, asylum seekers are brought to InterAid for an interview with one of that organization's counselors. This aspect of the process is not directly a part of status determination, but is used to identify at-risk asylum seekers or those with acute assistance needs. It is significant that UNHCR in Kampala (in contrast to UNHCR in Nairobi) was sensitive to the need to identify at-risk refugees, and therefore inserted this step into the process. InterAid explained which services the social workers might refer asylum seekers to as a result of the intake interview:

> At the second interview here at InterAid with intake counselors we identify women with children, the seriously ill, unaccompanied minors, and people with security problems. We provide emergency assistance—either cash, medical assistance, [or] placements in security houses. [338]

However, it was not evident to Human Rights Watch that all at-risk individuals do indeed receive the necessary assistance or referrals as a result of their interviews at InterAid. Four of the seventy refugees interviewed by Human Rights Watch in Kampala had received any assistance as a result of the intake interviews. UNHCR reported assisting only two hundred and seventy-four "security and medical cases, women-at-risk and special protection cases" in 2001.[339]

Interview with UNHCR Protection Officer

After the asylum seeker has been interviewed by one of InterAid's intake counsellors, he or she is interviewed by UNHCR. This is the first time that the merits of the individual case for asylum are considered in any detail, and the UNHCR interview is held usually a few days after the InterAid interview.

UNHCR protection officers spend anywhere from twenty minutes to several days assessing the merits of a particular case. Once UNHCR has seen an individual applicant, the file is sent on to the Office of the Prime Minister. In most cases, UNHCR recommends that OPM grant *prima facie* status to refugees fleeing war; this is the case with the majority of Sudanese or Congolese refugees. However, in other cases, OPM will consider the merits of the case.

---

[338] Human Rights Watch interview with InterAid, Kampala, Uganda, April 8, 2002.
[339] *See* UNHCR, *Community Services Report*, 2001.

Interview with the Office of the Prime Minister

OPM considers the merits of all cases that are not obvious *prima facie* cases. Those who can be granted individual refugee status are given that status, but before they are given the necessary documents, the refugees have to sign an agreement stating that they will be completely self-sufficient if they choose to live in Kampala. This is very problematic as many refugees are fleeing to the city for their protection, and yet do not have the means to survive by themselves.

Those asylum seekers who may have had a history of imprisonment, and basically all asylum seekers from Rwanda and Burundi, those with complicated stories, and those who were under suspicion for whatever reason are referred to the Special Branch, the security wing of the Ugandan police, for an interview.

Interview with the Special Branch

The Special Branch has no adjudicative function in the status determination process. Its role, as explained to a Human Right Watch researcher, is to prepare notes on an individual asylum seeker's case for the consideration of the REC.[340] Despite this seemingly innocuous role, the Special Branch is not a clerk's office for the REC, it is the security arm of the Ugandan police department. The Special Branch is charged with the task of "collect[ing] and process[ing] intelligence on suspect persons, organisations or activities that could threaten [Uganda's] national security and public safety, or likely to cause a breach of peace."[341] Given this function of the Special Branch, asylum seekers are especially frightened of appearing before it, a subject that is addressed more fully below.

Asylum seekers who are referred to the Special Branch are given a personal biographical information form that they can fill out and return. When the form is returned, they undergo an interview with one of four officers who staff the Special Branch. During the interview, the officers at the Special Branch do not consider the notes prepared by UNHCR on the individual applicant's case. Instead, they only review notes prepared by the Old Kampala police and OPM while preparing their own notes on the individual's case. It is on the basis of the notes prepared by the Special Branch that the individual's case is considered by the REC.

---

[340] Human Rights Watch interview with officer at the Special Branch, Kampala, Uganda, April 16, 2002.
[341] *See* "Facts About the Ugandan Police," (available at http://www.police.go.ug/intelligence.html).

Decision by the Refugee Eligibility Committee (REC)

The members of the REC include officials from nine government ministries and the senior protection officer of UNHCR (in an advisory capacity). The REC considers the totality of the file as prepared by the police, OPM and the Special Branch. UNHCR attends the meetings of the REC with its own notes from its interviews with refugees, but it can only advise the Committee and has no voting rights. Moreover, asylum applicants or their representatives have no right to appear before the REC and the deliberations and decisions are based on documentary evidence only.

Applicants who are granted status may present their reasons for preferring to remain in Kampala. If these reasons are accepted, as already noted the refugee must sign an agreement indicating that he or she will not rely on NGOs for assistance and will be completely self-sufficient. If the reasons are rejected, or if the refugee does not agree to self-sufficiency, he or she is directed to go to one of the refugee settlements. Applicants who are denied status have no right to appeal the decision of the REC. A review may be requested, but "usually only if there is new information for REC to consider."[342] Rejected applicants are given ninety days to leave Uganda.

Mandate Status from UNHCR

In rare, and often high-profile cases, UNHCR grants refugees in Kampala status under the agency's "mandate."[343] However, because the Ugandan government usually has already rejected these cases, UNHCR normally must search for resettlement opportunities for these mandate refugees in a third country of safety.

Resettlement Referrals

Once their status has been recognized, refugees living in Kampala may raise their need for resettlement with the Ugandan government or with UNHCR. The Ugandan government also refers cases it has identified as being in need of resettlement directly to UNHCR. Only those cases warranting additional review will be examined for possible referral according to criteria established in UNHCR's *Resettlement Handbook*. A threshold inquiry is whether the refugee is vulnerable in the country of first asylum. If he or she is found to be vulnerable, then refugees fulfilling one of eight criteria may be referred. These criteria are: legal and physical protection needs, survivors of violence and

---

[342] Human Rights Watch interview with Ugandan government official, Office of the Prime Minister, Kampala, Uganda, April 8, 2002.
[343] *See* note 172, above, for a discussion of UNHCR mandate status.

torture, medical needs, women-at-risk, family reunification, children and adolescents, elderly refugees and refugees without local integration prospects.[344]

UNHCR then refers the potential case for resettlement to one of several resettlement governments. The governments accepting the highest numbers of refugees from East Africa are the United States, Canada, Australia, and Norway.

---

[344] *See* UNHCR, *Resettlement Handbook*, Chapter 4.

PROTECTION FAILURES IN THE STATUS DETERMINATION PROCESS

Responsibility for Status Determinations

It is the responsibility of the government of Uganda to assess the status of refugees in its territory. UNHCR's ExCom has reiterated this responsibility of governments on several occasions by stating "the importance of establishing and ensuring access consistent with the 1951 Convention and the 1967 Protocol for all asylum seekers to fair and efficient procedures for the determination of refugee status."[345]

The fact that the government of Uganda is involved in the status determinations for asylum seekers is a mixed blessing. Uganda's neutrality is sometimes in doubt when the individual asylum seekers arriving in Uganda come from countries in which Uganda has a clear foreign policy or military interest.

However, Uganda has gone a long way towards establishing and ensuring access for the determination of refugee status. Procedures are in place, and police officers and ministers work on a daily basis to process asylum seekers' applications. The importance of guaranteeing the efficiency and fairness of these procedures has been reiterated by UNHCR's ExCom on several occasions.[346] The ways in which the government is falling short of these standards will be discussed in the following sections.

UNHCR also has a role to play in status determinations. In government-run procedures, such as those established in Uganda, UNHCR assumes more of a capacity-building and even "watchdog" role over the process. The agency has a responsibility to ensure that "normal procedural safeguards" are in place during status determinations.[347] All states parties to the Refugee Convention, including Uganda, should "give favorable consideration to UNHCR participation" in status determination.[348] Uganda has allowed UNHCR to play its capacity building and watchdog role to some extent. However, given the fears of bias and lack of confidentiality held by refugees in Uganda, UNHCR could do much more to fulfill this role and to build confidence among refugees in Uganda.

---

[345] *See*, e.g. ExCom Conclusions on International Protection Nos. 71, 74, 87.
[346] *See*, e.g. ExCom Conclusions No. 71, 1993, and 82, 1997.
[347] *See* UNHCR, *Follow-up on Earlier Conclusions of the Sub-Committee on the Determination of Refugee Status, inter alia, with Reference to the Role of UNHCR in National Refugee Status Determination Procedure,* UN Doc. EC/SCP/22, August 23, 1982, para. 8.
[348] *See* UNHCR, *Status Determination Handbook* para. 193.

Procedural Deficiencies in the Status Determination Process
Lack of Adequate Information
According to the Refugee Status Determination Handbook, applicants for refugee status should "receive the necessary guidance as to the procedure to be followed."[349] Contrary to this standard, asylum seekers in Kampala do not receive information about the legal standards or procedures that will be followed in their cases. As a result, many refugees in Uganda are poorly informed about the asylum determination process, which contributes to the fear and confusion it can engender in some asylum applicants. Asylum applicants are also confused about the institutional affiliations of the officers interviewing them, and the legal standards or procedures applicable to their cases. Human Rights Watch interviewed one refugee who thought the Ugandan Police working at Old Kampala Police Station were staff of UNHCR,[350] and several others who thought that the UNHCR protection officers who conduct interviews at the NGO InterAid were staff members of InterAid and not of UNHCR.

Failures of Accessibility: Fear of Registering
The status determination process is particularly inaccessible to Somali refugees. Of nine Somali refugees interviewed by Human Rights Watch, only two had undergone the status determination process. The others refrained from having their refugee status assessed because they were afraid of the first step in the process – registering with the Ugandan police. The reasons for this fear in the Somali community could be the result of any one or a combination of several factors. First, Somali refugees are poorly informed about what actually transpires during registration with the police. For example, Samatar B., a middle-aged man whose wife was killed in Somalia, had fled with ten children, all of whom were sleeping with him in a crowded room that they shared with several other refugee families. He told a Human Rights Watch researcher, "I have been here for three years. I do not go to the police... they will ask me for documents."[351]

Second, Somalis are afraid of the process because so many passed through Kenya, and fear that their cases will be rejected on secondary movement grounds (a subject that is discussed more fully in Part IV, below). Third, Somalis are simply afraid of being arrested or otherwise harassed by the police if they go to register. This is not surprising given that Somali refugees are often caught up in police swoops conducted in neighborhoods in Kampala heavily

---

[349] *See* UNHCR, *Status Determination Handbook* para. 192(i).
[350] Human Rights Watch interview with refugee, Kampala, Uganda, April 11, 2002.
[351] Human Rights Watch interview with refugee, Kampala, Uganda, April 16, 2002.

populated by refugees. For example, a middle-aged woman named Awa H. who was given a place to sleep by other Somalis living in Kampala explained, "I came one year ago because of civil war and insecurity from Kenya to here.... The problem I have is that I am unwelcome here... I didn't go to the police. If I go there, they will lock us in!"[352]

Interpretation Problems

Given the brevity of the initial interviews conducted at Old Kampala Police station, many refugees are fearful that the notes are incomplete and they worry that these notes remain with their files throughout the process. Some refugees raised doubts as to whether discrepancies between these notes and the later interviews could impact the outcome of a particular individual's case. Refugees were particularly worried because the police officers conducting the interviews do not speak their language, for example, French or Kinyarwanda.

Moreover, Human Rights Watch documented several problems with the quality of interpretation during the UNHCR interviews. Both UNHCR and InterAid explained that the interpreters available for the social worker interviews and the UNHCR status determination interviews came from one of two sources. Either the refugees bring the interpreters themselves, or an InterAid interpreter is provided for them.[353] However, UNHCR was candid with Human Rights Watch that the quality of interpretation at InterAid is "a bit of a problem."[354] The Director of InterAid supplied more information about the interpreters "provided" when he told Human Rights Watch that "for translations we usually choose a translator at random from among the refugees, or refugees can bring their own translator."[355] Choosing a translator at random from a group of waiting refugees creates serious security risks

Accounts from refugees substantiate this problem. Eddy L., a Congolese refugee explained, "translations are poor. One refugee I know told HCR that someone wanted to kill him, and the translator translated this as 'someone wanted to kill someone else.' . . . Sometimes they look for another refugee to do the translations, which can create security problems."[356]

Another applicant who had been a human rights activist in his country of origin described the problems he had with interpretation:

---

[352] Human Rights Watch interview with refugee, Kampala, Uganda, April 16, 2002.
[353] Human Rights Watch interview with representative of UNHCR, Kampala, Uganda, April 16, 2002.
[354] Human Rights Watch interview with representative of UNHCR, Kampala, Uganda, April 8, 2002.
[355] Human Rights Watch interview with representative of InterAid, Kampala, Uganda, April 8, 2002.
[356] Human Rights Watch interview with refugee, Kampala, Uganda, April 8, 2002.

I registered with the police on December 5, 2000. On
December 6, 2000 I had my interview with InterAid. After
that interview, they closed for the holidays. On January 6,
2001 I had an interview with the JPO [the UNHCR Junior
Protection Officer]. The interpreter was badly prepared, and
the JPO doesn't speak French. They referred me to the REC,
but I asked the [UNHCR] why should a human rights activist
go before the REC? [UNHCR] did another interview with me.
This time, he asked me to speak in English – which was very
difficult for me. I still have had no answer from them on my
case.[357]

Asylum seekers also complained of interpretation problems at OPM and
the Special Branch. One Rwandan told a Human Rights Watch researcher, "I
had problems with the translator [at OPM] and I couldn't explain myself very
well."[358] One Rwandan who had requested an interview in Kinyarwanda was
refused by the Special Branch, and his claim for refugee status was later
rejected.[359]   When a Human Rights Watch researcher inquired about the
procedures followed during interviews at Special Branch, we were told,

Sometimes we take one hour to make the interview. At other
times the interview is as short as ten to fifteen minutes. We
usually speak to them in Swahili. If someone doesn't speak
Swahili we try as much as possible to get interpreters. We
have some staff who speak Kinyarwandan.   Somalis are
difficult to interview, sometimes we need to use other Somali
refugees. Interpreters are expensive. Some come with their
own interpreters.[360]

---

[357] Human Rights Watch interview with refugee, Kampala, Uganda, April 10, 2002.
Another asylum seeker from Eritrea told a Human Rights Watch researcher, "I already
did my interview with InterAid [interviewee meant UNHCR]. They asked me why I
don't go back to Eritrea. I try my best with the translator, but it is not easy and they did
not even talk with me for twenty minutes." Human Rights Watch interview with refugee,
Kampala, Uganda, April 12, 2002.
[358] Human Rights Watch interview with refugee, Kampala, Uganda, April 15, 2002.
[359] Human Rights Watch interview with refugee, Kampala, Uganda, April 9, 2002.
[360] Human Rights Watch interview with officer at Special Branch, Kampala, Uganda,
April 16, 2002.

Hasty interviews and poor interpretation fall far short of the Refugee Status Determination Handbook's standards, which state:

> It should be recalled that an applicant for refugee status is normally in a particularly vulnerable situation. He finds himself in an alien environment and may experience serious difficulties, technical and psychological, in submitting his case to the authorities of a foreign country, often in a language not his own. His application should therefore be examined within the framework of specially established procedures by qualified personnel having the necessary knowledge and experience, and an understanding of an applicant's particular difficulties and needs.[361]

> These basic requirements, which reflect the special situation of the applicant for refugee status, to which reference has been made above, and which would ensure that the applicant is provided with certain essential guarantees, are the following: The applicant should be given the necessary facilities, *including the services of a competent interpreter*, for submitting his case to the authorities concerned.[362]

Delays at the Refugee Eligibility Committee

The most common problem refugees experience with REC is delay. Several refugees interviewed by Human Rights Watch had to wait without status for several months while REC considered their claims.

For example, Jean-Baptiste C., a male refugee from the DRC fled from Bukavu because of problems with the RCD said, "On September 28, 2000 I was arrested by RCD security, where I was kept in an unknown place until December 27, 2000." He was then transferred on December 29, 2000 to the central prison in Bukavu. He was suspected of working against the RCD, because there had been a big "explosion" [grenade attack] in Bukavu about three weeks before September 28, 2000 that killed several people.[363] Jean-Baptiste told a Human Rights Watch researcher,

---

[361] *See* UNHCR, *Status Determination Handbook* para. 190.

[362] UNHCR, *Status Determination Handbook* para. 192(v) (emphasis added).

[363] There were reports of a grenade attack on a charity fair being held in Bukavu at the end of August 2000. The explosion killed at least seven people and injured another forty-three. In September, fighting in the region continued to cause civilian deaths. Mai-Mai warriors ambushed and shot at a bus on its way to Bukavu, killing at least fourteen people and wounding six others. *See* Associated Press Newswires, "Seven Killed, 43 Injured in

> I had nothing to do with [the outbreak in fighting]. I was
> beaten in jail and they broke my teeth. They asked me
> questions and I didn't have the answers and that was why they
> first took me into custody. They killed people every day in
> that prison, and they didn't allow visitors to come. My wife
> paid money for my food but I didn't get to see her at all…. On
> January 13, 2001 I was allowed to pay $900 (USD) for my
> provisional bail. I have no record of this payment because
> they refused to give me a receipt, instead they wrote that I paid
> $100 (USD) bail.[364]

After several other incidents in which Jean-Baptiste's property was
destroyed and his life was threatened by the military in Congo, he fled to
Uganda. On September 13, 2001 Jean-Baptiste C. was interviewed at OPM and
he was referred to the Special Branch. Jean-Baptiste told Human Rights Watch
what happened next,

> I was so tired of waiting for appointments like that, so I
> decided to speak with an intermediary to try to get an
> appointment sooner. I paid [U.S]$45 to get an appointment
> sooner with the Special Branch. On October 1, 2001 I was
> given that appointment. However, the officer I spoke with
> only talked to me for five minutes. At first I was happy
> because I thought that the money was working. He said I
> would have a decision in one month.[365]

Jean-Baptiste was issued a letter on September 11, 2001 that stated "while
your case awaits the REC decision, this letter serves as a provisional
identification and will expire three months from today." The expiration date
was extended twice, first to November 2, 2001 and later to December 4, 2001.
Four months later, Jean-Baptiste told Human Rights Watch he was afraid to go

---

Grenade Attack During Charity Fair," August 28, 2000; PANA Daily Newswire, "14
Killed in Bukavu Ambush," September 13, 2000.
[364] Jean-Baptiste's bail document reveals that he was released on the following
conditions: 1) payment of $100 (USD), 2) ordered not to leave Bukavu, 3) ordered not to
cause a public disturbance, 4) ordered to appear at the Magistrate-Instructeur's office
every Friday and Tuesday [notes taken by Human Rights Watch directly from the bail
document].
[365] Human Rights Watch interview with refugee, Kampala, Uganda, April 10, 2002.

back to OPM to have his documents extended yet again. As of April 2002 he still had not heard anything about the REC's decision in his case. [366]

Uganda's Political and Military Interests – Potential for Bias
Fear of Bias at the OPM and the Special Branch

Many of the fears and problems asylum seekers experience while moving through Uganda's status determination process can be attributed to Uganda's political and military roles in their countries of origin. One Congolese refugee told a Human Rights Watch researcher, "People are afraid to declare themselves to the police because Uganda is fighting a war in our country."[367]

Specific bias concerns arise for many refugees when they present their claims to OPM or the Special Branch. Several Sudanese refugees interviewed by Human Rights Watch said that they were accused by OPM officials of fleeing a "just cause" when they decided to leave the SPLA and the SPLA-controlled camps. Similar accusations were leveled against those who expressed fears of forced recruitment by the SPLA.[368] For example, Abdu T., a twenty-five-year-old Sudanese man fled from southern Sudan after his family had been attacked because they were a part of the Muslim minority in the south. In 1992 his father had been abducted because he opposed the SPLA and he was known as a leader in opposition to the SPLA. He told a Human Rights Watch researcher,

> A faction wanted to recruit me in 1995 when they took my mother. I was tortured because I refused to fight. The SPLA said I was a spy of the Arabs and they kept me underground and tortured me until December 28, 1995. Then, they took me with them to work for them. They made me work with the relief trucks, to unload supplies. I worked like that for a long time....[369]

Abdu went to InterAid on January 6, 1996 and received his referral letter from UNHCR to OPM. Then he went to OPM. Abdu said,

> The [OPM] officer who interviewed me started to threaten me and to ask "why don't I return to Sudan to fight?" He didn't give me any documents and we spoke for only fifteen minutes.

---

[366] Human Rights Watch interview with refugee, Kampala, Uganda, April 10, 2002.
[367] Human Rights Watch interview with refugee, Kampala, Uganda, April 8, 2002.
[368] Human Rights Watch interview with refugee, Kampala, Uganda, April 9, 2002.
[369] Human Rights Watch interview with refugee, Kampala, Uganda, April 13, 2002.

> [He] told me to go to the camp, but [the SPLA] will abduct me
> from those camps. They know I ran away from them, but they
> also know the case of my father very well because he is well-
> known in the opposition. I said I would not go and I stayed
> here just with that asylum seeker document through 1997 and
> 1998.[370]

The case of Olivier C., introduced previously, illustrates some of the
problems Rwandan asylum seekers have in presenting their claims to both OPM
and the Special Branch. Olivier's family had been subject to persecution in
Rwanda because of their political activities. He told a Human Rights Watch
researcher that Rwandan agents had arrested and beaten him, holding him
incommunicado for close to one year. Olivier told Human Rights Watch about
his interview with OPM,

> I had problems with the translator and I couldn't explain
> myself very well. They stopped asking me questions and
> listening when I told them about what happened at the
> Rwandan's house. They didn't take notes when I started to
> talk about the beatings. They said they didn't want to hear
> about the beatings. The OPM said I was lying about my
> arrest. They said, "how can [the Rwandans] arrest you, what
> do they want with you? You are still very young!"

> I was then asked to go for an interview with the Special
> Branch. I did that interview on January 10, 2002. At that
> interview I was very afraid. They gave me a form to fill out
> that asked about my identity, my family, my tribe, which
> border I crossed, etc... I did the interview for about one hour.
> Three people interviewed me there. They asked me why I left
> and what job I did in Rwanda. There was no interpreter there
> and one man said he understood Kinyarwanda and translated
> for the others but he didn't understand me very well at all. I
> tried to explain that I fled because of my family, because of
> the problems of my family. It is not only my problems, but
> now they have become my own problems because of my
> family.[371]

---

[370] Human Rights Watch interview with refugee, Kampala, Uganda, April 13, 2002.
[371] Human Rights Watch interview with refugee, Kampala, Uganda, April 15, 2002.

As of April 2002, Olivier C. had not received any updates on the status of his case.

In addition, sometimes the security function of the Special Branch makes refugees so fearful that they do not give the officers all the facts upon which a decision can be made. For example, Béatrice K. (introduced previously) was interviewed by the Special Branch in February 2001. She did not tell them her story because she was too afraid. So they rejected her and they said her case was "not understandable."[372] Béatrice K. admitted to a Human Rights Watch researcher that she gave unlikely reasons for her flight. She told Human Rights Watch, "The Rwandan refugees are not accepted in this country as refugees. They are made to wait a long time at REC. They remain there. The government does not provide a place for them."[373]

The fears of bias that refugees such as Olivier and Béatrice have are supported by some recently publicized high-profile cases. Unlike Olivier and Béatrice, though, UNHCR took an active role in advocating on behalf of the rights of approximately forty-five RPA officers who had fled Rwanda for Uganda in late 2001 in order to seek asylum.[374] While the government and UNHCR were considering their refugee status, the Ugandan government arrested and detained a number of the officers. Subsequently, the governments of Uganda and Rwanda established a Joint Verification Team (JVT) to determine whether either of the countries was training the others enemies (rebels and dissidents) in their territory or in the eastern region of the DRC.[375] The JVT was organized after a high-profile mission by the United Kingdom's Secretary of State for International Development, Clare Short, under the auspices of the British High Commission, and was comprised of the deputy head of Central Military Intelligence (CMI), a military attaché from the British High Commission, and several Rwandan officers. The JVT presented the names of the defectors to Rwandan President Kagame at a joint meeting in London.

The exercise resulted in endangering refugees because the JVT, under the auspices of the British government, shared information about asylum seekers with high-ranking country of origin officials. Since the three governments were the "examiners" of these asylum seekers' claims, this seriously undermined the confidentiality of the officers' asylum applications and constituted a breach of refugee law by all governments involved. UNHCR's Refugee Status

---

[372] Human Rights Watch interview with refugee, Kampala, Uganda, April 11, 2002.
[373] Human Rights Watch interview with refugee, Kampala, Uganda, April 11, 2002.
[374] *See* Uganda Gives UN List of Renegade Rwandans, *New Vision,* (Kampala, Uganda) October 31, 2001.
[375] *See*, e.g. BBC Monitoring Service: Africa, "Government 'Protests' Against Uganda Defence Minister's Remarks," February 27, 2002.

Determination Handbook states unequivocally that, "It will be necessary for the examiner to gain the confidence of the applicant in order to assist the latter in putting forward his case and in fully explaining his opinions and feelings. In creating such a climate of confidence *it is, of course, of the utmost importance that the applicant's statements will be treated as confidential and that he be so informed.*"[376]

The UNHCR protested the JVT's operations on these grounds, but the information had already been shared between the governments. In addition, the Joint Verification Commission went to the refugee settlements looking for Rwandans. UNHCR told a Human Rights Watch researcher that the activities of the JVT were "unacceptable and [we] intervened with the U.K."[377]

Eventually, two-thirds of the Rwandan officers were given status and resettlement referrals. About one third were considered "Ugandans who didn't want refugee status."[378] As of April 2002, those who had been recognized as refugees were under twenty-four-hour house arrest in Kampala.[379] UNHCR explained to a Human Rights Watch researcher that Uganda's "Central Military Intelligence is providing protection to those who were recognized, and some are slated for resettlement."[380] However, as of June 2002 it was still not clear what had happened to those who allegedly "didn't want status." In addition, UNHCR was encountering difficulties in finding a third country that would be willing to accept the officers who had been referred for resettlement.[381]

The Ugandan government was also accused of bias in its treatment of approximately forty Rwandan students who sought asylum in December 1999.[382] The students fled Rwanda because they refused to study in French – a fact that neither the Ugandan government nor UNHCR considered as adequate grounds for asylum. However, when the issue became the subject of public debate and the students' demonstrations were covered in the press, UNHCR determined that

---

[376] *See* UNHCR, *Status Determination Handbook* para. 200 (emphasis added).

[377] Human Rights Watch interview with UNHCR official, Kampala, Uganda, April 8, 2002.

[378] *See* BBC Monitoring Service: Africa, "UNHCR May Relocate 'Renegade' Rwandan Soldiers," November 2, 2001; BBC Monitoring Service: Africa, "Over 30 Former Rwandan Army Officers Rounded Up," November 9, 2001; Xinhua News Agency, "Uganda to Hand Over 30 Rwandan Army Deserters to UNHCR," November 10, 2001.

[379] Human Rights Watch interview with UNHCR, Kampala, Uganda, April 13, 2002.

[380] Human Rights Watch interview with UNHCR, Kampala, Uganda, April 8, 2002.

[381] *See* Asia Intelligence Wire, "UNHCR Cannot Find a Home for Kampala and Kigali Dissidents," April 22, 2002.

[382] *See* BBC Monitoring Service: Africa, "UN Refugee Agency Refuses to Assist Asylum-seeking Rwandan Students," December 17, 1999; BBC Monitoring Service: Africa, "Group of Asylum-seeking Rwandan Students 'Disappear,'" December 24, 1999; BBC Monitoring Service: Africa, "Stranded Rwandan Students Rap Rwandan Vice-President Kagame," January 31, 2000.

the *sur place*[383] effect of the publicity made it impossible for the students to safely return to Rwanda. The government of Uganda disagreed and continued to insist that the students would be safe upon return. UNHCR eventually made arrangements for the students to be resettled in a third country since Uganda would not accept them. While the students waited to travel, the government finally agreed to provide them with twenty-four-hour security protection.[384]

Conclusion

Uganda has established procedures for the determination of refugee status, and has therefore gone a long way towards fulfilling its obligations as a state party to the Refugee Convention. However, as this section has demonstrated, there are several problems with the status determination system. Many of the most grievous are linked to the lack of confidence that refugees coming from the DRC, Sudan, and Rwanda have in the Ugandan government. The role of Uganda in regional conflicts causes these refugees to doubt the impartiality of the decision-makers involved.

Moreover, asylum seekers are ill-informed about the process and about what to expect at each stage. The quality of the determinations is also being harmed by the perceived or real bias on the part of the government, since many asylum seekers refuse to disclose the details of their cases. Improved

---

[383] A person who was not a refugee when she left her country, but who becomes a refugee at a later date, is called a refugee "sur place." UNHCR's Status Determination Handbook notes that, "a person may become a refugee 'sur place' as a result of his own actions [among other enumerated reasons], such as associating with refugees already recognized, or expressing political views in his country of residence." *See* UNHCR *Status Determination Handbook* para. 96.

[384] Human Rights Watch interview with UNHCR, Kampala, Uganda, April 8, 2002.

information and transparency would also enhance asylum seekers' confidence in the integrity of the system.

Finally, procedural problems such as the use of entirely inappropriate interpreters, or none whatsoever, and the lengthy delays asylum seekers experience once their cases are referred to the Special Branch and REC are of serious concern. With such major flaws in the system, Uganda is falling short of making "prompt determination[s] of refugee status in fair procedures."[385]

---

[385] *See* ExCom Conclusion No. 71, 1993 at para (k).

PART III: CAMP CONFINEMENT POLICIES IN KENYA AND UGANDA

Both Kenya and Uganda have adopted policies that require most refugees to live in refugee camps, or settlements, as they are called in Uganda. These policies have been decided and are implemented by each of these governments in collaboration with UNHCR. Refugees living in urban areas are violating this requirement. As a result, refugees are vulnerable to the kinds of human rights abuse documented in the two previous sections of this report, such as police harassment, arrest, detention, and in Kenya even refoulement after being charged with illegal entry.

Several of the refugees interviewed for this report arrived in Nairobi or Kampala after spending some time in refugee camps. While it has often been assumed that refugees flee to cities for economic reasons,[386] the following sections outline the most common reasons refugees gave to Human Rights Watch for leaving camps. What these sections show is that the decision to leave a camp is not necessarily taken lightly, and that the camp confinement policies of Kenya and Uganda are sometimes forcing people to live in places they find terribly unsafe.

After analyzing the reasons why some refugees feel compelled to leave camps, the camp confinement policies of Kenya and Uganda will be briefly described. Finally, the legality of camp confinement policies is examined under international human rights standards.

WHY REFUGEES LEAVE KENYA'S REFUGEE CAMPS

Inadequate Humanitarian Assistance in Camps

Kenya's refugee camps are located in some of the most inhospitable desert areas of the country. The camps are notorious for their extreme heat, lack of vegetation, scorpion infestation, and proximity to Kenya's borders with Somalia and Sudan. In addition, rations in Kenya's two camps—Dadaab and Kakuma—have fallen well below UNHCR's and the World Food Programme's (WFP) recommendations. WFP and UNHCR recommend that refugees should receive 2,100 kilocalories per day, although this amount may be reduced when refugees have access to other means of survival.[387] WFP was distributing between 1,400

---

[386] *See*, e.g. UNHCR, "Policy and Practice Regarding Urban Refugees: A Discussion Paper," October 1995 (noting that "urban refugees and asylum seekers tend to be influenced by some of the same push and pull factors" as "unequal development and a growing North-South divide" and a "growth in economically-driven migrations.").
[387] WFP/UNHCR revised their *Guidelines for Estimating Food and Nutritional Needs in Emergencies* in 1997 to reflect recommendations made by the World Health

and 1,600 kilocalories in Kakuma camp and 1,400 in Dadaab in the first four months of 2002.[388] In February 2002, the WFP lacked the funds and food donations necessary to meet the nutritional requirements of refugees. This lack of food or money to buy it caused the WFP to warn that "almost 220,000 refugees in Kakuma and Dadaab refugee camps in Kenya face malnutrition and a wider humanitarian crisis unless urgent contributions are received."[389]

Refugees in both Kakuma and Dadaab have a difficult time finding enough firewood for their cooking and sanitary needs. UNHCR has put innovative programs in place to try to supply the needed wood for refugees first in Dadaab and later in Kakuma camp, but they are falling far short of their targets.[390] In early 2002, UNHCR was only able to supply 30 percent of the refugees' firewood requirements, causing refugee women and girls to walk long distances to secure the necessary wood.[391] The need to travel such long distances alone or in small groups puts women and girls at great risk of sexual violence, a major human rights problem that Human Rights Watch and other organizations have called attention to for several years.[392] The collection of wood has also caused numerous conflicts with the communities surrounding the refugee camps.[393] For

---

Organization. According to these guidelines, "in the first stages of an emergency situation, the average estimated per capita energy requirement of 2,100 kilocalories will be used to expedite decisions about the immediate initial provision of food. As soon as some demographic and food security information can be collected, the calculation for the amount of food aid required should be adjusted accordingly." *See* WFP/UNHCR, *Guidelines for Estimating Food and Nutritional Needs in Emergencies*, 1997. The Sphere Project also uses 2,100 kilocalories as the reference point, and suggests that the initial value could be reduced depending on the given situation. *See* The Sphere Project, *Humanitarian Charter and Minimum Standards in Disaster Response*, 2000.

[388] *See* BBC Monitoring International Reports, "Kenya: About 220,000 Refuges Face Malnutrition Threat," February 23, 2002.

[389] Ibid.

[390] The Dadaab Firewood Project, also called The Energy Management and Environmental Rehabilitation Project, is a project to distribute firewood to refugees in camps near Dadaab, in Northeastern Province of Kenya. It was initiated by the United States government, which provided 1.5 million dollars to the UNHCR in late 1997 in response to the high risk of rape and sexual assault experienced by refugee women and girls when collecting firewood in the bush. There is a similar program in Kakuma camp. *See* also UNHCR, Evaluation and Policy Analysis Unit, *Evaluation of the Dadaab Firewood Project, Kenya*, June 2001.

[391] Human Rights Watch interview with NGO personnel, Kakuma camp, Kenya, April 23, 2002.

[392] *See* "Seeking Protection: Addressing Sexual and Domestic Violence in Tanzania's Refugee Camps," Human Rights Watch/Africa, October 2000.

[393] Firewood shortages are a widespread problem. *See*, e.g. "UNHCR deplores killing of four Somali refugees in Mandera," UNHCR Press Release, May 16, 2002; "Commission Allocates 2.5 Million in Humanitarian Aid for Drought-Affected Populations in Kenya," EU Press Release, March 19, 2002.

example, in March 2002 a court injunction barred UNHCR and NGOs operating in Dadaab camp from collecting firewood in Kenya's Garissa district.

Attacks and Insecurity in Camps

Both Kakuma and Dadaab camps have serious law and order problems, with incidences of violence occurring regularly in and near to the camps.[394] In fact, one paper in UNHCR's New Issues in Refugee Research states, "it is impossible to quantify the amount of violence which takes place in and around Kenya's refugee camps. But... incidents involving death and serious injury take place on a daily basis."[395]

The Sudanese rebel group the SPLA influences the governance of Kenya's camp, and is known to operate in Kakuma.[396] A human rights organization told Human Rights Watch, "in Kakuma refugees have the opportunity to elect their representatives. However, the SPLA influences this process so that in some parts of Kakuma the chairmen are appointed by [Sudanese rebel leader John] Garang."[397] The presence of SPLA leaders in the camps may at times be linked to camp violence. In 1999, the murder of an SPLA commander in Chukudum, Eastern Equatoria, southern Sudan, spurred riots in Kakuma that left five refugees dead and two hundred injured.[398]

The presence of Ethiopian security and former Derg[399] officers in Kenya's refugee camps is another source of fear. One refugee told a Human Rights Watch researcher, "I know people taken from Nairobi and from the Kakuma

---

[394] *See,* e.g., U.S. Department of State, *Country Reports on Human Rights Practices,* 2001 at 16.

[395] Jeff Crisp, "A State of Insecurity: the Political Economy of Violence in Refugee-Populated Areas of Kenya," *Working Paper No. 16,* December 1999 at 2.

[396] Human Rights Watch interview with representative of international NGO, Nairobi, Kenya, April 24, 2002.

[397] Human Rights Watch interview with representative of Kampala-based NGO, April 11, 2002.

[398] A Bor Dinka SPLA commander and his men clashed with a Didinga SPLA commander and his men in the Didinga town of Chukudum in 1999, leading to the death of the Bor Dinka commander. Many years of tension between the Didinga and the Bor Dinka there, where the SPLA at one time located its headquarters, culminated in open warfare, with the Didinga taking to the hills and seeking weapons from the government garrison in Kapoeta to the northeast. The Dinka refugees in Kakuma tried to take revenge on the Didinga refugees in Kakuma. The Dinka are the largest group in Kakuma, far outnumbering the Didinga. Many such ethnic conflicts inside southern Sudan have spilled over to clashes in refugee camps in neighboring countries. *See HRW World Report 2000* (covering the events of 1999) p. 81. *See* also BBC Monitoring Service, "Rival Groups Turn Refugee Camps into Battleground," February 1, 1999.

[399] From 1974 to its overthrow in 1987, Ethiopia was ruled by Major Mengistu Haile Mariam and the Derg government. During this time the government was responsible for egregious human rights abuses.

camp by Ethiopian security. They just disappear. Who knows where they are now?"[400] Another Ethiopian said, "my case is very serious, and I do not want to go to the camp. In both places, Kakuma and Dadaab there are soldiers and security agents. They may kill me; those camps are so close to the border. So many times soldiers cross over to search for their opponents."[401]

One senior NGO staff member from Kakuma camp confirmed to Human Rights Watch that the proximity of the camp to the border was a major source of insecurity,

> The location of the camp is very insecure. It is close to three borders. Ethiopian government forces have been present in the camp. Many former Ethiopian officers are vulnerable. The SPLA also enters the camp. We can notice changes in the camp composition based on how the fighting is going in the south in Sudan.[402]

New refugee arrivals from Somalia were encamped so near to the Somali border that two women and two children were killed when fighting broke out in Bulo Hawa, Somalia on May 15, 2002.[403]

The insecurity in Kenya's camps does not only come from proximity to the border, rebel groups and the work of security agents—ordinary crime also takes its toll. Banditry, property destruction, and violent clashes between the local population and refugees are common,[404] and UN and government sources allege that small arms traffickers operate in Dadaab camp.[405] In addition, sexual violence is an ongoing problem. Refugee women reported seventy incidents of rape in Dadaab in the first eleven months of 2001, according to UNHCR. In Kakuma, nineteen cases were reported in the first six months of 2001.[406]

---

[400] Human Rights Watch interview with refugee, Nairobi, Kenya, April 17, 2002.

[401] Human Rights Watch interview with refugee, Nairobi, Kenya, April 5, 2002.

[402] Human Rights Watch interview with representative of international NGO, Nairobi, April 24, 2002.

[403] See BBC International Monitoring, "Four Refugees Said Killed Following Faction Fighting Near Kenya-Somalia Border," May 16, 2002.

[404] See, e.g., UNHCR 2002 Global Appeal, "Kenya Chapter," 2002, at 83; BBC Monitoring Service: Africa, "Senior UN Official Says Refugee Camps 'Are a Bandits Paradise,'" November 25, 2000.

[405] See Kathi Austin, "Armed Refugee Camps: A Microcosm of the Link Between Arms Availability and Insecurity," Workshop on International Law and Small Arms Proliferation, Washington, DC, February 6, 2002 (presentation at a workshop organized by the U.S. Social Science Research Council's Program on Global Security and Cooperation).

[406] See, e.g., U.S. Department of State, Country Reports on Human Rights Practices, 2001, p. 16.

Insecurity for Particular Individuals

While some refugees are afraid of conditions in the camps because of generalized insecurity, others have individual reasons for fearing the camps because their ethnicity or their previous political or religious affiliations, or those of family members, make them targets for ongoing persecution. In Kakuma camp, Human Rights Watch interviewed Othman B., a Somali refugee who had been plagued by insecurity in both Dadaab and Kakuma camps. His story illustrates how the presence of arms, politically- and ethnically-based hostility, and inadequate law enforcement can create a deadly combination for some refugees:

> We came to Dadaab camp in 1992, but we faced the same problem there as we did in Somalia. We come from a minority tribe called the Geri tribe.[407] My father was a leader for our tribe and was always working for the rights of the Geri. In 1999 my father and uncle were shot and killed in Dadaab camp [complex].[408] Two others were seriously wounded. We were always reporting on our security problems before this happened, and after it happened they finally believed us. Because of these problems, they transferred us to Nairobi where UNHCR looked at our situation and they decided to send us to Kakuma camp. However, the same people have come after us here. I was attacked first in 2000 and most recently when I went to get medical treatment at the clinic in June 2001 I was attacked again. After these incidents, every time I need to pass out of the protection area[409] for medical treatment I worry . . . will I come back to my family? We have recently had news that another of our relatives was attacked and shot in Dadaab. They have started to hunt us down wherever we are in Kenya. I am not a free person here [in Kakuma protection area]. All the time, I just sit here. It is not good for your health; it is like someone in prison.[410]

---

[407] The Geri tribe, along with the Gebra, is a nomadic sub-group of the Oromo.

[408] On January 21, 1999 four men and two boys were killed and twenty-five wounded in Dadaab's Hagadera refugee camp *See* Inter Press Service, "Kenya: Fears of Inter-Clan Violence in Somali refugee camp," February 7, 1999.

[409] The "protection area" of Kakuma Camp is a cluster of tents surrounded by stakes and ten strands of barbed wire located near a police depot. UNHCR places individuals or families with security problems in the protection area.

[410] Human Rights Watch interview with refugee, Kakuma Camp, Kenya, April 23, 2002.

Ethnic Tensions or Discriminatory Treatment in Camps

Refugees often bring the prejudices and conflict plaguing their home countries with them to refugee camps. The resulting violence and discrimination can sometimes make life in the camps unbearable for at-risk or minority groups. In a lengthy interview with a Human Rights Watch researcher, several staff members of international relief NGOs working in Kenya's Kakuma camp outlined the most common forms of discrimination and violence in that refugee community (since Uganda also hosts refugees from each of the nationalities discussed, some of the same ethnic/political forces are also at play in Uganda's refugee communities):

> Sudanese who are aligned to the "Arab" population [referring to northern Muslim Arabic-speaking Sudanese who control the government of Sudan] are assaulted for being anti-SPLA. Those [southern Sudanese] believed to be against the SPLA are attacked and some have even been killed.[411] Young Sudanese girls who refuse arranged marriages are also at risk of violence and shunning. . . Rwandan refugees, particularly the Tutsi, have suffered from harassment and stonings in Kakuma camp. Any refugees with mixed marriages suffer a lot of problems, especially Rwandan Hutu with Tutsi.... There are inter-clan tensions and violence amongst the Somalis,[412] and the Banyamulenge[413] face discrimination from other Congolese.[414]

---

[411] The case of the disappearance of Dr. Karlo Madut from a Ugandan refugee camp, which led to his presumed death at the hands of the SPLA, is discussed in *Human Rights World Report 1998* (Events of 1997), p. 75.

[412] Several agencies report inter-clan struggles among Somali refugees and four fires that happened in the Somali area of the Kakuma camps in early 2000. *See* UNHCR, "UNHCR Briefing Notes: Kenya, Afghanistan, North Caucasus, Kosovo (Yugoslavia)," March 7, 2000.

[413] The Banyamulenge are ethnic Tutsis who live in Eastern DRC, in the province of South Kivu, and have a historic tie to Rwandan Tutsis. The Banyamulenge have been persecuted since Mobutu's time in power, and have faced repeated attempts to expel them from the region. In 1999, the Congolese government launched another campaign to expel the Banyamulenge from Congo, accusing them of sparking the war that began in 1998. The Banyamulenge have endured much discrimination at the hands of Congolese governments, although others among them have also been responsible for massacres and fighting throughout the eastern region. Some analysts also argue that Rwanda has used the Banyamulenge to further its own agenda in the region, and relations between these two parties have fluctuated throughout the years of fighting. *See* Alison des Forges, "Refugees in Eastern Zaire and Rwanda," Congressional Testimony, December 4, 1996;

Interviews with refugees in both Kenya and Uganda demonstrate the accuracy of this assessment. For example, discrimination against Banyamulenge and between Hutu and Tutsi were often mentioned. A Congolese man from the Banyamulenge ethnic group had been placed in the protection area of Kakuma camp because he had been violently attacked by other Congolese living there. His brother, who had fled to Nairobi, told a Human Rights Watch researcher, "all the Congolese want to kill him there."[415]

As mentioned above, Sudanese girls who refuse familial instructions to marry are often at risk in Kenya's refugee camps, where they can be easily found and abducted or otherwise forced to go through with the marriage. Awut S. is a sixteen-year-old Sudanese girl who fled Sudan in 1992. Awut was placed in the protection area of Kakuma when she refused to marry a man in Sudan who paid 150 cows to her uncle who moves between Kakuma and Sudan, for her dowry. She told a Human Rights Watch researcher,

> I don't want to get married. I don't have money. We just have nothing. I have been in this place [Kakuma protection area] since May 10, 2000. My uncle is so angry with me he beat Mom . . . he beat Mom until she was admitted to the hospital [in Kakuma camp]. He tried to catch me when I went to school. I am staying here because I have no place to go. I cannot go to school when I am here. I am missing my school so much. I cannot ever leave this place to go to school because my uncle is looking for me. I cannot walk outside the fence. He does not know that I am here.[416]

Finally, an international humanitarian agency told Human Rights Watch that refugees known to be or suspected of being homosexual are also at particular risk of physical and sexual assault.[417]

Reuters, "Governor Says Zaire Army has Duty to Evict Tutsis," October 9, 1996; Reuters, "Ethnic Fighting Erupts in Eastern Zaire," October 19, 1996; Inter Press Service, "Campaign Launched to Rid Congo of Ethnic Tutsis," July 13, 1996; Agence France-Presse, "Conflict in the DR Congo Since 1998," February 20, 2002.
[414] Human Rights Watch interview with representative of international NGO, Kakuma Camp, Kenya, April 23, 2002.
[415] Human Right Watch interview with refugee, Nairobi, Kenya, April 21, 2002.
[416] Human Rights Watch interview with refugee, Kakuma Camp, April 23, 2002.
[417] Human Rights Watch correspondence with international NGO, July 26, 2002.

Lack of Appropriate Education

In Kenya, secondary education is provided in the camps.   However, refugee youth in Kenya who fled from the Great Lakes region are reluctant to move to the camps because they want to continue their education in French.   In addition, Ethiopian refugees in Kenya who were university students in Addis Ababa[418] were distressed by the fact that they had missed at least a year of their university education while living in the camp.   One refugee university student in Kakuma camp said, "we have learned nothing in this place other than how to be hungry and we have nothing other than time."[419]   At the time of Human Rights Watch's interview, most of the Ethiopian university students had been informed by UNHCR that they had been accepted to study at the University of Nairobi and were waiting to leave to take up their places.

Inadequate Medical Care

Some refugees with medical problems never consider going to a camp, as they believe they must live close to hospitals and to access to medicines only available in the city.   This is true for many HIV-positive refugees, and for refugees with other serious conditions such as physical handicaps, tuberculosis, or heart disease.

UNHCR and camp authorities sometimes send refugees in need of medical care to Nairobi.   When a particular refugee cannot be adequately treated in one of the camps, UNHCR and both the Ugandan and Kenyan governments officially recognize that this is a legitimate reason for a refugee to leave the camps and seek treatment in the city.   A twenty-year-old Somali woman explained to a Human Rights Watch researcher that when she was diagnosed with tuberculosis in 2001 in Kakuma camp, she was transferred to Nairobi for treatment.   She told Human Rights Watch that UNHCR in Nairobi gave her TB

---

[418] The Ethiopian student protests in Addis Ababa began on Monday, April 9, 2001. When students pressed their demands for reinstatement of the student council and monthly student magazine, and the replacement of the armed campus security (police) officers with civilian guards, the minister of education issued an ultimatum threatening students who did not return to classes with police force. The security forces' efforts to enforce the ultimatum, coming on the heels of continuing police use of violence to quash student protests, set off the clashes on April 17 and 18 at Addis Ababa University. The riots, which began as a protest for academic freedom, spiraled out of control, and in the aftermath Human Rights Watch accused the Ethiopian authorities of having used excessive force against the students. *See* "Ethiopia: Government Attacks Universities, Civil Society," Human Rights Watch academic freedom press release, May 10, 2001. *See* also BBC Monitoring Service: Africa, "Students Continue Boycotting Classes, Meeting With Minister Fails," April 17, 2001; Associated Press, "Riot Police Injure More Than 50 Protesting Students," April 11, 2001. BBC Monitoring Service: Africa, "Minister in Talks With University Students to Defuse Tension," April 12, 2001.

[419] Human Rights Watch interview with refugee, Kakuma Camp, Kenya, April 23, 2002.

tablets and shillings for her subsistence: first Ksh.2,000 (U.S.$26) each month, then Ksh.1,500 (U.S.$19), and then Ksh.1,000 (U.S.$13). She said, "The doctor told me I had to take nice food with those tablets, but where would I get that nice food? I just went from place to place begging for food and sometimes people would give it to me and sometimes they would not. It was like that, from day to day."[420]

Some refugees believe that their health is so much at risk in the camps that they find a way to leave without permission. An Ethiopian refugee who had polio and had both legs in braces explained why he left Kakuma camp for Nairobi, "...it is too hot there, the heat made me sweat and that caused rashes and sores to develop where my braces rub against my legs. I lost my resistance there. I just could not stay."[421] One disabled refugee said that UNHCR reassured him when he expressed reservations about being able to survive in the camp that, "there are many handicapped people there even worse off than you." After four days in Kakuma, the refugee decided he could not stay. He told a Human Rights Watch researcher, "the other handicapped people there in Kakuma are wounded soldiers. Some of them have their families with them and the rest of their bodies [apart from their injuries] are very strong. They are not like me—they can even carry water for themselves without help. They are stronger than me."[422]

---

[420] Human Rights Watch interview with refugee, Nairobi, Kenya, April 5, 2002.
[421] Human Rights Watch interview with refugee, Nairobi, Kenya, April 4, 2002.
[422] Human Rights Watch interview with refugee, Nairobi, Kenya, April 4, 2002.

WHY REFUGEES LEAVE UGANDA'S CAMPS

Inadequate Humanitarian Assistance, Medical Care, and Education in Camps

Unlike Kenya, refugees in Uganda are given access to land for cultivation, and local government leaders sometimes agree to extend to refugees whatever public services are available in the surrounding villages. The Ugandan government calls the refugee camps "settlements" in order to communicate this integrationist policy intention. It is partly for this reason that UNHCR has commended Uganda on its "friendly" refugee policy.[423]

Refugees are given small plots of land to cultivate in order to promote self-sufficiency. However, refugees do not have clearly defined property rights since, according to Uganda's constitution land is owned by the "people of Uganda"[424] – and who "the people" are is not a settled question in Ugandan law. The settlement system was intended by UNHCR and the government of Uganda to create sustainable refugee communities that eventually could be integrated into the local economy and government. However, the full integration of the refugees into local communities has not so far been possible. UNHCR has only attempted to hand one refugee settlement over to the full control of the government of Uganda, and it was a dismal failure.[425] In 2002, UNHCR was still administering the camp.

Despite this more open approach, refugees who spend significant periods of time in the camps in Uganda complained to Human Rights Watch of food

---

[423] *See* e.g. "UNHCR Hails Policy on Refugees," *New Vision* (Kampala, Uganda), March 22, 2002.

[424] *Constitution of Uganda*, Article 237.

[425] Kiryandongo is located in the Masindi district, in the northeast corner of Uganda, and is a camp for Sudanese refugees. There were two reasons for the UNHCR impetus for withdrawing from the camp: budget and funding shortfalls, and the need to prove the rhetoric that Kiryandongo was one of the most successful settlements in Africa by withdrawing and demonstrating that the refugees were self-sustaining. The Ugandan government objected because they did not want to absorb the costs of caring for the refugees, and the Masindi district officials did not want to extend their services to the refugees. UNHCR ordered InterAid to wind up their activities by January 1997 and withdraw from the camp, and the handover was set to occur in an unofficial manner on January 8, 1997. In the end, the Ugandan government refused to be party to any handover, and UNHCR did not even go to the camp on that day, although InterAid did cease social services in the camp. From 1998 through 2002, UNHCR and Ugandan government officials were still in discussions about the handover. *See* Tania Kaiser, "UNHCR's Withdrawal from Kiryandongo: Anatomy of a Handover," *UNHCR New Issues in Refugee Research, Working Paper No. 32*, October 2000.

shortages.[426] Several refugees became concerned about food when their young children were diagnosed as anemic.   Bak S., a Sudanese man who was interviewed by a Human Rights Watch researcher in the Kabowa neighborhood of Kampala in a crowded shelter he shared with twenty other families explained:

> You do not get enough food there [in the camp]. You get very little oil and no salt. My child was malnourished in that camp, and he was diagnosed as anemic. I went to UNHCR and they gave me only Ush.500 [U.S.$0.27] for medicine, but he did not get better. I took him to the hospital in the camp, but it was so congested my boy could not even lie down. I tried to argue that I needed to bring him to Kampala for treatment. The people in the hospital said, "how did you let your child become like this?" What could I say? They could not treat him and he died because of this.[427]

Refugees in Uganda told Human Rights Watch that the camps do not provide adequate secondary education opportunities for adolescents.[428] Many refugee families living in the camps lack income-generating opportunities that would enable them to pay the secondary school fees, which are charged to

---

[426] A relief agency providing food in the camps decided on a policy of self-reliance for the refugees in Adjumani. They cut food supplies and the refugees protested, arguing that the land was not fertile. They took their case to OPM and UNHCR but there was no change in the policy so that many, mostly of Madi origin, from two or three camps returned to Nimule in southern Sudan, a Madi area. Human Rights Watch interview with an education and relief worker, Kampala, Uganda, July 22, 2002.

[427] Human Rights Watch interview with refugee, Kampala, Uganda, April 9, 2002.

[428] In Uganda, primary education is free for citizens through seventh grade. The same curriculum, also free to refugees, is used for Sudanese refugees, and they may, if permitted by local Ugandan officials, sit for a primary leave seven (PL7) certificate. Uganda requires fees for higher-level schools. Upon completion of secondary school, graduates may sit for an all-level or ordinary exam (O-level), after which one is qualified for public service jobs.   The Jesuit Refugee Service supported nursery, primary and secondary education to refugees as well as nationals in Moyo and Adjumani camps by providing "monthly incentives for staff, funds for classroom supplies and administrative costs."   See Jesuit Refugee Service, *2001 Report* p. 12 (available at http://www.jesref.org/resources/ar2001.pdf). According to UNHCR, 88,891 children are enrolled in education programs in Ugandan camps (including nursery, primary, and secondary). UNHCR states that efforts are underway to harmonize the refugee primary education programs with the local education system. Income-generating activities in the camps also led to more parents being able spare children from agricultural tasks and to afford secondary school fees. For the lower education levels, the ratio of males to females was good, but for secondary and vocational education the percentage of female attendance was much lower than that of males. See UNHCR, *2001 Global Report*, p. 189.

Ugandans and refugees alike. Rebecca B., a Sudanese girl living in Adjumani camp was propositioned many times by a man who was paying her school fees and who also wanted to make her his wife. Her brother told a Human Rights Watch researcher, "she refused him and he stopped paying for her. But now he is very angry with her and I don't know what will happen."[429] Another Sudanese refugee woman told a Human Rights Watch researcher, "in the camps they provide education up to grade seven, but after that it is up to you."[430]

Some refugees have multiple reasons for leaving the camp. Jebeda F., a fifty-seven-year-old Sudanese woman brought her grandchildren to Kampala. She described all the reasons she felt she and her family had to leave Kyangwali camp in southwestern Uganda:

> I was in Kyangwali for five years. There you find the tse tse fly and the mosquito. For so long we had to stay in that camp without any results. We could not pay for the school—it costs Ush.20,000 [U.S.$11] a term! We have no school uniforms, no books. We came to Kampala to escape that sickness and to satisfy those needs. The digging [agriculture] in that camp is not enough to satisfy your needs. We get malaria and sleeping sickness there…. Then we had problems between us. The refugees came from Congo, Rwanda, Somalia and they had conflicts between them. We would get only eight kilos of grain per person per month and one quarter liter of oil, and one point eight kilos of peas. The rest we had to get from digging. And the food they gave us—we would fight for this food between each other. We would take pangas and arrows and spears and fight. Most of the Sudanese who come to Kampala are very young. They are escaping that life.[431]

Attacks and Insecurity in Camps

The Lord's Resistance Army (LRA, a Ugandan rebel group—see above), has periodically attacked refugee camps in northern Uganda for several years.[432]

---

[429] Human Rights Watch interview with refugee, Kampala, Uganda, April 13, 2002.

[430] Human Rights Watch interview with refugee, Kampala, Uganda, April 9, 2002.

[431] Human Rights Watch interview, Kampala with refugee, Uganda, April 15, 2002.

[432] See Action by Churches Together, "Appeal for Sudanese Refugees Resettlement," April 27, 1998 (reporting that "The district including local national and refugee settlements is subject to intermittent insecurity primarily caused by Lords Resistance Army rebels infiltrating from adjoining Gulu district […] All project supplies en route to Adjumani have to travel through war torn Gulu district under infrequent military escorts

Approximately 120 Sudanese refugees have been killed by rebel attacks since 1996, including three who died during 2001.[433] Also in 2001, more than "1,000 refugees temporarily fled their settlement site because of rebel attacks during the year, and thirteen refugees were abducted before being released."[434] The camps in northern Uganda are particularly vulnerable to recruiting raids by LRA forces. Adolescents have been abducted, forced to fight, and forced into sexual slavery as well as manual labor. A September 2001 report estimated that 11,000 young people were abducted by the LRA since 1986, of which 5,000 are known to have escaped.[435] A recent report by Uganda's Refugee Law Project explained the pattern of LRA attacks in Adjumani,

> Rebels enter the settlement [at night], refugees are captured and bound, the houses and fields are looted of food, pots, clothes, and other household items, and refugees are stripped and forced to carry the loot as they are marched to [the forest].[436]

The LRA attacks on northern Uganda and the refugee camps there declined after an Ebola hemorrhagic fever outbreak in Gulu in late 2000. The LRA withdrew to their base camps inside Sudan-government-controlled territory and did not have a presence in northern Uganda until mid-2002, after the Ugandan People's Defense Force (UPDF) eliminated the LRA presence in southern Sudan, with the permission of the Sudan government.

LRA forces again stepped up attacks on refugee settlements in northern Uganda starting from mid-2002. In an attack on the Maaji settlement in early July six refugees and one UPDF soldier were killed.[437] Rebel forces looted and burned homes, schools and other public areas causing over half of the 12,000

[...] Seven project trucks and several light vehicles were destroyed by LRA rebels who attacked the LWF/UNHCR compound in October 1996.") The burning of UN vehicles was also reported in the press. See, e.g. Pan African News Agency, "Rebels Kill Ugandan Army Captain, Burn U.N. Vehicles," October 15, 1996. Sudanese refugees were killed by the LRA in Achol-pii camp in the northern Kitgum district of Uganda. See Reuters, "Ugandan Rebels Attack Refugee Camp, Kill 91," July 15, 1996.

[433] *See* U.S. Committee for Refugees, *Current Report (2002),* (available at http://www.refugees.org/world/countryrpt/africa/ uganda.htm).

[434] Ibid.

[435] *See* Women's Commission for Refugee Women and Children, *Against all Odds: Surviving the War on Adolescents,* September 2001, p. 15.

[436] "Refugees and the Security Situation in Adjumani District," *Refugee Law Project Working Paper No. 2,* June 2001.

[437] *See* "Uganda: Five refugees killed in LRA attack," IRIN, July 10, 2002.

refugees in the area to flee. In early August an LRA raid on the Achol-pii settlement resulted in the death of at least thirty-eight people, including refugees and six Ugandan nationals.[438]   Four local aid workers were also kidnapped during the pre-dawn incident; they were released unharmed one week later.[439] Reports by UNHCR staff in northern Uganda estimated that 24,000 refugees fled the settlement and that refugees were fired upon by the LRA as they fled.[440] Relief efforts for the refugees continued, including efforts to relocate them to another camp, despite the fact that the LRA warned relief agencies to cease their work with refugees in northern Uganda.[441]

A Sudanese widow named Mary A.[442] who was living in Kampala with her two small children told a Human Rights Watch researcher several reasons why she was afraid to go to Achol-pii camp. Given the July and August attacks, it appears her fears were justified.

> They told me they will take me to Achol-pii camp. But Kony
> [Joseph Kony, the leader of the LRA] comes and fights with
> the people there, and I refused that camp because it still has its
> own war.[443]

Located in western Uganda, Kyangwali camp has long been the site of attacks by another rebel group operating in the late 1990s and early 2000s in that part of Uganda, the Allied Democratic Forces (ADF). In addition, in April 2002, violent clashes broke out between groups of refugees in Kyangwali.[444] In

---

[438] *See* "Uganda Rebels Force 24,000 Refugees to Flee UN Camp," New York Times on the Web, August 5, 2002; "Refugees killed, aid workers kidnapped as Ugandan rebels raid Sudanese settlement," *UNHCR News Story*, August 5, 2002.

[439] *See* Agence France Presse, "Ugandan Rebels Release Four Kidnapped Aid Workers," August 12, 2002.

[440] *See* e.g. "Twenty-four thousand Refugees Flee Rebel Attack," IRIN, August 5, 2002.

[441] *See* Agence France Presse, "LRA Rebels Want Relief Agencies, Refugees out of Northern Uganda," August 10, 2002.

[442] Human Rights Watch interview with refugee, Kampala, Uganda, April 12, 2002.

[443] Human Rights Watch interview with refugee, Kampala, Uganda, April 12, 2002. There have been many attacks over the past five years by the Lord's Resistance Army in Achol-pii camp and its surroundings. In July 1996, 110 refugees were killed by LRA rebels, in January 1998 another three refugees were wounded, and in July 2000, LRA rebels based in Sudan attacked the camp and killed three refugees and burnt down about 80 huts. *See* IRIN, "Weekly Roundup," January 16-22, 1998; Xinhua News Agency, "Rebels Attack Camp in Uganda," August 13, 2000. Also, in its 2000 Global Report, UNHCR states that there were 30 attacks on camps in the Moyo and Adjumani districts throughout the year, pointing to a sharp increase in insecurity in the region. *See* UNHCR, *2000 Global Report*, December 2001.

[444] *See* "Trouble Brewing in Refugee Camps," *Monitor* (Kampala, Uganda), April 17, 2002. *See* also BBC Monitoring Service: Africa, "Ethnic Clash Said Brewing in Refugee

late May 2002, clashes between two ethnic groups of Sudanese refugees resulted in the burning of fifty refugee shelters in Kiryandongo camp.[445] Refugees learn of these attacks either through first-hand experience or, if they have never lived in camps, from others who have. One refugee told a Human Rights Watch researcher, "I can't go to the camp, what will I do in the camp? I won't have security in the camp. There is no food in the camp. And Kyangwali is near the place where the rebels are."[446]

Finally, the SPLA has thoroughly infiltrated the camps for Sudanese and also targets them for forced recruitment or sweeps for "deserters,"[447] sometimes with assistance from the UPDF.[448] One local human rights organization explained,

> The SPLA influence is very strong in the [Sudanese] camps. There are informers in the camps and there is a problem with forced recruitment. Uganda turns a deaf ear to refugees with this problem.... [The] SPLA stays in the camps with their guns and uses the camps for rest and recovery and to plan.[449]

Abdu T., introduced previously, told a Human Rights Watch researcher why he resisted UNHCR's attempts to transfer him to the camps in Uganda from Kampala. He had been abducted by the SPLA and forced to work as a laborer and porter when he was living in Sudan before fleeing to Uganda, "They told me

---

Camp in West," April 17, 2002; BBC Monitoring Service, "Rebels Attack Refugee Camp in West," September 7, 2000 (reporting that in September 2000, ADF rebels attacked the refugee settlement killing two people).

[445] See "Riot Police Rushed to Quell Refugee Camp Riots," New Vision (Kampala, Uganda), May 29, 2002.

[446] Human Rights Watch interview with refugee, Kampala, Uganda, April 10, 2002. In April 2002, there were reports of clashes between the Congolese and Sudanese refugees who were allegedly threatening each other and preparing weapons for attack. See BBC Monitoring Service: Africa, "Ethnic Clash Said Brewing in Refugee Camp in West," April 17, 2002. Also, the BBC reported that in September 2000, ADF rebels attacked the refugee settlement killing two people. See BBC Monitoring Service, "Rebels Attack Refugee Camp in West," September 7, 2000.

[447] The SPLA does not maintain a large standing army. It recruits new soldiers and searches for those who have returned home in the lulls between military engagements in the south as well as in refugee camps in Uganda and Kenya. It uses violence when other methods do not work.

[448] See e.g., BBC Monitoring, "University Report Accuses Army of Abetting Sudanese Rebel Recruitment," August 1, 2001 (reporting on an incident in which eighty-one male Sudanese were rounded up by the SPLA from Adjumani district with the assistance of the UPDF. Forty Sudanese were ultimately taken to Sudan.).

[449] Human Rights Watch interview with NGO staff member, Kampala, Uganda, April 11, 2002.

to go to the camp, but the SPLA will abduct me from those camps. They know I ran away from them, but they also know the case of my father very well because he is well-known in the opposition [to the SPLA]."[450]

When asked whether the Ugandan government recognizes that some refugees flee the camps because of insecurity, one Ugandan government official told a Human Rights Watch researcher, "we don't think refugees' fears of the camps are genuine, they are running from the camps."[451] Although the security situation in the camps in Arua district improved somewhat in 2001,[452] the onslaught of violent attacks in Maaji and Achol-pii camps by the LRA in mid-2002 meant that the situation remained extremely insecure elsewhere.

Insecurity for Particular Individuals

Sometimes a particular individual's political background is the reason for the security problems that he or she experiences in the camps. While living in the DRC, Etienne K. was asked by Rwandan military to participate in a plot to overthrow the government of Rwandan President Kagame that was allegedly supported by the government of Uganda. After resisting and revealing the plot, he fled to Uganda and was followed and attacked in Kampala. Eventually, he moved to Kyangwali camp.

However, Kyangwali camp was also unsafe for Etienne. In March 2001, Mr. X, a major who had been involved in the coup conspiracy, came to live in Kyangwali camp. Etienne was immediately afraid that Mr. X would take revenge against him for revealing the coup plot, so he told the camp "commandant" (a term commonly used in Uganda and appearing in Ugandan law)[453] and the protection officer. They questioned Mr. X. about his military background, which he then admitted. UNHCR and the camp commandant did nothing further about the situation. Afraid that Mr. X. would take revenge, Etienne then told UPDF headquarters about Mr. X. Etienne told a Human Rights Watch researcher what happened next,

> On May 11, 2001 a Ugandan military called [Mr. Z] came to my place in the evening and said, "I want to see Etienne." I said that is me and immediately he pointed his gun at me and

---

[450] Human Rights Watch interview with refugee, Kampala, Uganda, April 13, 2002.

[451] Human Rights Watch interview with Ugandan government official, Office of the Prime Minister, Kampala, Uganda, April 8, 2002.

[452] Human Rights Watch interview with U.S. Embassy official, Kampala, Uganda, April 11, 2002. *See* also "Refugees in Arua District: A Human Security Analysis," *Refugee Law Project Working Paper No. 3*, September 2001.

[453] *See* text accompanying note 490, below, for a discussion of the provisions of Ugandan law establishing the "camp commandants."

told me to walk in front of him. I asked why, and he said, "if you don't do what I say, I will kill you right here." When we left he said, "this is the end for you." . . . Luckily it was dark, and in the forest, and I ran away.[454]

Etienne decided to leave Kyangwali camp soon after this incident occurred.

Mahret Z., an Eritrean woman described mistreatment she suffered in Uganda's Nakivale Camp at the hands of Ethiopian refugees, who were in the majority. She said,

At night when I was sleeping [in Nakivale Camp] some people burned my house down in 1999…. There were people against me in that camp because I am Eritrean. The police didn't help me either. The second time six people started beating me and one of those men raped me. They hit me very hard on the head. That beating is in my file in the camp, but I kept the raping between me and God. It happened on December 22, 2000. After that when I went to food distributions they would beat me. On August 15, 2001 they beat me, and threw me to the ground in a bad place where there were many sharp things and there is still something in my [left] shoulder from that beating… They refused to give me a chance to travel out of that camp…. I decided I had to leave that place, and I came to Kampala in October 2001.[455]

Several other women refugees cited fears of sexual violence as a reason for not going to one of Uganda's camps. For example, Mary A., introduced previously, told a Human Rights Watch researcher, "[I]f they send me to one of those camps with the Congolese—if I have to stay among them—I know they

[454] Human Rights Watch interview with refugee, Kampala, Uganda, April 10, 2002. The next morning Etienne went to the camp commandant to report the incident. They went together to the UPDF headquarters. Mr. Z was identified and admitted he had been paid U.S.$300 to kill Etienne. But Mr. Z refused to admit who had paid him. So the UPDF soldiers beat Mr. Z, trying to get him to disclose the name of the person behind the assassination, but he refused. As a result, he was detained and transferred to Kampala where he remained in custody as of April 10, 2002. After Mr. Z had been arrested, some UPDF soldiers came later to Etienne and offered him money, suggesting he should change the story so Mr. Z could go free. Etienne refused, so they threatened him saying "you will drink blood."
[455] Human Rights Watch interview with refugee, Kampala, Uganda, April 12, 2002.

will cause me problems. They will beat me like they have beaten me before. They do not understand that in my culture you cannot have sexual relations when you have such a small child. They do not pay attention to my culture."[456]

Finally, Angeline Y. recounted to a Human Rights Watch researcher that the UNHCR Protection Officer told her she should go to the camp, but she refused, saying there is a lot of sexual violence there. He laughed and said, "You can find a husband there."[457] She was very upset about this and was too angry to even answer. She continually repeated to Human Rights Watch, "does he think this is why I am here?"[458]

---

[456] Human Rights Watch interview with refugee, Kampala, Uganda, April 12, 2002.
[457] Human Rights Watch interview with refugee, Kampala, Uganda, April 10, 2002.
[458] Human Rights Watch interview with refugee, Kampala, Uganda, April 10, 2002.

RESPONSIBILITY FOR CAMP CONDITIONS

Host Governments

Host governments are primarily responsible to provide refugees with adequate assistance and the means of survival. However, in developing countries such as Kenya[459] and Uganda,[460] governments may be unable to meet the needs of large numbers of refugees and will require the help of the international community, including UNHCR. That help has not always been forthcoming for refugees in East Africa. In 2002, UNHCR required U.S.$27,000,000 to run its programs in Kenya and by mid-year the agency had only received $13,000,000.[461] In Uganda, UNHCR required $16,000,000 to run its programs and the agency had only received $10,000,000 by mid-2002.[462]

Given these funding shortfalls, the international community is partially responsible for the lack of adequate food and other assistance for refugees described above. For example, food distributions in the camps in Kenya have fallen far below UNHCR/WFP nutritional standards,[463] and urgent pleas for contributions have not yet been answered.[464]

Host governments such as Kenya and Uganda are also responsible for ensuring security in refugee camps and for providing avenues of redress to victims of violence. Both governments bear responsibility for locating refugee camps near borders, thereby allowing rebel groups and security agents to infiltrate and de-stabilize camp security. By locating camps where they have, Kenya and Uganda have contravened their obligations under the OAU Refugee Convention.[465]

Host governments are also required to take "all necessary measures to ensure that the civilian and humanitarian character of refugee camps... is

---

[459] The size of the refugee population in Kenya as compared with the per capita GDP of the country indicates that Kenya bears the "tenth worst burden" of refugees in the world. *See* UNHCR, *Global Report 2001*, at 31.

[460] The size of the refugee population in Uganda as compared with the per capita GDP of the country indicates that Uganda bears the "ninth worst burden" of refugees in the world. *See* UNHCR, *Global Report 2001*, at 31.

[461] *See* UNHCR *Mid-Year Progress Report*, 2002.

[462] *See* UNHCR *Mid-Year Progress Report*, 2002.

[463] *See* WFP/UNHCR, *Guidelines for Estimating Food and Nutritional Needs in Emergencies*, 1997. *See* also above note 387.

[464] *See* WFP, *Updates on Selected Relief Operations*, "Kenya Chapter," 2002 (noting that "unless urgent food pledges are received soon, WFP will be obliged to reduce the ration scale to 1,119 kcal per person per day in June 2002).

[465] Kenya and Uganda are required to, as far as possible, "settle refugees at a reasonable distance from the frontier of their country of origin." OAU Refugee Convention, Article 2(6).

maintained,"[466] and to investigate crimes in refugee camps and provide access to courts for redress.[467] Kenya has made some improvements in these areas, by increasing the presence of trained police and by prosecuting some criminals; however, the rate of conviction for the crime of rape still remains very low.[468] And while Uganda does station UPDF officers to oversee security in the refugee camp districts, the day-to-day security is most often provided by so-called local defense units, which are not as well trained, and often deployed in low numbers.[469]

UNHCR

Although UNHCR's mandate is to protect refugees and to seek durable solutions to refugee situations, it has increasingly become involved in the delivery of humanitarian assistance. In fact, UNHCR argues that it is often through the provision of assistance that it has access to and is best able to protect refugees.[470] Moreover, UNHCR's statute requires it to facilitate the coordination of relief efforts for refugees.[471] As a result, UNHCR has overarching responsibility for the assistance programs in camps, which are often run by NGOs contracted as implementing partners to the agency. UNHCR recognizes that it "is responsible for ensuring that the... immediate material needs of the refugees are met in an effective and appropriate manner."[472] Unfortunately, given the inadequate food relief distributed to refugees in Kenya and Uganda, UNHCR was not meeting this responsibility. Again, the failures were not only the agency's responsibility. WFP, responsible for delivering food supplies, reported that in Uganda it "will be running out of... food commodities between May and October 2002, which will adversely affect the refugees."[473] As mentioned above, this is largely due to lack of international funding for assistance programs.

---

[466] See ExCom General Conclusion on International Protection No. 77, 1995, para. q.

[467] See "Personal Security of Refugees," ExCom Conclusion No. 72, 1993.

[468] Human Rights Watch interview with UNHCR officials, Nairobi, Kenya, April 18, 2002.

[469] See e.g. Refugee Law Project, *Refugees and the Security Situation in Adjumani District*, June 2001, p. 8.

[470] See Executive Committee of the High Commissioner's Programme Forty Fifth Session *Note on International Protection* A/AC.96/830, September 7, 1994, paragraphs 14-18.

[471] See *Statute of the Office of the United Nations High Commissioner for Refugees*, General Assembly Resolution 428(V), December 14, 1950.

[472] UNHCR, *Handbook for Emergencies*, January 1, 2000, p. 4.

[473] WFP, *Updates on Selected Relief Operations*, "Uganda Chapter," 2002.

UNHCR is charged by its own guidelines and by numerous ExCom conclusions to develop and implement "practical measures"[474] to "provide effective physical protection to asylum-seekers and refugees."[475] And, for example, the agency has promulgated detailed guidelines on preventing sexual violence against refugee women in camps.[476] UNHCR has taken some appropriate measures in Kenya, for example, by creating the "protection area" in Kakuma camp and by instituting the firewood program in both Kakuma and Dadaab. However, both of these innovations are limited in their effectiveness. Located near a police post and surrounded by barbed wire, the "protection area," does provide some protection. But at the same time, refugees living there are suffering from a severe deprivation of freedom of movement, and children are being denied access to education. Finally, addressing the protection concerns of 100,000 individual refugees is extraordinarily difficult when UNHCR has only one protection officer working in the camp, which was the case in Kakuma until July 2002.[477]

While the Ugandan government has a primary responsibility to bring to an end attacks on refugee camps in Uganda, UNHCR also has a responsibility to deal with the consequences of such attacks. In an effort to fulfill this responsibility, UNHCR devoted itself in mid-August 2002 to transferring more than 20,000 refugees who had fled the attacks to safer camps in Kiryondongo and Kyangwali.[478]

When host governments such as Kenya or Uganda insist on confining refugees to camps, UNHCR sometimes goes along with the policies because they are more convenient or cost-effective; and at other times because the agency believes it will put the very principle of asylum at risk if it opposes camp confinement. UNHCR is sometimes stuck between the rock of unpleasant camp confinement policies and the hard place of governments refusing to host any refugees at all if camps are not used. However, because UNHCR is mandated to provide protection to all refugees (regardless of where they are living), the agency must take notice when confinement to refugee camps constitutes a protection problem. One senior staff member of an NGO said,

---

[474] *See* "Personal Security of Refugees," ExCom Conclusion No. 72, 1993, at para f.
[475] Ibid. at para d.
[476] *See,* e.g., *UNHCR Guidelines on Prevention and Response to Sexual Violence Against Refugees,* 1995.
[477] Human Rights Watch correspondence with international NGO, July 26, 2002. Another international NGO staff member explained that there had also not been a Senior Protection Officer in place in Kakuma during 2000 and 2001. Human Rights Watch interview with international NGO staff member, Nairobi, Kampala, April 24, 2002.
[478] *See* "Final Move to Start Soon for Displaced Refugees in Uganda," *UNHCR News Story,* August 16, 2002.

> The location of camps is very poor, and if people had better legal rights, they could integrate better. However, there is such a problem of donor fatigue. The camps should not be located so far away from major trading centers.... The refugees are becoming refugees from UNHCR since they are not being attended to appropriately. Some of these people have lived in camps for more than ten years.[479]

Since UNHCR runs the refugee camps and settlements in Kenya and Uganda, the agency should work with the governments concerned to put standard procedures in place so that refugees may apply for permission to leave camps on any of several clearly established grounds. In addition, when camps are not safe and where conditions are life threatening, and when governments consider urban refugees to be impermissibly present in the city, the agency's protection mandate requires it to push Kenya and Uganda to acknowledge that "freedom of movement is the rule under international law and restrictions should be the exception."[480]

---

[479] Human Rights Watch interview with international NGO staff member, Nairobi, Kenya, April 24, 2002.
[480] *See* UNHCR, *Policy on Refugees in Urban Areas*, December 12, 1997, para. 3.

CAMP CONFINEMENT POLICIES

Kenya's Camp Confinement Policy

In Kenya, refugees are required by an unwritten executive policy, which started in 1991, to reside in Dadaab camp or in Kakuma camp. The camps have been in place for more than eleven years.[481] The minister responsible for internal security has been granted the power to enact a policy for "requiring aliens to reside and remain within certain places or districts."[482] However, under law such a policy may only be enacted "when a state of war exists... or when it appears that an occasion of imminent danger or great emergency has arisen."[483] Neither the Minister nor parliament has ever promulgated laws or regulations to enact the encampment policy. Nevertheless, a camp confinement policy exists and is enforced on a daily basis.

While administrative exceptions to the camp confinement policy appear to exist, they—like the confinement policy itself—are not enacted into law or regulation. According to UNHCR, the exceptions have been developed through consultations with Kenya's Ministry of Home Affairs.[484] Apparently, the following categories of refugees may fit within one of these administrative exceptions to camp confinement:

- refugees undergoing resettlement interviews or processing;
- refugees who require specialized medical or psychological care not available in camps;
- refugees who are pursuing educational opportunities not available in camps; and
- refugees with serious security problems in camps.

However, refugees are completely unaware of these exceptions. In fact, even staff members of large international NGOs working in Kakuma camp

---

[481] *See* Arthur C. Helton, *The Price of Indifference*, 2002 at 156 (noting that the camps for Somali refugees in Kenya "were established in the early 1990s: Ifo in September 1991, Dagahaley in March 1992 and Hagadera in June 1992."); Lutheran World Federation, "Kakuma Refugee Camp," 2002, available at: www.lwfkenyasudan.org (explaining that "LWF/DWS was invited by UNHCR in mid-1992 to help establish a refugee camp at Kakuma (north west Kenya) in response to an influx of an estimated 30,000 Sudanese refugees fleeing fighting in Southern Sudan and entering Northern Kenya through the border town of Lokichoggio.").
[482] *See* Aliens Restriction Act, Article 3, May 1973.
[483] *See* Aliens Restriction Act, Article 3, May 1973.
[484] Human Rights Watch interview with UNHCR officials, Nairobi, Kenya, April 18, 2002.

informed Human Rights Watch that they were not aware of any exceptions to the camp confinement policy.[485] There are also no regularized procedures before impartial decision makers in which individuals may apply to be considered for one of the exceptions, and the camp authorities, who do occasionally grant travel permission, exercise completely unfettered discretion in deciding who among the refugees will be allowed to leave the camps.

Finally, the Kenyan police are not informed of any accepted exceptions to the camp confinement policy.[486] As a result, police in Kenya regularly enforce the policy without exceptions. In fact, the policy is used as a rationale for police harassment even if a refugee has been granted permission to leave the camp. As a senior member of an NGO working in Kakuma camp explained, "There is a major problem with the police along the way from Kakuma to Nairobi. They subject people to harassment and physical violence even when they have travel permits."[487] Refugees are often ordered by police to return to camps without any inquiry into whether a particular refugee fits within one of the exceptions to the confinement policy. One refugee who had faced serious security problems in a camp was arrested by an officer who angrily shouted at him, "you are supposed to be in the camp – so what are you doing here? Go to the camp!"[488]

Uganda's Camp Confinement Policy

In Uganda, refugees are required to live in camps that have been in place since the late 1980s, hosting mostly Sudanese refugees.[489]

Uganda's laws provide for its camp confinement policy in more detail than Kenya's. Uganda's 1960 Control of Aliens Act (CARA) provides for the confinement of refugees in settlements. The Minister in charge is enabled to appoint a Director of Refugees, who in turn may designate particular places in Uganda as refugee settlements and appoint "settlement commandants."[490] CARA also provides that the Minister may "by order in writing" direct refugees or classes of refugees to reside in a refugee settlement or in "such other place in

---

[485] Human Rights Watch interview with staff member of international NGO, Nairobi, Kenya, April 24, 2002.
[486] Human Rights Watch interviews with Kenyan police officers, Nairobi, Kenya, April 18, 2002.
[487] Human Rights Watch interview with staff member of international NGO, Nairobi, Kenya, April 24, 2002.
[488] Human Rights Watch interview with refugee, Nairobi, Kenya, April 4, 2002.
[489] See Zachary Lomo, Angela Naggaga, Lucy Hovil, "The Phenomenon of Forced Migration in Uganda: an Overview of Policy and Practice in an Historical Context," *Refugee Law Project Working Paper No. 1*, June 2001 at 5 (recalling that "[s]ince 1988 approximately 150,000 Sudanese refugees have been resident in the West Nile districts" of Uganda).
[490] See CARA, Article 5(b).

Uganda as may be specified in the order."[491] A refugee who violates such an order "shall be guilty of an offence."[492] It prohibits refugees from leaving or attempting to leave settlements without the permission of the settlement commandant and makes it an offence for any person to harbor a refugee outside of the settlements.[493] CARA does not provide for any exceptions to the requirement that refugees reside in settlements.

As in Kenya, the exceptions to the camp confinement policy in Uganda are not enacted into law and are implemented by an ad hoc administrative policy. In an interview with the Office of the Prime Minister, the exceptions to Uganda's camp confinement policy were described as follows:

> There are some [refugees] with security reasons for not being in the camp, and there are others who don't integrate easily into camps like the particularly vulnerable, professionals, those who are chronically sick. There are others who have security problems in the camps but in the city people have security problems too. We use our administrative powers to allow people to stay [in Kampala].[494]

The Directorate of Refugees, within the Office of the Prime Minister, sets policy for the camps, and it works in concert with UNHCR. However, the day-to-day business in the camps and the direct power over who may leave the settlements rests at the unfettered discretion of the camp commandant. Many refugees fear the camp commandants, who often exercise their authority in an arbitrary fashion.[495] In addition, many refugees in Uganda do not know that there are exceptions to the camp confinement policy.

---

[491] See CARA, Article 8(1).

[492] See CARA, Article 8(5).

[493] See CARA, Section 17(3), Section 13.

[494] Human Rights Watch interview with Ugandan government official, Office of the Prime Minister, Kampala, Uganda, April 13, 2002.

[495] Camp commandants are sometimes accused of abusive behavior as well. At Kyangwali settlement, a refugee alleged that the camp commandant raped a Congolese refugee woman. UNHCR was investigating, but later refugees reported that the camp commandant was freed by the police and threw himself a party to celebrate. Human Rights Watch interview with NGO, Kampala, Uganda, April 9, 2002. See also Refugee Law Project, Refugees in Arua District: A Human Security Analysis, September 2001 at 12-14 (noting that "[refugees] saw the authorities as not only unfair, but as a direct threat to themselves.").

EXAMINATION OF CAMP CONFINEMENT POLICIES UNDER INTERNATIONAL LAW

For both Kenya and Uganda, the relevant international law applicable to refugees can be found in the 1951 Convention Relating to the Status of Refugees and its Related Protocol (the "Refugee Convention"), the OAU Refugee Convention, and the ICCPR.

Once an individual has entered a country and has been recognized on either a *prima facie*[496] or individualized basis as a refugee, his or her rights and duties as a refugee under international law do not change based on whether he or she is located in a city or a refugee camp. The same international standards, originating from the Refugee Convention or the OAU Refugee Convention or other forms of human rights law,[497] apply irrespective of where a refugee lives within a particular country.

The Refugee Convention affords refugees the right to freedom of movement, subject to any restrictions applicable to aliens generally in the same circumstance.[498] While the Refugee Convention provides for this right, it has been better elaborated upon and is more protective[499] in the ICCPR, which is complementary to the Refugee Convention on this subject, and to which both Kenya and Uganda are parties.[500] The Human Rights Committee has recognized that the ICCPR must apply "without discrimination between citizens and

---

[496] *See* note 18, above for a definition of *prima facie* refugees.

[497] UNHCR's ExCom has reiterated the importance of respecting other human rights of refugees, not merely those established in the Refugee Convention, on numerous occasions. *See*, e.g. "Conclusion on Safeguarding Asylum," ExCom Conclusion No. 82 (1997) para. (vi) (reiterating "the obligation to treat asylum-seekers and refugees in accordance with applicable human rights and refugee law standards as set out in relevant international instruments.").

[498] *See* Refugee Convention, Article 26. It should be noted that neither Kenya nor Uganda has enacted general limits on freedom of movement applicable to all aliens in the same circumstances.

[499] UNHCR notes that "when both the 1951 Convention and an international human rights treaty deal with a particular right affecting refugees (for example, the right to form associations) and the human rights treaty offers more generous protection.... The general rule to apply... is that the provision which is most generous should prevail." The only possible exception, UNHCR notes, is when a very general and more generous provision is in a human rights treaty and that provision is unclear as to whether it benefits refugees. *See* UNHCR Training Module, "Human Rights and Refugee Protection: Part I," October 1995, p. 47. This latter exception cannot apply to the ICCPR's freedom of movement provision since it is more specific than the provision in the Refugee Convention, and it clearly applies to all non-citizens, including refugees.

[500] Kenya acceded to the ICCPR on May 1, 1972 and Uganda acceded on June 21, 1995. It should be noted that other rights set forth in the ICCPR are not necessarily more protective or detailed than those in the Refugee Convention.

aliens."[501] The term "aliens" includes asylum seekers and refugees. The Committee further notes that, "Aliens have the full right to liberty and security of the person.... They have the right to liberty of movement and free choice of residence.... These rights of aliens may be qualified only by such limitations as may be lawfully imposed under the Covenant." [502]

Camp Confinement Policies as a Violation of Freedom of Movement
The ICCPR provides for the principle of freedom of movement[503] in the following manner:

> Everyone lawfully within the territory of a State shall, within that territory, have the right to liberty of movement and freedom to choose his residence.[504]

This right to freedom of movement can only be restricted as "provided by law" if "necessary to protect national security, public order, public health, or morals, or the rights and freedoms of others."[505]

In sum, the right can be understood in the following manner:

- Every non-citizen (including an asylum seeker or refugee) who is lawfully present in a country must enjoy the right to freedom of movement;
- Limits enacted in law can be placed on this right if a non-citizen is not lawfully present;
- Limits enacted in law can be placed on this right if a non-citizen presents a threat to national security, public order, public health, etc.;
- Governments cannot discriminate between the freedom of movement rights of non-citizens and citizens, unless non-citizens present a threat to national security, in which case the limits on the right must be enacted in law; and

---

[501] See "The Position of Aliens Under the Covenant", CCPR General Comment 15, 1986 para. 2.
[502] Ibid.
[503] The Refugee Convention provides in its Article 26 that: "Each Contracting State shall accord to refugees lawfully in its territory the right to choose their place of residence and to move freely within its territory, subject to any regulations applicable to aliens generally in the same circumstances."
[504] See ICCPR, Article 12(1).
[505] See ICCPR, Article 12(3).

- Governments cannot discriminate between the freedom of movement rights of different categories of non-citizens.

UNHCR's ExCom has encouraged "States to intensify their efforts to protect the rights of refugees. . .to avoid unnecessary and severe curtailment of their freedom of movement."[506]

The Lawful Presence of Refugees in Kenya and Uganda

Non-citizens who enter Kenya or Uganda must have their status as refugees recognized before they can be considered lawfully present in either country. In the case of asylum-seekers who enter either Kenya or Uganda unlawfully (which many do), the Refugee Convention does allow for restrictions on the movement of asylum seekers if necessary until their status is assessed.[507]

As described more fully above, Kenya and Uganda each have two methods for recognizing the status of refugees. First, refugees who are fleeing events disturbing security in their countries of origin are recognized as refugees under the OAU Refugee Convention. The OAU Refugee Convention expands the definition of refugees to include persons compelled to seek refuge from "external aggression, occupation, foreign domination, or events seriously disturbing internal order in either part or the whole of [the] country of origin." Both Kenya and Uganda have implemented their obligations under the OAU Refugee Convention by affording *prima facie*[508] status to all refugees fleeing Sudan and Somalia, as well as to some fleeing Ethiopia and Congo.

Second, refugees may be recognized through UNHCR-run or government-run individualized determinations.

Uganda acknowledges in its domestic law and policy that individual refugees recognized either on a *prima facie* basis or through individual determinations are lawfully present. In Kenya, the government has requested UNHCR to conduct individual determinations on its behalf and the government has officially recognized that Somalis and Sudanese are *prima facie* refugees. Therefore, as in Uganda, refugees recognized as such either on a *prima facie* basis or through UNHCR individual determinations are lawfully present in Kenya. Once they are lawfully present in either Kenya or Uganda, refugees are entitled to the right of freedom of movement under the ICCPR.[509]

---

[506] *See* ExCom General Conclusion on International Protection No. 65 (1991) at (c).
[507] *See* Refugee Convention, Article 31(2).
[508] *See* note 16, above.
[509] According to international standards, Kenya and Uganda also cannot distinguish between *prima facie* refugees of a particular nationality and refugees of other nationalities recognized through individual determinations in domestic legislation, without violating the conclusions of CERD that "legislation concerning asylum must treat

Balancing the National Security Concerns of Kenya and Uganda

Kenya and Uganda justify limits on the freedom of movement of refugees by asserting that refugees present a threat to the national security of Kenya or Uganda.[510] It is not altogether evident that the concentration of refugees into large and long-standing camp settings near to borders, in places within easy reach of armed groups and small-arms traders, actually addresses the security concerns. By placing refugee camps so close to the borders with Sudan (in the case of Uganda) and with Sudan and Somalia (in the case of Kenya), the countries have contravened the OAU Convention, which requires governments to, as far as possible, "settle refugees at a reasonable distance from the frontier of their country of origin."[511] In addition, security risks are heightened by the simple fact that camps are set up in a single location, where sometimes hostile ethnic or national groups must live together and where rebel leaders know they can launch recruiting raids or find humanitarian assistance.[512]

National governments have considerable discretion as to what constitutes a threat to national security. However, the ICCPR requires that in the absence of a derogation during a time of public emergency,[513] limits placed on freedom of movement in the name of national security must be "necessary."[514] In order to determine whether something is "necessary," the severity of the security concerns must be weighed against the severity of limits on freedom of movement. The primary means by which such limits can be balanced against

---

all asylum-seekers equally without regard to national origin." If *prima facie* refugees (who come mostly from Sudan and Somalia) are afforded fewer rights than individually recognized refugees, the principle of non-discrimination between non-citizens is violated.
[510] *See* e.g. BBC Monitoring Service: Africa, "Kenyan President Warns Police, Prison Officers Against Violating Human Rights," June 15, 2002 (reporting that Kenyan President Daniel arap Moi "expressed concern at the infiltration into Kenya by refugees, many of who [sic] were not regularized by the UN High Commissioner for Refugees (UNHCR). 'This has caused a serious security situation in the country as some of the refugees brought with them firearms,' [Moi] said."); Xinhua News Agency, "Ugandan, Rwandan Presidents to Meet Again," November 23, 2001 (noting that the presence of Rwandan army officers in Uganda had led to "strained relations" between Rwanda and Uganda and promises between the two governments "not to harbor dissident groups seeking to destabilize relations between the two countries.").
[511] OAU Refugee Convention, Article 2(6).
[512] *See* the detailed discussion of these security problems in camps at pages 73-74 and 79-81, above.
[513] *See* ICCPR, Article 4.
[514] ICCPR, Article 12(3).

the national security concerns at stake is through legislative debate, which is one reason why the ICCPR requires that such provisions be enacted "in law."[515]

Neither Kenya nor Uganda have enacted legislation to identify the security concerns of either of the host governments and provide for limits on refugees' freedom of movement tailored to the need to address those concerns. Instead, both governments have adopted unwritten ad hoc policies that allow for exceptions to the camp confinement rule. The presumption for legislators should be that people are not confined to camps, except for reasons that fully meet the international standard, and to which there should be appropriate exceptions and procedures put in place to determine impartially whether an individual fits within one of the exceptions. If Kenya and Uganda did so, the human rights of refugees would be better respected.

Camp confinement policies impose an extreme limit on refugees' freedom of movement, and while recognizing legitimate security concerns of the governments involved, without providing a framework for the policy in law, the policy violates freedom of movement under the ICCPR.

Long-term Camp Confinement Policies as Analogous to Arbitrary and Indefinite Detention

Camp confinement policies are not the same as arbitrary and indefinite detention. However, there are some important comparisons to be drawn that should guide governments when confining refugees to camps. The ICCPR sets forth the following protection against arbitrary and indefinite detention:

> Everyone has the right to liberty and security of person. No one shall be subjected to arbitrary arrest or detention. No one shall be deprived of his liberty except on such grounds and in accordance with such procedures as are established by law.[516]

Similarly, the African Charter on Human and Peoples' Rights states that, "Every individual shall have the right to liberty and to the security of his person. No one may be deprived of his freedom except for reasons and conditions

---

[515] The Human Rights Committee (the UN body charged with interpreting and enforcing the ICCPR) has stated that States parties to the ICCPR "shall guarantee [the right of freedom of movement] to everyone lawfully within the territory of the State and thus, States parties must, if necessary, amend their domestic legislation accordingly." *See* Commission on Human Rights, *Report of the Special Rapporteur on the Rights of Non-Citizens*, E/CN.4/Sub.2/2001/20 at para. 52.

[516] *See* ICCPR, Article 9(1).

previously laid down by law. In particular, no one may be arbitrarily arrested or detained."[517]

The ICCPR also requires that detained individuals have access to a court to determine the lawfulness of the detention:

> Anyone who is deprived of his liberty by arrest or detention shall be entitled to take proceedings before a court, in order that that court may decide without delay on the lawfulness of his detention and order his release if the detention is not lawful.[518]

The right to be free from arbitrary and indefinite detention is not dependent upon whether an individual is lawfully present in a country. UNHCR has repeatedly reminded governments that the detention of asylum seekers, some of whom may enter a country unlawfully, is inherently undesirable.[519] Refugees should not be arbitrarily detained.

Camp Confinement Compared with Detention

Interpreting the Refugee Convention and norms of international human rights law, UNHCR's *Revised Guidelines* define detention as "confinement within a narrowly bounded or restricted location, including prisons, closed camps, detention facilities or airport transit zones, where freedom of movement is substantially curtailed, and where the only opportunity to leave this limited area is to leave the territory."[520] In addition, UNHCR *Guidelines* state that, "persons who are subject to limitations on domicile and residency are not generally considered to be in detention." [521]   Finally, UNHCR notes that, "the cumulative impact of the restrictions as well as the degree and intensity of each of them should also be assessed." [522]

Under UNHCR's definition, camp confinement policies in Kenya and Uganda could be considered a form of detention. While the camps are not completely closed, freedom of movement is "substantially curtailed." For many refugees, the only opportunity to leave the camps will come when they agree to

---

[517] *See African Charter on Human and Peoples' Rights*, OAU Doc. CAB/LEG/67/3/Rev.5, Article 6.
[518] *See* ICCPR, Article 9(4).
[519] *See* UNHCR Revised Guidelines on Applicable Criteria and Standards Relating to the Detention of Asylum Seekers, February 1999, para. 1 (noting that "the detention of asylum seekers is, in the view of UNHCR inherently undesirable.").
[520] Ibid.
[521] Ibid.
[522] Ibid.

repatriate, or "leave the territory." However, UNHCR does note in the above definition that persons limited in their "residency" are not generally considered to be in detention, which appears to distinguish camp confinement from detention. At the same time, the camp confinement policies do have a marked "cumulative impact" on the lives of refugees, which UNHCR suggests "should be assessed."

By way of comparison with other governmental policies, governments from Côte d'Ivoire to Thailand have hosted large numbers of refugees in camp settings. Particularly well-known camps of the "closed" variety were set up for the hundreds of thousands of Cambodian refugees who fled first to the border areas of Cambodia and later to Thailand in the late 1970s and early 1980s. Thailand, which unlike Kenya and Uganda is not party to the Refugee Convention, insisted in 1984-5 that the camps for Cambodians should be closed.[523] Thai ranger unit[524] personnel were stationed around the camps to monitor the refugee's movements. In addition, internal political pressures kept refugees from fleeing the camps.[525]

However, permission to leave the camp could be bought with a bribe, and refugees were able to leave after bribing officials on a periodic basis. Refugees often left the camps to search for food, to visit family inside Cambodia and to travel to market centers in nearby villages.[526] However, living in nearby Thai villages was not an option and refugees always had to return to the camps. Finally, while bribes could be paid, sometimes travel outside the camp came at a very high price. Thai officials were known to shoot and kill refugees found outside the camps.

In contrast to the above, the recognized best practice is for camps to be "open" so that refugees can travel in and out freely—which refugees living in Kenya or Uganda simply cannot do. For example, Côte d'Ivoire has hosted large populations of refugees in some four hundred and fifty sites within its *zone d'accueil*.[527] The zone is a swath of territory, located in the west of the country, in which individual refugees can choose to live anywhere—in a more rural setting or an urban environment—within the designated area.

The official policy of the governments of Kenya and Uganda is that the refugee camps are "closed." Refugees are not allowed to settle elsewhere in Kenya or Uganda or even to travel in and out of the camps. Of course, the fact

---

[523] *See* Tony Jackson, *Just Waiting to Die?*, Oxfam, 1987 at 1.
[524] Ibid. at 5.
[525] *See* e.g. Dr. Josephine Reynell, *Socio-Economic Evaluation of the Khmer Camps on the Thai/Kampuchean Border*, Refugee Studies Programme, 1986, p. 6 (stating that "the camps are closed not only because of Thai policy but also because of Khmer policy.").
[526] Id. at 26.
[527] *See* e.g. UNHCR, "Cote d'Ivoire," *UNHCR Global Report 2002*.

that Uganda grants refugees access to small portions of land for cultivation alters the degree to which refugees feel compelled to leave the settlement areas. And in practice in both countries, some refugees do move in and out of the camps, but always facing the risk that their lack of permission to travel or live (even for short periods of time) anywhere else in Uganda or Kenya makes them vulnerable to police harassment and even arrest and deportation. Few refugees are able to convince the camp authorities in either Kenya or Uganda to grant them official permission to travel out of the camps.

Camp Confinement Compared with Arbitrary Detention
The Human Rights Committee has stated that "arbitrary detention" arises not only when there is no law allowing for it, but also when there are elements of inappropriateness, injustice, lack of predictability or disregard for due process of law.[528]

The Working Group on Arbitrary Detention has adopted a series of principles to govern the detention of non-citizens (including refugees). Principle Six requires that the decision to detain a non-citizen "must be taken by a duly empowered authority with a sufficient level of responsibility and must be founded on criteria of legality established by the law."[529]

The confinement of refugees in camps in Kenya and Uganda is analogous to arbitrary detention because the procedures and standards by which an application for leave to depart from the camp are not known to the refugees, and are arbitrarily implemented by camp authorities. If the Kenyan and Ugandan governments enacted exceptions to the camp confinement policy into law, and implemented standard procedures by which refugees could apply for permission to leave the camp, they would go a long way towards bringing their camp policies into line with international human rights standards.

Camp Confinement Compared with Indefinite Detention
The camp confinement policy is also of concern because refugees have been confined to camps for such a long period of time—in Kenya for eleven and in Uganda for fourteen years. The Working Group on Arbitrary Detention has stated in its Principle Seven that in all cases in which a non-citizen is detained, "[a] maximum period should be set by law and the custody may in no case be unlimited or of excessive length."[530] In one decision of the Working Group, it

---

[528] See Womah Mukong v. Cameroon, Communication No. 458/1991, U.N. Doc. CCPR/C/51/D/458/1991, August 10, 1994.
[529] See Report of the Working Group on Arbitrary Detention, U.N. Doc. E/CN.4/2000/4, December 28, 1999.
[530] Ibid.

was held that three Cuban nationals who had been detained in the United States for over ten years violated the prohibition against arbitrary detention in international human rights law.[531]

In addition, the U.S. Supreme Court has held that non-citizens cannot be indefinitely detained when they cannot be returned to their own country.[532] The two individual non-citizens at issue in the case had been held in non-criminal detention for eight and five years, respectively.

Moreover, the serious problems refugee children face after several years of living in camp confinement were resoundingly criticized by ExCom when it

> [n]oted with serious concern the detrimental effects that extended stays in camps have on the development of refugee children and called for international action to mitigate such effects and provide durable solutions as soon as possible.[533]

While there is no clear rule as to the permissible length of time, courts and human rights bodies have found detention particularly suspect when there is no end in sight.[534] Like the non-citizens ordered released by the U.S. Supreme Court, many of the refugees living in Kenya and Uganda in long-term camp situations have no prospects of returning home. In addition, they have no prospects of being allowed to better integrate into Kenyan or Ugandan society.

In its Principle Seven, the Working Group on Arbitrary Detention has stated that governmental custody "may in no case be unlimited." The refugees living in Kenya and Uganda's camps are facing unlimited time in custody, making the fact of their camp confinement a human rights concern. It is for this reason that Human Rights Watch recommends that a time limit on refugees' presence in camps—after which they could apply to leave if they could show that their prospects for safe repatriation are few—be considered and implemented by the governments of Kenya and Uganda.

Conclusion

As this section has discussed, confinement in camps constitutes a serious limitation on refugees' freedom of movement. While governments do have the ability to determine whether the presence of refugees constitutes a national

---

[531] *See* Decisions and Opinions Adopted by the Working Group on Arbitrary Detention, U.N. Doc. E/CN.4/1998/44/Add.1, November 3, 1998.

[532] *See Zadvydas v. Davis*, 121 S.Ct.2941 (2001).

[533] *See* "Refugee Children," ExCom Conclusion No. 47 (1987) para. (m).

[534] The European Court of Human Rights has held that holding of asylum seekers risks becoming a "deprivation of liberty" when it is "prolonged excessively." *See Amuur v. France*, 22 EHRR 533 (1992).

security threat, that threat must be balanced against refugees' freedom of movement rights. Any limitations on those rights must be proportionate to the threat, and must be enacted in law. Moreover, Kenya and Uganda's camp confinement policies are analogous to arbitrary and indefinite detention. First, the camp confinement policies could be considered a form of detention. Second, the policies are arbitrary because refugees are not informed about the procedures and standards by which an application for permission to leave the camp can be made, and camp authorities arbitrarily grant permission. Finally, the fact that some refugees have been confined to the camps for more than a decade, in a situation where they have few prospects of returning home, makes the policies analogous to indefinite detention.

PART IV: POLICY CONSIDERATIONS

UNHCR'S 1997 URBAN REFUGEE POLICY
Introduction
UNHCR has a clear mandate to protect refugees, including those living in urban areas. In December 1997 UNHCR introduced its *Policy on Refugees in Urban Areas* (Urban Refugee Policy). The policy is based on a blanket assumption that most refugees should not be moving to or living in urban areas. In many places, UNHCR policy-makers at the field level have embraced this assumption. The Urban Refugee Policy makes two misguided assumptions about urban refugees:

- They are too reliant on UNHCR assistance; and
- Many of them should not be in urban areas, either because they have moved without authorization from a country where they found protection to another country (making them "irregular movers"); or because they have moved without authorization from elsewhere in the country of asylum.

In light of considerable evidence that these assumptions are unfounded, including the evidence contained in this report, Human Rights Watch recommends that the Urban Refugee Policy be substantially revised. Indeed, UNHCR's own Evaluation and Policy Analysis Unit (EPAU) has already come to this same conclusion on several occasions in thorough evaluations of UNHCR's urban refugee program in New Delhi[535] and Cairo,[536] in an evaluation of the implementation of the Urban Refugee Policy,[537] and in a report from a UNHCR/NGO workshop on this same subject.[538] Unfortunately, the EPAU's recommendations have not yet been implemented by UNHCR.

The most fundamental problem in the Urban Refugee Policy continues to be its lack of detailed protection recommendations. Instead, the policy focuses almost exclusively on assistance and ignores the very real protection needs of refugees in urban areas. As a result urban refugees, such as those interviewed

---

[535] *See* UNHCR, *Evaluation of UNHCR's Policy on Refugees in Urban Areas: A Case Study Review of New Delhi*, November 2000.
[536] *See* UNHCR, *Evaluation of UNHCR's Policy on Refugees in Urban Areas: A Case Study Review of Cairo*, June 2001.
[537] *See* UNHCR, *Evaluation of the Implementation of UNHCR's Policy on Refugees in Urban Areas*, December 2001.
[538] *See* UNHCR, *UNHCR Policy on Refugees in Urban Areas, Report of a UNHCR/NGO Workshop*, August 2002.

by Human Rights Watch in Kenya and Uganda, are falling into a protection vacuum.

Earlier Drafts of the Urban Refugee Policy
UNHCR began work on an urban refugee policy following recommendations from its Inspection and Evaluation Service in October 1995. An earlier draft of the policy was completed in March 1997, but this was heavily criticized both internally and externally. The major criticism centered on the unfounded core message—that it was either overtly illegal, or against efficient program management, for refugees to reside in urban centers. UNHCR's policy conclusion was unabashedly to reduce programs for urban refugees and to prevent refugees from locating in urban environments:

> This [1997] policy is likely to result in a more restrictive approach to the provision of care and maintenance assistance than hitherto and requires a more active approach to durable solutions, including containment of future irregular movement.[539]

Critique of UNHCR's Current Urban Refugee Policy
In response to these criticisms, UNHCR re-issued the policy in December 1997. Important improvements were made. For example, the second paragraph of the new Urban Refugee Policy gives renewed emphasis to UNHCR's protection responsibilities towards urban refugees:

> UNHCR's obligations in respect of international protection are not affected by either the location of the refugees of the nature of the movement to that location. In a number of countries, asylum seekers arrive directly in urban areas. Whatever the nature of the movement or legal status of a person of concern to UNHCR in an urban area, the overriding priority remains to ensure protection.[540]

However, this commitment is undermined by UNHCR's statement in the first paragraph that the policy seeks to address "the provision of assistance to...refugees in urban areas, [and] the problems that may be created by *unregulated* movement to urban areas, whether this movement takes place

---

[539] See UNHCR, *Comprehensive Policy on Urban Refugees*, Geneva, March 25, 1997, introductory note, para 4.
[540] See UNHCR, *Policy on Refugees in Urban Areas*, December 12, 1997, para. 2.

within the country or from another country where the refugee had found protection."[541] Thus, the concept of "irregular movers" to urban areas remains even in the revised policy.

Over-Reliance on UNHCR Assistance

The Urban Refugee Policy begins its discussion of assistance by stating that "there are many examples of problems and long-standing demands on UNHCR resources as a result of assistance programmes in urban areas."[542] The policy also focuses on means by which assistance programs can avoid long-term dependence and promote self-reliance, which are both understandable goals for any development initiative.

However, the policy also states "UNHCR may, however, limit the location where UNHCR assistance is provided. Where refugees are assisted in settlements or camps outside urban areas, UNHCR should provide assistance in urban areas to refugees from the same country of origin only with the agreement of the government and if there are compelling reasons[543] to do so."[544] The underlying message of this statement is that when refugees from the same country of origin are living in camps and in cities, UNHCR should assist them mainly in camps, particularly if the host government prefers them to live there.

Human Rights Watch believes that this policy runs counter to UNHCR's core mandate to provide protection to refugees wherever they are living. Neither the Refugee Convention nor UNHCR's Statute allow for a distinction to be made between the rights of refugees based upon their location in a camp or an urban setting. While many governments, such as Kenya and Uganda, have policies in place to limit the presence of refugees in urban environments, it is too often the case that UNHCR unreservedly accepts these policies, rather than advocating for the rights of refugees wherever they are under human rights and refugee law. UNHCR should be pushing governments like Kenya and Uganda to respect refugees' rights to freedom of movement and to provide protection and assistance to refugees in cities like Nairobi and Kampala.

Moreover, Human Rights Watch has found that refugees in urban areas have chronic assistance needs. Refugees in Nairobi and Kampala suffer from

---

[541] Ibid. para. 1.

[542] Ibid. para. 5.

[543] The "compelling reasons" UNHCR lists are: specific protection or security problems faced by an individual or his or her family in the settlement or camp; pre-arranged movement to an urban area for the duration of health care or for reunion with family members legally resident in the urban area; and assistance in achieving a durable solution, where this is possible in the urban area. *See* UNHCR, *Policy on Refugees in Urban Areas*, December 12, 1997, para. 4.

[544] *See* UNHCR, *Policy on Refugees in Urban Areas*, December 12, 1997, para. 3.

unsafe housing, inadequate food, and lack of access to basic medical care. Far from reducing assistance to urban refugees, as the Urban Refugee Policy advises, UNHCR should be increasing assistance to refugees in urban areas who are desperately in need.

The policy's recommendation that where refugees from the same country of origin are living in camps and in cities, UNHCR should only provide assistance to refugees in urban areas under compelling circumstances and with the express permission of the government is also problematic and contradicts other aspects of the Urban Refugee Policy. For example, the policy asserts that "a refugee in an urban area should have neither more nor less chance of resettlement than he or she would have had in a refugee camp in the same country."[545] Yet it was clearly the case in Uganda, for example, that *prima facie* refugees living in Kampala had less access to UNHCR and to resettlement opportunities.

Finally, in its analysis of planning assistance programs, the Urban Refugee Policy incorrectly assumes that "the majority of refugees in urban areas are generally male."[546] UNHCR's EPAU has consistently questioned the accuracy of this statement.[547] The assumption that refugee women and children are in the minority in urban areas has led directly to insufficient attention being paid to their particular protection and assistance needs. UNHCR recognizes this when it recommends that "particular attention must... be paid to identifying the[] needs [of women, adolescents, and children]."[548]

"Irregular" Movers

More than one-third of the Urban Refugee Policy is focused on the problem of "irregular movement,"[549] which is a term used in the policy to describe the concept of "secondary movement," for reasons not related to protection. The policy begins its discussion with protection concerns - it states that: "a refugee who is compelled to move because of specific protection or security problems in his or her previous country clearly cannot be considered to have found protection there."[550]

However, the remainder of the discussion focuses on means by which UNHCR can "discourage" irregular secondary movement. The policy states that while UNHCR's obligation to protect irregular movers is unchanged, the agency

---

[545] Ibid., para. 10.
[546] Ibid., para. 8.
[547] *See* also UNHCR, *Evaluation of the Implementation of UNHCR's Policy on Refugees in Urban Areas*, December 2001, para. 12.
[548] *See* UNHCR, *Policy on Refugees in Urban Areas*, December 12, 1997, para. 8.
[549] Eight of the Policy's twenty-one paragraphs discuss this issue.
[550] *See* UNHCR, *Policy on Refugees in Urban Areas*, December 12, 1997, para. 13.

"does not have an obligation to provide assistance to refugees after irregular movement on the same basis as it would have had there been no irregular movement."[551]

There is an assumption in the policy that the majority of urban refugees are irregular movers, but this is not substantiated anywhere in the policy and was not borne out by Human Rights Watch's own investigation into urban refugees in East Africa. Of the 150 refugees interviewed by Human Rights Watch, at most five were irregular movers, or persons who had already accessed protection through UNHCR's offices or obtained refugee status in a previous country of asylum. As already noted, many of these people had serious security reasons for moving from one country to another.

In addition, the overwhelming attention paid in the Urban Refugee Policy to the impropriety of irregular movement fails to recognize the nature of refugee movements in countries like Kenya and Uganda.[552] In these two countries and many others, the complexity of protection and assistance problems, the strong desire to reunite with family members, the realities of modes and paths of transport, and the panoply of actors who pose security threats all mean that refugees may have compelling reasons to move from one country to another.

The Urban Refugee Policy states that when determining the status of an individual who has moved from a first country of asylum, UNHCR staff should take into account the "specific protection or security problems" an alleged secondary mover may have faced in her first country of asylum before deciding whether or not to afford refugee protection.

But assessing the nature of the threats a refugee may have faced and the quality of the protection obtained only adds an additional labor-intensive layer to the determination process—one that in a city like Nairobi is already fraught with delays and staffing constraints. Perhaps partly because of these constraints, UNHCR protection officers do not always apply the protection standards articulated in the Urban Refugee Policy to potential "irregular" movers and, instead, summarily order them returned to the first country of asylum. As discussed below, Human Rights Watch documented problematic instances in which the policy against irregular "secondary movements" was applied to individuals both in Kenya and Uganda.

---

[551] See UNHCR, *Policy on Refugees in Urban Areas*, December 12, 1997, para. 18 (emphasis added).

[552] Such a policy focus on stopping irregular movers in their tracks also avoids ExCom's advice that humane treatment for refugees and asylum seekers should still be ensured "because of the uncertain situation in which they find themselves, [they] feel impelled to move from one country to another in an irregular manner." *See* "Problem of Refugees and Asylum-Seekers Who Move in an Irregular Manner from a Country in Which They Had Already Found Protection," ExCom Conclusion No. 58, 1989, para. c) iv).

Moreover, the Urban Refugee Policy focuses exclusively on modalities for sending "irregular" movers back to their countries of first asylum,[553] while completely ignoring the important question of how to provide adequate protection in the new country of asylum to those urban refugees who have legitimate security rationales for leaving their countries of first asylum.

Finally, the policy states that while UNHCR's protection duties vis-à-vis irregular movers remain the same, assistance may be scaled back. Yet this belies UNHCR's own frequently cited assertion that protection is most effectively provided through assistance.[554] In this report, Human Rights Watch has shown how urban refugees are suffering protection problems, such as rape, because of their lack of access to assistance, such as adequate housing.

Urban Refugees: A Policy Blind-Spot

Urban refugees are consistently ignored and policies in place for them sometimes contradict UNHCR's other policies and guidelines on protecting refugees, especially those on refugee women and children. The underlying assumption in many of these policies appears to be that refugees either live in camps, or if they are in an urban environment they are located in the developed world, where a number of governments have put in place sophisticated policies. Where urban refugees in developing countries are considered it is always with the assumption that they are there improperly.

For example, UNHCR's *Guidelines on the Protection of Refugee Women* make detailed recommendations on planning for the delivery of assistance within and the layout and location of refugee camps. Similar recommendations are not made for assistance programs or housing arrangements for women refugees in urban centers.[555] UNHCR's comprehensive discussion of physical and sexual attacks and abuse considers the problem in camps, and then jumps to a discussion of refugee women, presumably in industrialized countries, who are located in detention facilities.[556] Physical and sexual abuse of women refugees in urban environments is not considered. The few instances in which urban refugee women are directly addressed falter on the assumption that these women are improperly present in cities. For example, the policy accurately links the problem of prostitution with the illegal status of urban refugee women, without

---

[553] *See* UNHCR, *Policy on Refugees in Urban Areas*, December 12, 1997, para. 18.
[554] *See* Executive Committee of the High Commissioner's Programme Forty Fifth Session *Note on International Protection* A/AC.96/830, September 7, 1994, paragraphs 14-18.
[555] *See* UNHCR's *Guidelines on the Protection of Refugee Women*, July 1991, p. 29-30.
[556] Ibid. p. 31.

making targeted recommendations to ameliorate that illegal status in domestic law.[557]

In addition, *UNHCR's Guidelines on Prevention and Response to Sexual Violence Against Refugees*, acknowledges that refugees may be in camps or urban situations.[558] However, when discussing the various kinds of environments in which refugee women are at risk of attack, attacks near or in the "homes" of refugee women are discussed,[559] and problems in camps are discussed.[560] Nowhere is the obvious point made that refugee women sleeping on the streets due to lack of housing are particularly at risk of sexual violence.

Moreover, UNHCR's *Guidelines on the Protection and Care of Refugee Children*, fail to make explicit the agency's protection responsibilities for refugee children in urban environments. The agency's *Guidelines on Policies and Procedures in Dealing with Unaccompanied Children Seeking Asylum* are mostly directed at governments in the industrialized world, and they fail to mention UNHCR's responsibilities in its own status determinations, or the particular factors that arise when refugee children are seeking asylum in urban environments in the developing world. For example, the *Guidelines* fail to recognize that unaccompanied refugee children may not be identified when large numbers of refugees are seeking access to UNHCR's office in urban areas. Neither do the *Guidelines* recognize that unaccompanied refugee children may be seeking asylum and making decisions on behalf of several other younger siblings who may not be represented at the proceedings.

Finally, UNHCR does not compile comprehensive statistics on urban refugees. In those countries in which field offices do collect statistics on urban refugees, the focus is on those refugees who are registered with UNHCR and/or who are receiving UNHCR assistance.[561] Refugees not receiving UNHCR assistance, those who have been unable or unwilling to register, and those who are located in other urban environments within the same country are invisible and almost completely forgotten.

---

[557] Ibid. p. 40.
[558] *See* UNHCR, *Guidelines on Prevention and Response to Sexual Violence Against Refugees*, 1995, p. 5.
[559] Ibid. p. 5.
[560] Ibid. p. 9.
[561] *See* UNHCR, *Evaluation of the Implementation of UNHCR's Policy on Refugees in Urban Areas*, December 2001, para. 11.

POLICIES AGAINST SECONDARY MOVEMENT
The European Genesis of Policies Against Secondary Movement

In the course of our research in Kenya and Uganda, Human Rights Watch discovered that the governments of Kenya and Uganda, as well as UNHCR are increasingly applying policies against "secondary movement" in their status determinations. Generally speaking, these policies prohibit asylum seekers from accessing a country's refugee status determination procedures if, prior to arrival in that country, they traveled (made a "secondary movement") through another country where they did or could have applied for refugee status and/or obtained protection. In such cases, the policies provide that the asylum seeker should be returned to the latter country to seek protection there, though protection is by no means guaranteed.

Policies against secondary movement are rooted in Europe's "safe third country" policies, which emerged with the advent of two European treaties: the 1985 Schengen Agreement[562] and the 1990 Dublin Convention.[563] Their signatories sought to counteract the greater openness of Europe's internal borders brought about by the European Union by limiting the movements of asylum seekers and other migrants. The Council of Ministers for Immigration added a third layer to European safe third country policy in 1992, with its Resolution on a Harmonized Approach to Questions Concerning Host Third Countries.[564] The Resolution calls for the return of asylum seekers to any available *non*-E.U. "host third country" if a given asylum seeker will not face torture or a threat to her life or freedom there.

---

[562] *Agreement Between the Governments of the States of the Benelux Economic Union, the Federal Republic of Germany and the French Republic on the Gradual Abolition of Controls at the Common Frontiers* (the Schengen Agreement), June 14, 1985, 30 I.L.M. 73. The Schengen Agreement was designed to eliminate European border controls of all sorts, and was later buttressed by the 1990 Convention Applying the Schengen Agreement. *Convention Applying the Schengen Agreement of 14 June 1985 Between the Benelux Economic Union, the Federal Republic of Germany and the French Republic, on the Gradual Abolition of Checks at their Common Borders*, June 19, 1990, 30 I.L.M. 84. Article 29(2) of the Schengen Convention reads that "[e]very Contracting Party shall retain the right to refuse entry or to expel any applicant for asylum to a Third State on the basis of its national provisions and in accordance with its international commitments."
[563] Convention Determining the State Responsible for Examining Applications for Asylum Lodged in One of the Member States of the European Communities, (the Dublin Convention), June 15, 1990, 30 I.L.M. 427. *The Dublin Convention*, which superceded the Schengen Convention's asylum provisions, elaborated that an asylum seeker should always be returned to her country of first asylum within the European Union, where the domestic status determination procedures of that country will then govern her claim.
[564] Resolution on a Harmonized Approach to Questions Concerning Host Third Countries, Nov. 30 – Dec. 1, 1992, Doc. 4464/1/95 CIREA 3.

As a result, European governments routinely return asylum seekers to countries they have traveled through. In some cases, once they reach those "transit countries," asylum seekers are at risk of being deported once again to a state that does not have adequate refugee protection mechanisms in place and/or a state that has not even agreed to consider the claims of the particular individuals to be returned.

Individual European and other Western governments, such as the United Kingdom[565] and Australia,[566] have incorporated policies against secondary movement into their domestic laws as well. As of late September 2002, the U.S. and Canada were also considering such a policy.

Critique of Secondary Movement Policies

Most fundamentally, policies prohibiting secondary movements put asylum seekers at risk of being refouled to face torture and/or other serious harm. Refoulement can occur when a refugee is returned to any place where her life or freedom is at risk—that place could be her home country, but it could also be *any other country* she is sent back to. As a result, countries that expel asylum seekers to countries from which they have made a secondary movement risk violating their non-refoulement obligations. Human Rights Watch, the European Council on Refugees and Exiles, and many others have repeatedly criticized the clear risk of unlawful refoulement fostered by Europe's safe third country policies.[567] The Executive Committee of UNHCR has alluded to this risk as well, asserting that "notions such as ... 'safe third country' ... should be

---

[565] The United Kingdom's 1999 Immigration and Asylum Act, for example, specifies that an asylum applicant should be removed to an available third country if the Home Secretary certifies that country as one where her "life and liberty would not be threatened" for a Refugee Convention reason. *Immigration and Asylum Act*, 1999, c. 33, pt. I, § 11, entered into force October 2, 2000.

[566] In Australia, a federal court recently described its similar common law rule that expulsion "to a third country will not contravene Art 33 notwithstanding that the person has no right of residence in that country and that the country is not a party to the Convention, provided that it can be expected, nevertheless to afford the person claiming asylum effective protection against threats to his life or freedom for a Convention reason." *See Patto v. Minister for Immigration and Multicultural Affairs*, 106 F.C.R. 119, 131 (2000).

[567] Ibid. ("under the [European regime,] states can and do expel asylum seekers to 'safe third countries,' which in turn expel them to other countries, safe or not, and in some cases even back to their countries of origin, without there ever being any substantive review of the asylum claim"); European Council on Refugees and Exiles, *Safe Third Countries: Myths and Realities*, para. 32, *available at* www.ecre.org/positions/s3c.pdf ("the result is that an asylum seeker refused entry in country A and sent to country B may well also be refused entry in country B and sent to country C – which that country (B), but not country A - considers to be a 'safe third country'").

appropriately applied so as not to result in improper denial of access to asylum procedures, or to violations of the principle of non-refoulement."[568]

While supporters of restrictions on secondary movement often concede that return is never proper when refugees lives or freedom are put at risk, formal guarantees to this effect are rarely sufficient. As Human Rights Watch illustrates in this report, such guarantees are not rigorously applied, and the specific threats facing individual refugees in the first country they reach are not considered by decision-makers. As a result, many refugees slip through the cracks and are denied protection for secondary movement reasons, and are sent back to places where they are not in fact safe.

Secondary movement policies also needlessly interfere with family unity, contravening the Executive Committee's explicit command to receiving states "to facilitate family reunification of refugees on their territory, especially through the consideration of all related requests in a positive and humanitarian spirit."[569] As Human Rights Watch has noted in the European context, "[f]amily members that enter [the E.U.] by different travel routes or under authorization of different countries may be required by the Schengen and Dublin systems to go through the asylum procedure in different countries."[570] Moreover, those asylum seekers who leave their country of first refuge for a second country in order to reunite with family in the latter are similarly thwarted by secondary movement policies.

Problematic Use of Secondary Movement Policies in Kenya and Uganda
In Kenya and Uganda, individuals who have passed through a country where they are deemed to have had access to adequate protection are rejected by UNHCR or the government from having their status assessed and are instructed to return to that first country. Governments often argue that the policy is appropriate when refugees are simply moving to access better assistance, and Human Rights Watch did interview one twenty-one-year-old Somali woman whose decision to move on to Uganda from Kenya was based on her perception

---

[568] ExCom General Conclusion on International Protection No. 87, 1999. *See* also "Problem of Refugees and Asylum-Seekers who Move in an Irregular Manner from a country in Which They had Already Found Protection," ExCom Conclusion No. 58, 1989 (stating that asylum seekers may be returned to countries "where they have already found protection" if "(i) they are protected there against refoulement and (ii) they are permitted to remain there and to be treated with recognized basic human standards until a durable solution is found for them.").
[569] ExCom General Conclusion on International Protection No. 85, 1998. *See* also UNHCR, *Refugee Status Determination Handbook*, para. 181-88 (stressing the importance of preserving the family unity of refugees).
[570] *See* Human Rights Watch/Helsinki, *"France, Toward a Just and Humane Asylum Policy,"* Vol. 9, No. 12(D), October 1997.

that she would receive more assistance in Kampala.[571] But there are many other cases in which basic protection, rather than level of assistance, is the motive.

While UNHCR recognizes that the policy against secondary movement should *not* be applied to "a refugee who is compelled to move because of specific protection or security problems in his or her previous country,"[572] this provision does not appear to be consistently and carefully applied during status determinations in Kenya and Uganda.

In Kenya, the primary country from which refugees make secondary movements is Uganda. However, as noted previously in this report, Uganda is not always a safe place for refugees. Rwandan and Congolese refugees often move on to Kenya after having security problems in Uganda. Although UNHCR claims to take such security problems into account, so that individuals with serious security problems in Uganda will not be denied status or access to UNHCR in Nairobi,[573] Human Rights Watch learned of cases in which refugees were returned to Uganda even though they had grounds for fearing mistreatment there. Simon J., a Congolese refugee told the story of his brother-in-law who was afraid to stay in Uganda because of his family's work on behalf of the Banyamulenge, which had made him a target for police and military action in Kampala:

> My brother-in-law from Congo was sent [by UNHCR] back to Uganda, where he had spent time before. When he arrived in Kampala he was arrested by the police—twice. Eventually, he became so fed up with the life in Uganda that he returned to Congo, where he was held in prison for one year in Goma. Only the volcano[574] allowed him to be free again.[575]

Refugees facing serious security threats in Uganda have caught wind of the secondary movement policy in Kenya, and are unsure of whether they should try

---

[571] Human Rights Watch interview with refugee, Kampala, Uganda, April 16, 2002.

[572] *See* UNHCR, *Policy Refugees in Urban Areas*, December 12, 1997, para. 13.

[573] Human Rights Watch interview with UNHCR protection staff, Nairobi, Kenya, April 2, 2002.

[574] Mount Nyiragongo, ten kilometers north of Goma, began to erupt on January 17, 2002, and immediately began to engulf the town in a huge flow of lava. As of January 18, hundreds of thousands of refugees were streaming out of Goma into the safety of neighboring Rwanda. The destruction caused by the volcano left more than half a million people in the already poverty- and war-stricken region of Goma homeless. *See* Agence France-Presse, "Goma Burns as Tens of Thousands Flee Laval From African Volcano," January 18, 2002; AP, "Lava Consumes Congolese Town; Hundreds of Thousands Face Refugee Crisis," January 19, 2002.

[575] Human Rights Watch interview with refugee, Nairobi, Kenya, April 4, 2002.

to make their way to Kenya. Olivier C., introduced previously, who had been detained and beaten by Rwandan agents for several months in Kampala, had been told by other refugees that he could not go to Nairobi because he would just be sent back to Kampala. He had also been informed about the delays at UNHCR, and the problems of police harassment in Nairobi. But even these potential problems did not dissuade him from wanting to seek greater safety in Nairobi. He told a Human Rights Watch researcher,

> The life has become very difficult for me here. I am very afraid for my security. The Ugandans want to send us back to Rwanda. I am afraid of that. I am afraid here in Uganda and I want to go to Kenya because I am not secure here. I want to leave here and go somewhere safe.... I do not care about the life in Nairobi, I just want to leave this insecure place. I am afraid to go there and I am afraid to move around here. What can I do?[576]

Ugandan government officials told a Human Rights Watch researcher that Uganda had also begun applying policies against secondary movement. Since refugees from Ethiopia and Somalia must transit through Kenya to reach Uganda, they were the groups most often affected. However, as illustrated in the first part of this report, Kenya is an insecure place for many such refugees. In some cases when an asylum seeker has passed through Kenya or another ostensibly "safe" country, the individual is referred to the Special Branch and his or her file is considered by the Refugee Eligibility Committee.[577]

However, some asylum seekers are not even allowed to begin the status determination process. This is problematic since these refugees are not afforded the opportunity to explain whether they had security reasons for making the secondary movement. The Refugee Coordinator in the Office of the Prime Minister explained,

> People who pass through Kenya don't even bother to find UNHCR. For example, a Somali who passes through Kenya and just decides he wants to go to Uganda.... No! We will not take such an individual. We also won't take people from Burundi who pass through Rwanda.[578]

[576] Human Rights Watch interview with refugee, Kampala, Uganda, April 15, 2002.
[577] Human Rights Watch interview with representative of NGO, Kampala, Uganda, April 8, 2002.
[578] Human Rights Watch interview with official, Kampala, Uganda, April 13, 2002.

Refugees told Human Rights Watch that they were blocked from having their security concerns in the allegedly "safe" country considered at an early stage in the process. For example, Solomon O., a twenty-seven-year-old refugee from Ethiopia was not allowed to register with the Old Kampala police because he and his wife had spent two weeks living in Kenya. Solomon fled because his father, who was actively involved in the OLF had been killed and Solomon had been informed by the military that he was next. Solomon fled with his wife to Nairobi, where they lived from April 5, 2001 until April 20, 2001. He recounted what happened next:

> When I first reached Nairobi they told me to go to HCR, so I did and I received an appointment for two months later. But, I could not stay in Kenya. Everyone knows my picture and that I am wanted in Ethiopia. The Kenyan police will cause problems for me there too. I went to the police station here in Kampala and they refused to accept me, because of that time I spent in Kenya. My wife is pregnant and we have no place to sleep, we have to sleep outside near Old Kampala.[579]

Finally, Hiruy Z.'s story demonstrates the interrelationships between application of the policy against secondary movement and the serious human rights concerns that result from the delays and inefficiencies plaguing the UNHCR office in Nairobi. Hiruy Z. was born in 1964 and comes from Tigray, the northern part of Ethiopia. He was a member of the TPLF[580] and fought

---

[579] Human Rights Watch interview with refugee, Kampala, Uganda, April 9, 2002.

[580] In 1974 a military rebellion ended the Haile Selassie regime, ushering in a 17-year period of military rule lead by Marxist Lieutenant Colonel Mengistu Haile Mariam. Civil unrest and a worsening economy fueled the creation of several regionally/ethnically based opposition groups, including the Tigray People's Liberation Front (TPLF). Future Ethiopian Prime Minister, Meles Zenawi, joined the TPLF later in 1974 and the movement led several insurrections seeking the overthrow of Mengistu's socialist government, popularly known as "the Derg" (or "the Dergue"). The Central Committee constitutes the decision making core of the TPLF and, especially in the early stages of the movement, students made up a large part of the membership. In 1989, the TPLF merged with other opposition movements, including the Eritrean People's Liberation Front (EPLF) and the Oromo People's Democratic Organization (OPDO), to form a broader coalition -- the Ethiopian Peoples' Revolutionary Democratic Front (EPRDF). That year Meles assumed leadership of both EPRDF (also known as "the Front") and the TPLF. On May 21, 1991, with the central government on the verge of collapse and EPRDF gaining ground, Mengistu fled the country. EPRDF forces captured Addis Ababa on May 28 and established the Transitional Government of the new Federal Democratic Republic of Ethiopia (FDRE) with Meles and the TPLF at the helm. First-round

against Mengistu in 1980. In addition to his military training, he was trained in Sudan and Ethiopia by the TPLF's central committee in journalism and "political mobilization." From 1997 to 2000 he worked as a radio broadcaster and managed the Relief Society of Tigray, which distributed food to internally displaced persons.

In the last year of his work with the Relief Society, Hiruy discovered that the central committee was selling relief supplies intended for displaced persons in order to raise money to erect a *Sematat* [a ceremonial tower] to honor three deceased army officers. Around this time he also began reporting on incidents in the war between Ethiopia and Eritrea on the radio station, arousing the suspicion of his superiors. The TPLF began to monitor his activities very closely, and questioned him about the fact that his mother was Eritrean. On February 20, 2000 he was arrested and jailed in Mak'ele, Ethiopia. While he was imprisoned, Hiruy was beaten and told to admit that he was taking food from the Relief Society to pass to the Eritreans. On May 15, 2000 he was so weakened by the beatings and hunger that he fell ill. Blood was discovered in his stools. He was taken to the hospital for treatment and escaped because a friend of his family was working in the hospital. Hiruy told a Human Rights Watch researcher what happened after he first fled to Kenya—and then later, when he fled to Uganda:

> I arrived in Nairobi on July 16, 2000. I stayed in Eastleigh for two months. I went to UNHCR on July 19, 2000. I finally got my decision by April 2001. The decision said that I had to go to the Kakuma camp.... I was renting a room in a house very cheaply in Eastleigh. On the night of September 19, 2001, some Ethiopians entered my house and beat me. They took all my documents and even hurt my head, cutting it open with something sharp they were beating me with [a Human Rights Watch researcher viewed the scar on the side of Hiruy's forehead]. I passed out from the beatings.

---

elections held in 1992 failed to resolve regional/ethnic tensions and both Oromo and Eritrean movements withdrew from the EPRDF coalition, in 1992 and 1993 respectively. Meles has won all subsequent elections for Prime Minister and the Tigrayan dominated EPRDF holds 90 percent of the seats in the Council of Peoples' Representatives, primarily due to widespread boycotts of the elections by opposition groups. Differing opinions within the TPLF leadership about its relationship with the EPLF contributed to Ethiopia's war with Eritrea between 1998 and 2000. *See* The Economist Intelligence Unit Ltd. *Ethiopia – Political Forces*, April 10, 2002.

On the morning of September 20, 2001, in the very early morning, a friend found me lying on the floor, bleeding from my head. He helped me get up and he advised me strongly to leave Kenya. He gave me money for this. I decided I would try to stay in Nairobi, but to get better security from UNHCR. I first went to the Refugee Consortium of Kenya to get assistance on that day. They saw my injuries and gave me a slip of paper to refer me to UNHCR. The slip asked UNHCR to see me about security assistance and social assistance. When I waited for an appointment at UNHCR, they gave me an appointment for two weeks later. I complained. How could I wait that long? They told me, "you go back to RCK to solve your problem." I felt I had no option [but to travel to Uganda].

On September 24, 2001 I boarded a bus for Kampala.... When I finally got to Kampala, I did not even have a coin.

I reported to the Old Kampala Police on September 28, 2001. I slept there for two months outside. When the rain comes at night, it falls on me. When the cold comes, it comes on me. I gave the first interview at the police and then I went to InterAid for the interview. The other refugees had told me not to say that I had a mandate[581] already. I said to them that I didn't want to lie about my situation. I told them at InterAid that I had a mandate in Kenya. The UNHCR officer told me, "I will ask if you have a security problem. I will ask from UNHCR in Nairobi if they have a record of this." But, I knew UNHCR would not have a record of my beating because they never saw me on that day, they just gave me an appointment slip.[582]

Hiruy's status was not assessed by UNHCR as of April 2002 and he informed a Human Rights Watch researcher that he would not stay in Kampala if he did not receive status soon. Without status or adequate protection, he left Kampala in July 2002. His current whereabouts are unknown.

---

[581] *See* description of mandate or protection letters at note 172, above.
[582] Human Rights Watch interview, Kampala, Uganda, April 14, 2002.

RESETTLEMENT AS AN IMPORTANT PROTECTION TOOL
Resettlement Fulfills the Responsibility to Protect Refugees

Resettlement allows refugees whose lives are under threat in either Kenya or Uganda to reach a third country of safety. It can literally mean the difference between life and death. Governments and UNHCR have recognized this life-saving quality of resettlement on numerous occasions.[583]

Facilitating the resettlement of refugees from a country of first asylum where their lives are at risk is the responsibility of both UNHCR and the international community. Under its Statute, UNHCR is mandated to facilitate the resettlement of refugees as one of the three permanent solutions[584] to refugee situations. However, UNHCR cannot resettle refugees without the cooperation of other governments to take them in. The obligation of international cooperation stated in the preamble to the Refugee Convention is the basis upon which industrialized governments have accepted refugees for resettlement. In addition, refugee resettlement is often viewed as an important aspect of international responsibility sharing for the world's refugees. On several occasions UNHCR's ExCom has emphasized the importance of "[a]ctions with a view to burden-sharing... directed towards facilitating... resettlement possibilities in third countries."[585] When resettlement becomes the only viable "solution" for a particular refugee, the obligation on UNHCR and the international community rises in importance to become almost mandatory.

Unfortunately, given its crucial protection function, resettlement is only available to very small numbers of refugees each year. As a result, it addresses the protection problems of only a small fraction of the world's refugees. In 2001, the United States planned to resettle 70,000 refugees, with 20,000 coming from Africa—a continent with well over 3,000,000 refugees.[586] The U.S. resettlement numbers are usually higher than all the other resettlement countries—including Australia, Canada, and Norway—combined.[587] Although

---

[583] *See*, e.g. ExCom General Conclusion on International Protection No. 55, 1989, No. 67, 1991, para. (d).

[584] The three durable solutions to the problems of refugees are: voluntary repatriation, local integration, and resettlement. *See*, e.g. ExCom General Conclusion on International Protection No. 90, 2001, para. j (noting that "the ultimate goal of international protection is to achieve a durable solution for refugees," and commending "States that continue to facilitate these solutions, notably voluntary repatriation and, where appropriate and feasible, local integration and resettlement.").

[585] *See* note 26, above, for a discussion of the obligation of international responsibility sharing.

[586] *See* U.S. Committee for Refugees, *World Refugee Survey 2001*.

[587] *See* Arthur C. Helton, *The Price of Indifference*, 2002, p. 184.

most governments choose not to participate in resettlement at all, eighteen governments do offer annual resettlement places.[588]

The Process of Obtaining Resettlement

Asylum seekers in either Nairobi or Kampala must first be recognized as refugees through UNHCR-run, or government-run individualized procedures before they can be considered for a resettlement referral. Refugees living in camps are also considered for referrals, although camp-based refugees are often resettled on a group basis. For example, the U.S. is currently resettling Somali Bantu refugees from Kenya's camps. These refugees have not been chosen for individualized reasons (such as problems with security), but rather simply by virtue of being members in a group selected for resettlement by the U.S. government.

Once an individual living in an urban area has been recognized as a refugee, he or she may raise the need for resettlement with UNHCR, or in the case of Uganda, with OPM, which in turn can ask UNHCR to consider the individual for resettlement. UNHCR is also expected to identify resettlement cases of its own volition, without completely relying on refugees to self-identify. The role played by UNHCR is crucial to the process.[589] UNHCR identifies resettlement referrals according to criteria established in its *Resettlement Handbook*. A threshold inquiry is whether the refugee is vulnerable in the country of asylum. If he or she is found to be vulnerable, then referrals may be made for refugees with one of eight characteristics: legal and physical protection needs, survivors of violence and torture, medical needs, women-at-risk, family reunification, children and adolescents, elderly refugees and refugees without local integration prospects.[590] UNHCR then refers the potential case for resettlement to one of several resettlement governments. At both UNHCR and government levels, the process of reviewing cases for resettlement is very rigorous – only a tiny subset of the total number of refugees are ever resettled.

Once they are in receipt of a resettlement referral from UNHCR, resettlement governments have a great deal of flexibility in setting up their

---

[588] The eighteen governments who accept refugees for resettlement are: Argentina, Australia, Benin, Brazil, Burkina Faso, Canada, Chile, Denmark, Finland, Iceland, the Netherlands, New Zealand, Norway, Spain, Sweden, Switzerland, and the United States of America.

[589] ExCom has recognized the importance of UNHCR's role on numerous occasions. *See* e.g. ExCom Conclusion No. 90.

[590] *See* UNHCR *Resettlement Handbook*, Chapter 4. Since October 1995, UNHCR, resettlement governments and NGOs have gathered for annual consultations on resettlement at the Annual Tripartite Consultations on Resettlement (ATC). Under the auspices of the ATC, UNHCR developed its Resettlement Handbook in July 1997, which is used by UNHCR field offices and governments involved in the resettlement process.

programs. For example, the United States accepts refugees for resettlement on the basis of five processing priorities, ranging from priority one to priority five. Priority one covers cases that have been referred by UNHCR or identified by the U.S. embassy as individuals who are: facing compelling security concerns in the first country of asylum; in danger of refoulement; in danger of armed attack or physical violence; facing persecution as a result of political, religious, or human rights activities; women at risk; victims of torture or violence; physically or mentally disabled; in need of urgent medical care that could not be given in the country of asylum; and those individuals who do not have any other feasible "durable solution" options. Priority two offers places for refugees from particular countries of origin identified by the U.S. State Department. The Somali Bantu refugees, mentioned earlier, were one example of a priority two group. Priority three, four, and five are for family members of non-citizens legally present in the United States.[591]

Problems Plaguing Resettlement in East Africa
Continuing Problems in Nairobi: The Aftermath of the UNHCR Corruption Scandal

In 1999, evidence came to light that a criminal ring, including some UNHCR staff, had infiltrated UNHCR's office and corrupted its work on status determinations and referrals to resettlement. UNHCR asked the UN Office of Internal Oversight Services (OIOS) to investigate the allegations of corruption in October 2000. The report was published in December 2001. The investigations revealed that refugees had to bribe UNHCR staff between Ksh.50 and Ksh.100 (U.S.$0.60 – U.S.$1.28) to access the offices.[592] Later, refugees who wanted resettlement to a third country were asked to pay bribes ranging from U.S.$1,500 to $6,000 per refugee.[593] The criminal ring would arrange to substitute individuals, some of whom were not deserving of resettlement, in the place of deserving refugees.[594] In other cases, deserving refugees would have false "family members" added to their files.[595]

The criminal ring, involving more than seventy persons, established itself under a UNHCR "management structure" that allowed those "tempted to enrich

---

[591] See U.S. Committee for Refugees, "Description of U.S. Refugee Processing Priorities," Refugee Reports, Vol. 20, No.12, 1999. Available at: http://www.refugees.org/world/articles/usrpp_rr99_12.htm.
[592] See OIOS, Investigation Into Allegations Of Refugee Smuggling At The Nairobi Branch Office Of The Office Of The United Nations High Commissioner For Refugees, U.N. Doc A/56/733, December 21, 2001, para. 23.
[593] Ibid, para. 2.
[594] Ibid, para 26.
[595] Ibid, para 40.

themselves [to] do so with virtual impunity."[596]   At the same time, press accounts recognized that criminals were able to flourish because status determinations and referrals to resettlement were handled so poorly by UNHCR and were so fraught with delays that desperate persons had only one way out— bribery.[597]   Nine people, including three UNHCR staff members were arrested and charged with seventy-eight violations of Kenya's criminal laws in the spring of 2002.

In April 2002, Human Rights Watch discovered that serious protection problems stemming from the corruption scandal continued to reverberate throughout Nairobi's refugee community, particularly among asylum seekers and refugees whose files had been processed by one of the corrupt UNHCR officials.

As a result of the corruption scandal in the Nairobi office, which was previously handling all resettlement referrals from East Africa,[598] UNHCR in Nairobi froze all regular resettlement referrals starting from 2001, although urgent referrals continued.[599]   Given the freeze, UNHCR failed to fulfill its core protection mandate function of referring cases for resettlement. This constitutes a serious failure to perform the tasks entrusted to the agency by governments.[600] More importantly, it is putting refugees lives at risk.

The Presumption of "Tainted" Files
One group of refugees interviewed by Human Rights Watch had their files rejected for refusing to cooperate with corrupt officials and were continuing to

---

[596] Ibid, para 69.

[597] One press account from February 2001 told the story of Ahmed, who resorted to bribery because "[he] knew that [bribery] was the only way to achieve what years of going through official channels had failed to…. Corruption is reportedly so pervasive that refugees are unable to even enter the agency's Nairobi office without forking over baksheesh. 'You have to pay 50 shillings [U.S.$0.60] just to get inside the waiting room,' says Ahmed. 'I went to that office every day for three years and never even got an interview.'" See Europe Intelligence Wire via NewsEdge Corporation, "The Nairobi Connection: How U.N. Agents Bilk Refugees They Are Supposed to Help," February 21, 2001.

[598] This is partly because the major resettlement governments of the United States, Canada, and Australia all handle resettlement out of their Nairobi embassies.

[599] UNHCR in Nairobi referred four emergency and twenty-nine urgent resettlement cases in the five months since Human Rights Watch's visit to Kenya and Uganda in April 2002.

[600] UNHCR responded to Human Rights Watch's concerns about the post-corruption problems by stating, "following the resettlement scandal in Kenya, there was not only a total collapse of resettlement activities in Kenya but an equal collapse in staff morale, and that the recovery ground [sic] can only be achieved incrementally. How long this is supposed to take, remains the big question." UNHCR written comments to Human Rights Watch, October 8, 2002.

experience difficulties with their appeals. Refugees caught in this dilemma have spent years trying to remove the "taint" from their status claims. Many have lost all faith in the integrity of the UNHCR system. For example, Chaltu S., a woman refugee who was well known in Ethiopia as an artist and supporter of Oromo rights, fled after police harassed and detained her and her husband in Ethiopia. She arrived in Nairobi on August 29, 2000 and registered with UNHCR on August 30, 2000. She was finally seen by UNHCR on December 4, 2000. Chaltu S. said:

> I was rejected by an officer called Peter. I received the rejection letter on December 18, 2000. During the interview that officer asked me to add two more people to my case as my family so they could get their case assessed with mine. This would bring money to Peter and the translator told me that I could get money too. When I refused to add any additional people, they rejected me.
>
> Then I appealed to KHRC [the Kenyan Human Rights Commission] and RCK and to the Home Affairs office in Kenya. I was finally given a mandate in March 2001. But the mandate is for Kakuma.... When I go to HCR I have to wait a whole day. And the corruption is still there. It is like a virus, it is transmitted to every new officer who works there.[601]

Many refugees were frustrated that individuals who had bribed UNHCR officials, some of whom may not have even qualified for refugee status, let alone resettlement, had received prompt attention to their claims, whereas those who had resisted the corruption were still waiting for their cases to be processed. For example, Ibrahim H., a fifty-five year old Ethiopian man from the Bale Region of Ethiopia told a Human Rights Watch researcher:

> Those people who participated in the corruption have left. We are the people who have nothing. All this is done by UNHCR. My case is frozen by UNHCR. There are a lot of people who are like me.... Those people who were working properly have left. These days there is no-one there who is working properly. The money UNHCR is getting is in the name of the refugees. But, they are using the money of the refugees for

---

[601] Human Rights Watch interview with refugee, Nairobi, Kenya, April 24, 2002.

themselves. They are eating three meals a day, while we eat only one. I am not a false refugee. But the true refugee is not assisted by UNHCR. I have had only God's assistance, but none from human beings. [602]

Egregious Delays in Reviewing the "Backlogged" Files

Another group of 3,500 refugees had been waiting in legal limbo since 2001, while UNHCR attempted to put staff in place to re-examine all of their files. As of October 2002, only 225 cases had undergone a thorough eligibility interview and fifty of these cases were referred to resettlement. [603] UNHCR admitted that these "backlogged files" were still a serious problem, "The departure of the second protection officer was a major problem." [604] A senior U.S. resettlement official explained how many people destined for the U.S. were caught in the backlog:

> The [U.S.] backlog involves about 180-200 cases, each case is a family so it could involve close to 1,000 individuals.... [They] are still on hold because of their association with the corrupt JPO [Junior Protection Officer]. These cases need to be vetted. Some people need resettlement and without it don't have a way to get on with their lives. [605]

Ibrahim H's case, introduced above, is illustrative of the plight of other refugees who have been caught in limbo because of UNHCR's inability to thoroughly vet backlogged files. Ibrahim was imprisoned in Addis Ababa during the Derg [606] from 1981 to 1982. He was jailed for approximately six months during 1992-1993. Since he was an outspoken supporter of Oromo rights, Ibrahim was jailed again in Goba for the first six months of 1996, and then transferred and held for a year and a half in Addis Ababa Central Police Station. He had been tortured repeatedly during his detention:

---

[602] Human Rights Watch interview with refugee, Nairobi, Kenya, April 6, 2002.

[603] UNHCR written comments to Human Rights Watch, October 8, 2002. In these same comments, UNHCR noted that "[t]here are serious indications that most cases that have undergone the eligibility interview will be submitted for resettlement based on the compelling nature of their cases."

[604] Human Rights Watch interview with UNHCR, Nairobi, Kenya, April 18, 2002.

[605] Human Rights Watch interview with U.S. Embassy official, Nairobi, Kenya, April 18, 2002.

[606] From 1974 to its overthrow in 1987, Ethiopia was ruled by Major Mengistu Haile Mariam and the Derg government. During this time the government was responsible for egregious human rights abuses.

They tortured me and beat me and put my genitals in cold water. One day they forced me to dig a hole in the ground. I dug a big hole and then they shouted at me that that was where they would put my body after they killed me. I am existing now just because of God.[607]

Ibrahim arrived in Nairobi in 1999 where he was followed by security agents and arrested by Kenyan police, whom he believed were cooperating with the Ethiopian government. He was first referred to the camps, but because of security problems he remained in Nairobi and was referred for resettlement. However, his file was processed by one of the corrupt UNHCR officials. Therefore, his approval subsequently was revoked by the United States Immigration and Naturalization Service (INS). He explained,

> I received a notice to go to Westlands [UNHCR's office] on August 29, 2001. I was then asked to go there on September 8, 2001 and I was told my case would be cleared in one month. On September 29, 2001 I had to go back to UNHCR because I received a letter indicating that INS had revoked the conditional approval of my status. On October 26, 2001 I received the letter indicating that UNHCR would reconsider my case.... And up until now there is no solution for my case [Ibrahim has not yet traveled to the United States]. The man who should be assisted is not getting any assistance.... It is not possible to see [UNHCR protection staff]. It is not at all possible. If this is the case, to whom am I to tell my problems?[608]

Asad N. was born in Somalia in 1980 and fled after both of his parents were killed in 1991. Without family or close clan members to care for him, he told Human Rights Watch how he often felt marginalized within the camps he lived in. Since he was without close family relations and was from a minority tribe, his case was particularly well-suited for resettlement. A UNHCR field officer eventually recognized the urgency of his case, and he was referred for resettlement from Dadaab camp. Asad explained the labyrinthine processes he

---

[607] Human Rights Watch interview with refugee, Nairobi, Kenya, April 6, 2002.
[608] Human Rights Watch interview with refugee, Nairobi, Kenya, April 6, 2002.

had endured, only to end up as one of the cases in the "backlog," without any result:

> On February 11, 1999 the resettlement officers came to the [Dadaab] camp. They fixed names to the board. They put my name there. I was allowed to fill in the resettlement form. I stayed waiting until the end of the year. The field officer told me that my case was in Nairobi. Then on January 21, 2000 they came for a group of Sudanese. They said, "your form was lost and we will give you another one." I filled in that new form in January [2000]. On August 10, 2000 my name was on the board again and UNHCR was running the interviews. They told me that they had reached the number of people they needed to talk to and they didn't have room for me again.

> I waited until December 5, 2000 when I finally was allowed to do a screening interview with JVA [Joint Voluntary Agency – initial screening agency for U.S. resettlement]. On February 7, 2001 I had an appointment to see the INS. INS gave me a letter saying that my case was conditionally approved [under section 207(a)]. Then, I did a medical orientation and a cultural orientation session. On March 13, 2001 I did the first medical check, and then they sent me back to the [Dadaab] camp.

> On September 6, 2001 in Dadaab I was given a travel document to go to Nairobi to do an interview with the INS. The INS asked me three or four questions about whether I had paid money or was involved in corruption. I answered their questions. Then, on September 8, 2001 I received a "notice of revocation" of my conditional approval. This was for cases they thought were involved in the corruption, but I was not! Then, UNHCR said they wanted to send me back to the camp. It turns out that the resettlement officer who worked on my case was called Joseph and he was corrupt.[609]

---

[609] Human Rights Watch interview with refugee, Nairobi, Kenya, April 22, 2002.

As of April 2002, Asad N. had received no update on his case from UNHCR or the United States government.

Conclusion

The corruption scandal has caused serious problems in establishing an efficient and life-saving resettlement system for refugees in East Africa. Refugees in urgent need of resettlement have been waiting under risky conditions while the "taint" of the corruption continues to hamper the processing of their files.

UNHCR has always experienced difficulties in referring as many cases for resettlement as governments have requested from the agency.[610] Since the corruption scandal, UNHCR has completely frozen all regular resettlement referrals from its Nairobi office, although a very small number of urgent referrals have continued. Given the freeze, some embassies are looking for other ways to fill their resettlement quotas—and some of these adaptations may be improvements on the old system. NGOs are increasingly being used to fill the vacuum left behind by UNHCR. Referrals are also still being sent from UNHCR offices in other countries, such as Uganda. At the same time, however, this use of NGOs can easily constitute an improper delegation of UNHCR's core responsibility for resettlement referrals, discussed above. Most importantly, such measures cannot substitute for UNHCR's resumption of its core responsibility for resettlement referrals in Kenya.

Kampala: Inadequate Resettlement Referrals for Prima Facie Refugees

As was described previously, Uganda, in conformity with the OAU Refugee Convention,[611] has recognized as *prima facie* refugees persons fleeing civil war in Sudan and other serious disturbances to the public order. However, because *prima facie* refugees are provided refugee protection without having

---

[610] Human Rights Watch interview with embassy staff from major resettlement countries, Nairobi, Kenya and Kampala, Uganda, April 4 and 11, 2002. UNHCR explains its inability to fill governmental resettlement quotas in the following manner: "Governments are not always ready to adapt their quotas to rapidly changing needs, and often establish them in response to domestic interest groups, targeting specific nationalities. Resettlement countries may also turn down cases such as families with pressing medical problems, who may be more costly in terms of welfare payments, or who may have limited ability to integrate rapidly. In general, although some countries do accept difficult to place hardship cases, most resettlement countries prefer educated refugees with strong family and cultural links, an intact family structure, and a high likelihood of rapid integration. Such families may not always correspond to the pressing protection cases which UNHCR attempts to resettle." *See* UNHCR, "Protecting Refugees: Frequently Asked Questions," available at www.unhcr.ch (site visited August 17, 2002).
[611] *See* note 16, above.

their cases individually assessed, and instead are simply located as a group in camps, their individual security and protection needs are less likely to be addressed. As a result, they are less likely to have their cases considered for resettlement than refugees from other countries of origin who are able to access UNHCR and/or governmental status determination processes.

A governmental or UNHCR policy to afford lesser rights or protections to one group of refugees than another violates the principle of non-discrimination provided for in Article 3 of the Refugee Convention, which states, "The Contracting States shall apply the provisions of this Convention to refugees without discrimination as to... country of origin." Therefore, an individual refugee coming from a place such as Somalia or Sudan, who will automatically fulfill the requirements of the OAU Refugee Convention, must have the same opportunity to claim status under the Refugee Convention.[612] This is important because in both Kenya and Uganda only refugees fulfilling the Refugee Convention definition are considered for resettlement.

In Nairobi, the UNHCR office recognized the problematic discrepancy caused by the *prima facie* policy when the new senior protection officer arrived in November 2000. Protection staff were instructed to consider individual claims from Somali and Sudanese refugees. Apparently missing the point of the change in policy, a former UNHCR employee told a Human Rights Watch researcher, "When [the SPO] came he added eligibility interviews for Somalis and Sudanese, but this is a waste of time because these were *prima facie* cases."[613]

However, in Kampala, the policy had not changed at this writing. The only way a *prima facie* refugee can have his or her case assessed for status or resettlement is if he or she "self-identifies."[614] A senior UNHCR official implied that this policy was arbitrary when he told a Human Rights Watch researcher that "the REC['s] . . .work is very 'ad hoc' . . . They give *prima facie* status to Sudanese, but Rwandese and Congolese have their individual cases assessed."[615]

Sudanese refugees are the only group required by Ugandan administrative policy to register their security concerns and claims for resettlement with camp commandants. Therefore, all Sudanese refugees must convince camp commandants that their claims are legitimate in order to obtain a referral slip to

---

[612] The OAU Convention also provides for non-discrimination. Article 4 of the OAU Refugee Convention states that "Member States undertake to apply the provisions of this convention to all refugees without discrimination as to... nationality...."
[613] Human Rights Watch interview with former UNHCR staff member, Kampala, Uganda, April 18, 2002.
[614] Human Rights Watch interview with UNHCR staff, Kampala, Uganda, April 16, 2002.
[615] Human Rights Watch interview with UNHCR staff, Kampala, Uganda, April 8, 2002.

undergo status determinations in Kampala. Given the infiltration and power of the SPLA in the camps in Uganda, refugees were understandably reluctant to say that they wanted to leave due to opposition to or fear of the SPLA, much less to voice a need for resettlement on these grounds.

At the same time, Sudanese refugees who try to access status determinations in Kampala without referral slips are constantly being sent back to the camps.[616] This policy was made very clear in a public notice posted at InterAid's offices on February 7, 2001. The notice was posted around the time that many Sudanese refugees were trying to move to Kyangwali camp, because of rumors that resettlement could be obtained there. The notice (which is reproduced in full in Annex C) stated:

> The Government of Uganda has designated settlements in the North of the country for Sudanese refugees.... Asylum seekers with particular or specific protection needs should address their concerns to Offices in the Field before proceeding to Kampala.... UNHCR Kampala would not carry [sic] interviews for Sudanese entering the country through any of the border points in the North unless asylum [seekers] are referred to Kampala by our Offices. UNHCR would not facilitate transport of such asylum seekers back to settlements in the North.[617]

Some government officials recognized that Sudanese should be able to access the status determination procedures in Kampala and be referred on for resettlement. For example, one official involved in the status determinations told Human Rights Watch, "The Sudanese who arrive are highly mobile people. Some boys do run away from SPLA recruitment. Other refugees come here to seek resettlement. We can always check these stories with UNHCR to see what is going on in a camp."[618] Another said, "People coming from DRC and Sudan can make individual claims because they may present particular problems."[619]

---

[616] Human Rights Watch interviewed several Sudanese refugees who said they had been told to "go back to the border where you came from" when they tried to access the individual determination system provided by the government of Uganda, UNHCR and InterAid officers. Human Rights Watch interviews with refugees, Kampala, Uganda, April 15, 2002.
[617] UNHCR Notice No. 1/2001 (on file with Human Rights Watch).
[618] Human Rights Watch interview with Ugandan government official, Kampala, Uganda, April 8, 2002.
[619] Human Rights Watch interview with Ugandan government official, Kampala, Uganda, April 13, 2002.

While these words appear well-meaning, it is not clear how much they are put into practice—in February 2001 over 150 Sudanese refugees were instructed to return to the camps without a prior assessment of the security threats they faced.[620] In addition, of the more than thirty refugees interviewed by Human Rights Watch who had been able to make use of the resettlement referral process in Kampala, only one was Sudanese.

Other Reasons for the Malfunctioning Resettlement System
The resettlement system for refugees in East Africa is in trouble—and not just because of the corruption scandal or Uganda's *prima facie* policy. Governmental and UNHCR authorities are too slow in processing cases for refugee status and in referring cases on for resettlement. Once resettlement authorities receive a referral, a new set of bureaucratic delays arise. This is particularly worrisome given the extraordinary security problems faced by refugees and documented by Human Rights Watch in both Kenya and Uganda.

Resettlement governments are partly to blame for the current crisis. The bureaucratic steps involved in vetting resettlement cases has meant that refugees whose lives are at risk must remain living under dangerous conditions while their files are processed. For example, Human Rights Watch interviewed several refugees with serious security problems whose spouses had been found to be HIV positive. Their cases had been stalled for several months, and the governments concerned did not give the refugees conclusive information about what the HIV test results implied for their resettlement claims.[621]

But the most serious problems have occurred in the post-September 11 anti-immigrant environment. Governments such as the United States have instituted new security screening mechanisms for refugees. This slows down the approvals process considerably, especially since all male refugees between the ages of eighteen and forty-four are put through these additional checks by the

---

[620] *See* "Sudanese Asylum Seekers Stranded in Kampala," *Refugee Law Project Fact Sheet No. 1*, February 21, 2001.
[621] Both the United States and Canada require all applicants seeking permanent immigration, including refugees, to undergo an HIV test. For the United States, applicants testing HIV positive are nearly always denied immigration visas, but HIV positive status is not an automatic bar for refugees. *See* The Lesbian and Gay Immigration Rights Task Force, *LGBT Immigrants and the Law: Frequently Asked Questions*, available at www.lgirtf.org/faq.html. In Canada, refugees seeking permanent immigration who test HIV positive will not be denied due to this status. Canada generally only excludes those with HIV if it can be proven that that the individual will excessively burden publicly funded health services. All other immigrants are assessed on a case-by case basis. *See* Canadian HIV/AIDS Legal Network, *HIV/AIDS and Immigration: Frequently Asked Questions*, Third Revised Version, February 2002, available at www.aidslaw.ca/maincontent /issues/immigration.htm.

United States. Africans are disparately impacted by the additional screening. Out of 22,000 Africans authorized to travel to the United States during 2002, only 1,617 were admitted by early August 2002.[622] It was unlikely—even impossible—that the remaining 20,000 slots would be filled in the final two months of the fiscal year.[623] Other governments have been slow in processing resettlement cases. Perhaps the most egregious and well-publicized example of delays putting refugees at risk occurred when the Rwandan family, described on the first pages of this report, was brutally attacked after waiting eleven months for resettlement to Australia.[624]

Several of the refugees interviewed by Human Rights Watch for this report were in need of urgent resettlement action, but their cases were not being addressed or they were languishing in administrative delays. Unfortunately, neither UNHCR nor governments have responded with the kind of speed and flexibility required to address the individual security problems presented by

---

[622] Immigration and Refugee Services of America national telephonic briefing, August 15, 2002.

[623] Ibid.

[624] In the last six months of 2001 Australia granted 104 resettlement places for refugees from Nairobi. Of these, 50 percent took up to fifty-two weeks to process and 75 percent took up to sixty weeks, with the remaining 25 percent taking even longer. *See* Department for Immigration and Multicultural and Indigenous Affairs (DIMIA), *Report to the Australian Senate's Additional Estimates Hearing*, February 19 and 22, 2002. For its part, UNHCR explained to a Human Rights Watch researcher that delays in processing the Rwandan family's case were caused by the need to check the family's identity with the International Criminal Tribunal for Rwanda. Human Rights Watch interview with UNHCR official, Nairobi, Kenya, April 24, 2002.

refugees in Kenya and Uganda.[625] UNHCR's ExCom has recognized the need "for rapid and flexible response to UNHCR resettlement requirements in particular for vulnerable groups and emergency protection cases subject to refugee admission requirements of receiving States."[626] In addition, the United States has established clear guidelines for the rapid processing of resettlement claims from particularly at risk refugees. Unfortunately, these guidelines have only been used to resettle five at- risk cases from the entire continent of Africa since their establishment in 2001.[627]

Finally, protracted refugee situations such as those currently faced by Sudanese, Somalis, and some Rwandans in Kenya and Uganda puts enormous pressure on the resettlement option. When safe repatriation is not possible, and local integration is either non-existent (in the case of Kenya) or far from perfect (in the case of Uganda), resettlement seems the only viable means by which refugees can find a way to enjoy basic human rights.

---

[625] For its part, a UNHCR official in Kampala told a Human Rights Watch researcher that "in situations where people are at risk, we implement fast-track resettlement procedures. In some cases it can take only one to two weeks to remove someone from Uganda." Human Rights Watch interview with UNHCR official, Kampala, Uganda, April 8, 2002.

[626] See "Resettlement as an Instrument of Protection," ExCom Conclusion No. 67, 1991.

[627] Human Rights Watch interview with Resettlement NGO, New York, June 2002.

CONCLUSION

Refugees in Kenya and Uganda have fled persecution or civil war in their countries of origin. This report has shown that refugees suffer ongoing abuses of their human rights even after they reach their new countries of asylum. Many refugees flee from the insecurity and inadequate assistance that have been plaguing Kenya and Uganda's camps for years on end to Nairobi or Kampala, others arrive directly in these cities after leaving persecution and abuse at home.

Once in the city, refugees encounter overburdened agencies with neither the resources nor the ability to help all of them. Others find something much worse: governmental hostility to their presence in urban areas, vulnerability to rape or other forms of physical attack, police abuse, and harassment by agents from their countries of origin.

Kenya and Uganda's preference to house refugees in camps only exacerbates these problems. In Kenya, police continue to harass refugees arrested in the city and magistrates deport them, in violation of refugees' fundamental rights. And in Uganda, there is little investment in providing protection to urban refugees because they are expected to live in camps, or because the Ugandan government itself is the cause of refugees' insecurity.

The expectation that refugees will find all the protection and assistance they need in camps is contradicted by the problems documented in this report. However, the trend in Kenya at least is to make the confinement policy more stringent. Human Rights Watch was informed that the government of Kenya and UNHCR plan to transfer all status determination interviews from Nairobi to camps.[628] This will only compound the marginalization and vulnerability of newly-arriving asylum seekers in urban areas, increasing their risk of suffering human rights abuses similar to those documented in this report since they will have no place to turn to regularize their status.

The benign neglect or hostility of host governments; UNHCR's misguided urban refugee policy, insufficient funding, and unwillingness to challenge host government polices; and the ignorance of donor governments about the specific needs of refugees living in urban environments means that human rights abuses against urban refugees are in plain view, but remain "hidden" to those who have responsibility to take corrective action.

Yet there are also signs of hope, including UNHCR's new focus on the problem of "protracted refugee situations," or long-term refugee camp situations that Human Rights Watch has analogized to the problem of indefinite detention in this report. UNHCR is clearly looking for solutions for refugee groups, such

---

[628] Human Rights Watch interview with UNHCR officials, Nairobi, Kenya, April 19, 2002.

as those in Kenya and Uganda, with "no durable solution in sight."[629] In a recent policy document, the agency renews emphasis on the out-of-favor solution of local integration for long term refugee populations and also proposes that development assistance to countries of asylum should include a view of refugees as "agents of development."[630] In addition, the government of Uganda, by allocating land for refugees to cultivate and by allowing some refugees to work in urban environments, has recognized that refugees can contribute a great deal to the development of Uganda's economy.

While not all refugees have the need or desire to live in urban areas, there are several reasons why host governments, UNHCR, and the international community should allow some refugees to reside in Nairobi and Kampala, and why programs which cater to refugees' protection and assistance needs in the cities should be improved.

Long-term camp confinement imposes limits on freedom of movement that in and of themselves are serious violations of the human rights obligations of Kenya and Uganda. Governments and UNHCR should consider ways in which camp stays can be avoided for refugees who have few prospects of returning home, or for those with specific reasons for being in the city.

Allowing for the lawful presence of some refugees in urban areas could help, rather than hinder, both governments' ability to combat some forms of crime. If some categories of refugees had legal rights to remain in Kampala and Nairobi, the incentives for corruption, harassment, fraud, or other criminality would be reduced. When refugees in urban areas are registered, counted, and their presence is regulated, criminals will lose the ability to prey upon legitimate refugees, to masquerade as "refugees," or to counterfeit refugee documentation.

Moreover, cities are among the few places in developing countries where UNHCR and NGOs already have an infrastructure and offices, and where refugees can be included in overall development programming without creating the entirely false economy and environment of a refugee camp. The educational, infrastructure and employment needs in cities like Kampala and Nairobi are virtually endless. Promoting economic growth in urban areas would help refugees and nationals alike.

Finally, personal security problems facing urban refugees are also security risks for host governments. Stopping the activities of security agents in large cities would not only better protect the rights of refugees, but would improve the domestic security situation for Kenya and Uganda. Security fears also limit the economic contributions that refugees can make. Refugees in Kampala and

---

[629] *See* UNHCR Africa Bureau, Discussion Paper on Protracted Refugee Situation in the African Region, October 2001.
[630] Ibid.

Nairobi are often so afraid for their security that they do not venture out of their homes during the day, and therefore cannot work even when they have the permission to do so. Extremely well educated and highly skilled refugees often end up trapped in cramped shelters in urban environments. Both governments could make much better use of these refugees' skills in urban areas.

The first step towards stopping the police harassment, unsafe living conditions, arbitrary arrests, and physical insecurity of refugees living in Nairobi and Kampala would be to allow some categories of refugees to live there lawfully. At the same time, greater investments must be made in the refugee protection and assistance programs in urban areas that are currently overburdened and ineffective. This is why not only host governments and UNHCR, but also donor and resettlement governments have a very crucial role to play in improving the situation for urban refugees in Nairobi and Kampala.

ANNEXES

Kenya-Related Documents
Annex A: HRW's Letter to the Kenyan Government

HUMAN RIGHTS WATCH

350 5th Ave., 34th Floor
New York, NY 10118
Telephone: 212-290-4700
Fax: 212-736-1300
Website:http://www.hrw.org

VIA FACSIMILE
+41.22.731.2905
+254.2.218.811

Mr. Edward K. Rintaugu
Counsellor, Permanent Mission
Mr. Augstino Lomongin
Deputy Permanent Secretary, Home Affairs
Permanent Mission of the Republic of Kenya
to the United Nations Office in Geneva
1-3, Avenue de la Paix
1202 Geneva, Switzerland

July 22, 2002

Dear Sirs:

Further to my letter of June 25, 2002 in which I re-transmitted a list of questions originally prepared on April 19, 2002 regarding Kenya's policy on urban refugees for your consideration, I am attaching here some annotations to these questions, which may assist you as you finalize your responses. Please do not feel compelled to answer each sub-question, as I am aware of your time and staffing constraints. I am including the details here to give a clear sense of what issues we will be addressing in the report beneath each major heading.

In order to have the position of the government of Kenya included in this report, I will need to receive your responses no later than July 30, 2002. These responses can be sent via DHL or facsimile to the address / number indicated above. Alternatively, they can be sent via email to ▓▓▓▓▓▓▓▓▓▓▓▓

We are grateful for your assistance in this matter. Please do not hesitate to contact us should you have any questions or concerns.

Sincerely yours,

Alison L Pa

Alison Parker
Leonard H. Sandler Fellow on Refugee Policy
Human Rights Watch

Enc. [2 pages of annotated questions]

1. What is the position of the government of Kenya on the presence of asylum seekers and refugees in Nairobi?
   - If Nairobi is the first place these individuals arrive to?
   - If these individuals have been living in refugee camps in Kenya previously?
   - If these individuals have passed through Uganda or Tanzania?

2. What protection can the government of Kenya provide to refugees living in Nairobi?
   - Can refugees living in Nairobi seek the protection of the Kenyan police?
   - Are any other protection measures being taken?

3. Are police aware of the various documents that asylum seekers and refugees carry? Are these documents honored?
   - Are police trained in the principles of refugee law and are they trained to respect these documents?
   - Is there an official disciplinary procedure for police who extort money from or arbitrarily detain refugees?

4. What position does the government of Kenya take on instance of sexual violence against refugees in Nairobi and / or attacks against high-profile security cases, such as the April 17, 2002 attack on the Rwandan family housed in a UNHCR-run facility? Is the provision of designated areas in order to ensure the security of refugees in Nairobi or elsewhere in Kenya a priority?
   - Does protection against sexual or other forms of violence fall within the government of Kenya's work with refugees in urban areas?

5. What measures are being taken to prevent the "repatriation" of individuals arrested and charged with "illegal entry" to places where they fear persecution?
   - Are magistrates aware of the government of Kenya's nonrefoulement obligations and do they make adequate inquiries into an individual's fear of persecution prior to ordering their repatriation?
   - On April 18, 2002 Human Rights Watch interviewed a young Somali national at the Langata Police Station. He had served six months imprisonment on "illegal entry" charges and both officers present for the interview said they planned to repatriate him. The man indicated that he was a refugee, and said he did not want to go back because he was afraid and had no family left there. What can you say about cases like this one?
   - Human Rights Watch obtained official statistics from the Nairobi Provincial Police indicating that thirty-nine individuals were "repatriated" to countries known to produce refugees. In addition, UNHCR statistics indicated that one hundred and sixty four individuals were returned through Moyale to Ethiopia. How does the government of Kenya ensure that such people are not being returned to places where they fear persecution?

6. What position does the government of Kenya take on developing legal protections for asylum seekers and refugees within the domestic laws of Kenya?
   - Why is the draft refugee bill still languishing in parliament?
   - Can the government of Kenya estimate when it hopes to pass domestic refugee legislation?

- What is the reason for the delay in issuing new joint government / UNHCR refugee documentation?

7. What position does the government of Kenya take on the current efforts to harmonize refugee policies within Eastern Africa?
   - To what extent does the government of Kenya already communicate and coordinate with the governments of Uganda and Tanzania on refugee policy?
   - Is the recent revival of the ECA seen as an opportunity for a regional approach to refugee protection?

8. How does the government view the performance of the office of the United Nations High Commissioner for Refugees, and its implementing NGO partners in Kenya?
   - How would you describe the communication and working relationship between the government of Kenya and UNHCR?
   - Please comment on the capacity and effectiveness of UNHCR and partner NGOs, as well as their working relationship with the government of Kenya.

9. What position does the government of Kenya take on the freedom of movement of refugees and their enjoyment of other human rights, including provision of permission to work?

10. Would the government of Kenya consider becoming directly involved in the refugee status determination process? (i.e. through conducting status determinations by using its own legal officers)

11. What areas of concern to the government of Kenya relating the protection of the human rights of refugees would you like to see Human Rights Watch address?

Annex B: Sample Appointment Slip

come back Monday 12 June 200_
resettlemet

APPONTMENT FOR AN INTERVIEW WITH UNHCR

NAME: ▰▰▰▰▰▰▰▰▰▰▰▰▰▰▰

NO OF DEPENDANTS: _NONE_   MALE/FEMAL

NATIONALITY AND NO: CONGOLESE/CD ▰▰▰

DATE: 9/8/2000 13/04/2000: 8:00 HOURS
14/5/2000

PERSON TO BE SEEN:
UNHCR PROTECTION OFFICER   ☐ De C
UNHCR SOCIAL/SERVIC/EDUC. OFFICER   ☐
UNHCR REPATRIATION OFFICER   ☐
UNHCR RESETTLEMENT OFFICER   ☐
OTHERS: ☐

DATE: __83 - 03 - 2000__   TC to return ou
SIGNATURE: _____   26/05/2000

Uganda-Related Documents
Annex C: UNHCR's Posting on the Prima Facie Policy

NATIONS UNIES

HAUT COMMISSARIAT

POUR LES RÉFUGIES

Délégation pour l'Ouganda

Tel: 256 41 231231
Fax: 256 41 256989
Email: ugaka@unhcr.ch

UNITED NATIONS

HIGH COMMISSIONER

FOR REFUGEES

Branch Office in Uganda

P.O Box 3813

Kampala

07 February 2001

Our Code:
Your Code:
Notice no. 1/2001

TO ALL ASYLUM SEEKERS FROM SOUTH SUDAN REPORTING AT KAMPALA.
During the recent past few weeks, UNHCR has noticed an ever increasing number of
asylum seekers claiming to have entered Uganda through Moyo, Kitgum, Kotido,
Adjumani and Arua Districts in the North of Uganda. The asylum seekers hav .
claiming that they either are joining relatives in Kyangwali or want to settle in
Kyangwali settlement in Hoima District.

The Government of Uganda has designated settlements in the North of the country
for Sudanese refugees. Except for Kotido District, there are indeed refugee
settlements in all other Districts above mentioned. UNHCR as well as the office of
the Prime Minister has offices in all areas where settlements are loca ed.

Asylum seekers with particular or specific protection needs should address their
concerns to Offices in the Field before proceeding to Kampala. Family reunification is
also possible from settlement to settlement. However applications for Family
reunification should also be in the first place, lodged at the Field levels.

In consultations with The Governmentof Uganda , it has been agreed and it is hereby
directed that henceforth, asylum seekers should register in the OPM Offices and
UNHCR Offices nearest to the border where they have crossed.

For avoidance of doubt, the following table should be helpful:

ENTRY POINT-	REGISTRATION /REPORTING OFFICES
KOBOKO, ARINGA	ARUA
MOYO, NIMULE, JALEI	PALORINYA, PAKELE
MASINGO, PAJOK, CHUA, LOPODI	ACHOLI PII (PADER)
KITGUM	

UNHCR Kampala would not carry interviews for Sudanese entering the country
through any of the border points in the North unless asylum are referred to Kampala
by our Offices. UNHCR would not facilitate transport of such asylum seekers back to
settlements in the North.

Abel Mbilinyi

SENIOR PROTECTION OFFICER
BRANCH OFFICE, UGANDA
Cc: Inter Aid + Notice Board/ OPM/Field Offices

Annex D: Security Referral Correspondence

TELEX: ~ ~ ~1378 OPM
TELEFAX: 341139 OPM

In any correspondence on
this subject please quote No

THE REPUBLIC OF UGANDA

POST OFFICE BUILDING
YUSUF LULE ROAD.
P.O. BOX 341. KAMPALA, UGANI

OPM/R/⬛

ᵗʰ March 2002

The Representative
UNHCR
KAMPALA

(ETH)

Please find attached a case of insecurity reported to us by
Mr. ⬛ .

I suggest your protection office should analyse the case and take any
necessary action.

FOR: PERMANENT SECRETARY/DIRECTOR FOR REFUGEES

ORIGINAL

POLICE FOR:43

UGANDA POLICE

MEDICAL EXAMINATION REPORT

TO:

THE MEDICAL OFFICER,

POLICE SURGEON

SURE HOUSE BOMBO RD.

C.F.No. 49/9/12/2001

OLD KIRA Police Station

15/12/2001

Please examine ....

who is the ~~accused~~/complaint* in a ...... A.SSAULT ...... case and has been

sent to you on the ...... 17th DEC. ......, 20.01.. Please furnish a report as soon as possible
using the reverse side of this form. The duplicate should be retained.

It is particularly requested that you should distinguish between the degrees of injury which are quoted
from the Penal Code (Cap. 22 section 4) as s footnote overleaf. A note as to the kind of weapon by which
any injury (or injuries) may have been inflicted should be made; in the case of suspected alcoholism reasons
for the conclusions reached should also be given under "Remarks".

Signature ....

Rank .... P.C.

Date ...15/12/01.. Time ..12:00

*Delete whichever is not applicable.

[P.T.O.

Nature of each injury, whether cut, wount or bruise	On what part of the body inflicted	Size of each injury in inches (length, beradth and depth)	Classification
Old Lacerated wounds across the upper end of the (R) upper arm, 2. Cm long, scratched and the front of the (R) mid thigh, 1.0 cm scratched			Harm

REMARKS:

Consistent with assault with blunt implement.

Date ...12/12/2007...   Signature ...

                                 Designation ...

Notes - "Harm" means any bodily hurt, disease or disoder, whether Permanent or Temporary.
       "Grievous Harm" means any harm which amounts to a main or dangerous harm, or seriously or
       permanently injury to any internal or external organ, membrane or sense.
       ...us Harm" means harm endangering life.
       ... the destruction or permanent disabling of any external organ, membrane or senses.

NATIONS UNIES

HAUT COMMISSARIAT

POUR LES REFUGIES

Délégation pour l'Ouganda

Tel: 256 41 231231
Fax: 256 41 256989
Email: ugaka@unhcr.ch

UNITED NATIONS

HIGH COMMISSIONER

FOR REFUGEES

Branch Office in Uganda

P.O Box 3813

Kampala

⬛ March 2002

Our Code: UGA.M.PROT.⬛⬛⬛

Your Code:

Dear Mr. ⬛⬛⬛

Re: ⬛⬛⬛ (ETH)

We write with reference to your letter referenced OPM/R/   and dated March 2002, suggesting our protection office to analyse the case of insecurity reported to your office by ⬛⬛⬛ (Eth).

As we are all aware, the physical security of refugees is the responsibility of host nations. We would thus urge you to rather advise IC and subsequent ICs to utilise the state security apparatus which is the appropriate entity to ensure the security of all persons residing within the territorial boundaries of Uganda.

Your co-operation and understanding in this matter will be highly appreciated.

Yours sincerely,

for Senior Protection Officer

Office of the Prime Minister
Kampala

Policy-Related Documents
Annex E: UNHCR's Urban Refugee Policy

Annex

UNHCR Policy on Refugees in Urban Areas

OFFICE OF THE UNITED NATIONS HIGH COMMISSIONER FOR REFUGEES, GENEVA

Inter-Office Memorandum No.90/97
Field Office Memorandum No.95/97

To: All Directors of Operations,
The Directors of the Divisions of International Protection and
Operational Support.
All Heads of Sections/Desks/Units at Headquarters,
All Representatives/Liaison Offices in the Field

From: Sergio Vieira de Mello, Assistant High Commissioner

Dossier/File Code: ADM 1.1   Date: 12 December 1997

Subject: UNHCR Policy on Refugees in Urban Areas

1.   The "UNHCR Comprehensive Policy on Urban Refugees" dated 25 March 1997 was promulgated under cover of IOM/25/97, FOM/30/97 of 28 April 1997, and shared thereafter with a number of our NGO partners. While the central thrust of the policy - promote self-reliance and avoid dependency - has not been challenged, a number of colleagues and NGOs expressed concern at aspects of both the form and substance of other elements. In particular, it was felt that the policy was formulated in a manner that did not properly reflect its claim that refugee protection was the central consideration.

2.   The policy was reviewed in light of these concerns. It was concluded that, rather than amend the document to take account of them, it would be better to redraft and refocus the document. The attached document "UNHCR Policy on Refugees in Urban Areas", dated 12 December 1997, therefore supersedes that dated 25 March 1997, and is effective on receipt. The French text is also attached.

3.   The policy will be further revised as necessary in light of comments and suggestions received from UNHCR Offices and partners. Field offices are requested to share the attachment with relevant NGO or other partners and give them the opportunity to make comments and suggestions. These, together with any of their own, are to be forwarded to reach the Senior Community Services Officer, PTSS, by 31 March 1998. Comments and suggestions from colleagues at Headquarters are of course also welcome. The attachment is also being shared directly with those NGOs that were represented at an informal discussion on the issues on 10 October 1997, held within the framework of UNHCR's pre-EXCOM consultations with NGOs.

REFUGEES IN URBAN AREAS

4.   Since the promulgation of the earlier document, considerable progress has been made in a number of countries in reviewing and redirecting assistance in accordance with the policy, and in consolidating action that was already underway. Several workshops have also addressed the issues. In order to take stock of the situation and have a reference for measuring further progress, all country offices concerned are requested to provide the following information by 31 January 1998 on the situation as at 1 January 1998 with respect to refugees receiving material assistance from UNHCR in urban areas.

- a)   Total numbers by country of origin.
- b)   Numbers and gender, disaggregated by the following age groups: 0-4; 5-12; 13-17; 18-59; 60 and above.
- c)   Brief description of registration system and its effectiveness.
- d)   Of assisted refugees:
   - 1)   what percentage (or how many) are being resettled?
   - 2)   what percentage of the remainder are already largely self-reliant (that is not significantly dependent on UNHCR subsistence or other allowances, or are expected to have benefits cut or substantially reduced in the next 3 months)?;
   - 3)   what percentage are making progress to self-reliance (e.g. starting a small business, undertaking skills training)?;
   - 4)   what percentage, through vulnerability or other factors, are having difficulty in working towards self-reliance?;
- e)   Brief description of implementing arrangements for delivery of assistance and promotion of self-reliance.
- f)   Comments (optional).

5.   This report should be addressed to the SCSO, PTSS, by e-mail where possible (ashton@unhcr.ch).

Enclos.

UNHCR Policy on refugees in urban areas

Introduction

1.   The objective of this document is to provide clear guidelines for the provision of assistance to and the promotion of solutions for refugees in urban areas. It takes due account of both their specific situation and the problems that may be created by unregulated movement to urban areas, whether this movement takes place within the country or from another country where the refugee had found protection.

2.   UNHCR's obligations in respect of international protection are not affected by either the location of the refugees or the nature of the movement to that location. In a number of countries asylum seekers arrive directly in urban areas. Whatever the nature of the movement or legal status of a person of concern to UNHCR in an urban area, the over-riding priority remains to ensure protection, and in particular, non-refoulement and treatment in accordance with recognized basic human standards.

Residence in urban areas

3.   Freedom of movement is the rule under international law and restrictions should be the exception, though some restrictions - such as the location of refugees away from the border - respond to protection concerns. UNHCR should encourage the government to allow freedom of movement, and should promote the refugees' right to work and access to national services, wherever possible. In consultation with the government, UNHCR may, however, limit the location where UNHCR assistance is provided. Where refugees are assisted in settlements or camps outside urban areas, UNHCR should provide assistance in urban areas to refugees from the same country of origin only with the agreement of the government and if there are compelling reasons to do so.

4.   Such compelling reasons could include: specific protection or security problems faced by an individual or his or her family in the settlement or camp; pre-arranged movement to an urban area for the duration of health care or for reunion with family members legally resident in the urban area; and assistance in achieving a durable solution, where this is possible in the urban area.

Nature of assistance in urban areas

5.   There are many examples of problems and long-standing demands on UNHCR resources as a result of assistance programmes in urban areas that provided regular monthly allowances and refugee-specific services without ensuring that this support from UNHCR was indeed essential. Most such examples show an increasing involvement by UNHCR in the administration of assistance and rising overheads. There are also examples where UNHCR offices designed and implemented programmes for assistance in urban areas that did not create avoidable long-term reliance on UNHCR. There are recent examples of successful redirection of long-term care and maintenance programmes in accordance with the guidelines set out below.

6.   Assistance to refugees should be given in a manner that encourages self-reliance and does not foster long-term dependency. Where assistance has to be provided by UNHCR, care and maintenance assistance should be strictly limited to

those cases where early self-reliance is not possible, and the continuing appropriateness of this form of assistance must be confirmed at regular intervals. Services for those who are not yet self-reliant should be provided through support, where necessary, to national health and education services, not by the creation of parallel structures and special services for refugees. This support should be in the form of one-time assistance where possible, not open-ended commitment to recurring costs. UNHCR assistance that is selective - for example, access to higher education - should be made available only on the basis of the same criteria as apply for refugees elsewhere.

7.   Asylum seekers in urban areas should receive assistance from local authorities and institutions pending assessment of their claim. If no other source is available and if the asylum seeker would otherwise be unable to meet minimum needs, UNHCR may provide material assistance. In such circumstances, it should be limited to essential requirements and provided in a manner that does not raise false expectations of open-ended care and maintenance assistance if the claim is successful. Any such assistance should be subject to regular review if consideration of the claim is delayed, when UNHCR's own assessment of the status of the asylum seeker should be taken into account. UNHCR should, however, ensure that any specific needs of an asylum seeker as a result of the circumstances of his or her flight (for example, for health care and trauma counselling) are being met.

8.   Guidelines on how assistance programmes for refugees in urban areas should be developed are provided in the Community Services Guidelines, part 3, Urban Refugees - A Community-based Approach (May 1996). Guidelines on the promotion of self-reliance, employment and on microfinance are under preparation. Unlike other refugee populations, the majority of refugees in urban areas are generally male: the proportion of family groups is often lower than usual. While there may thus be fewer women, children and adolescents than normal, they can be even less visible than they are in some refugee camps and settlements. Particular attention must therefore be paid to identifying their needs, and also to identifying the needs of those who remain behind in urban areas - for example, the elderly, handicapped and those not eligible for resettlement - after others of their group have left.

Solutions for refugees living in urban areas

9.   Where voluntary repatriation is a viable option in the foreseeable future, this should be the preferred option, as for all refugees. Where this is not the case, or pending it, local integration if possible should be the objective of UNHCR assistance. The promotion of self-reliance should be undertaken accordingly, in a manner that will depend on local circumstances. This must respect the policies of the government while recognizing that many refugees, including many who have never received UNHCR assistance, are de facto locally integrated in urban areas.

10.   Any determination that resettlement is needed for individual refugees should be made with direct reference to the criteria set out in Chapter 4 of the Resettlement Handbook. The corner-stone of UNHCR's resettlement policy is the application of criteria that are consistent, both within a country and among countries with refugees from the same country of origin, with respect to an individual's circumstances. Thus a refugee in an urban area should have neither more nor less chance of resettlement than he or she would have had in a refugee camp in the same country, or in another country where protection had been found. Active and timely case finding by UNHCR, based on the consistent and transparent application of resettlement criteria, should

REFUGEES IN URBAN AREAS

remove the incentive for refugees to move to urban areas, and in particular to the capital, in search of resettlement.

11.   Irregular movement (see 13 below) to an urban area in another country in search of resettlement can in itself create a new situation where criteria for resettlement are met or more nearly met than was the case in the previous country. This may happen, for example, when he act of irregular entry creates a protection problem. Such cases create a dilemma for UNHCR: resettlement after irregular movement has been demonstrated to encourage more such movements, and may lead to increased reluctance of countries of resettlement to accept such refugees, particularly when this may be at the expense of those who have not moved. At the same time, the only alternative to resettlement in extreme cases may be prolonged incarceration in an immigration jail.

12.   Refugees who have moved irregularly to the country should not be submitted for resettlement (or given any prospects of resettlement) without the approval of the Resettlement Section, DIP. Such approval is likely only if it is determined that the person(s) would already have met the criteria for resettlement in their previous country. Approval would otherwise be conditional on the absence of any other means of resolving immediate protection problems.

Movement between countries

13.   The movement of refugees without the consent of the authorities concerned from a country where they had found protection to another country is often described as "irregular movement", and usually takes place to urban areas. Such movement may or may not have been legal: the key consideration is rather whether or not the refugee had found protection. A refugee who is compelled to move because of specific protection or security problems in his or her previous country clearly cannot be considered to have found protection there. Such persons should therefore be treated as if the present country is their first country of asylum, not as refugees whose movement was irregular.

14.   Irregular movements can put asylum and protection in the country of destination at risk for other refugees, and place demands on UNHCR's resources in the country of destination that far exceed those that would have been required in the previous country. Where voluntary repatriation was an option, irregular movement may make it less likely and more costly. Irregular movements tend to encourage others to follow.

15.   Working with the government(s) concerned, UNHCR should therefore seek to remove the incentive for and discourage irregular movement by:

   a)   ensuring proper protection and promoting durable solutions in countries of first asylum;

   b)   ensuring appropriate and consistent standards of assistance;

   c)   placing certain restrictions on assistance to refugees whose movement was irregular, and taking the special precautions with regard to their resettlement set out in paragraph 12 above;

   d)   supporting return to the previous country of asylum in certain clearly defined circumstances, as set out in paragraph 18 below.

Assistance after irregular movement

16.   UNHCR offices should first determine if the person is of concern to the Office. If the country of destination applies the same prima facie or group recognition as the country from which the irregular movement took place, or if the person was previously recognized (or not recognized) as a result of an individual determination by UNHCR, further action to determine status is not required. If the government of the country of destination has made a determination, this should be accepted unless UNHCR has reasons to undertake its own individual determination. If none of the above is applicable, there should be an individual determination of status by UNHCR in the present country. If the person is not found to be a refugee, any further action by UNHCR would be on the basis of good offices; issues related to the return of rejected cases are not covered herein.

17.   While, as explained in paragraph 1 above, UNHCR's protection obligations are unaffected by such movement, UNHCR does not have an obligation to provide assistance to refugees after irregular movement on the same basis as it would had there been no irregular movement.   With the obvious exception of life-saving assistance that is not available in time from any other source, or where the lack of UNHCR assistance would compromise protection, UNHCR should generally not provide direct individual assistance; persons whose movement to an urban area was irregular should use government services and their own resources whenever possible.   UNHCR assistance that is selective - for example, access to higher education - should not be made available.

Return after irregular movement

18.   UNHCR may promote the return of refugees who had found protection in a previous country provided certain conditions are met. Some conditions will be specific to the circumstances; the following are general conditions, likely to be applicable in all circumstances:

   a)   desire of the authorities in the present country to ensure return if possible;

   b)   sufficient evidence of stay in the previous country to satisfy that country;

   c)   assurance that protection will again be available after return;

   d)   readiness of the authorities in the previous country to readmit;

   e)   a determination by UNHCR that a durable solution is not possible in the present country.

It should be noted that Executive Committee Conclusion 58 on international protection states that return may take place if persons returned are "permitted to remain there and to be treated in accordance with recognized basic human standards until a durable solution is found for them."

Response to threats and violent protests

19.   Some refugees in urban areas have reacted with threats and violence to what they perceive as UNHCR's failure to meet their needs and/or expectations. Such

actions have taken forms that include hunger strikes, threats of suicide, and threatened or actual violence towards UNHCR and implementing partner staff and property, or towards other refugees who do not support the protests or the means used. A consistent, firm and fair implementation of the policies set out herein, and proper, timely and transparent information to the refugees on these policies - and on the constraints and limitations on UNHCR - are the best ways of ensuring that refugees' expectations are realistic, and thus preventing such actions.

20.   Where problems nevertheless occur, UNHCR should first establish whether the reaction of individual is due to psychological problems. If this is the case, these problems should be addressed. Where the refugees' concerns are legitimate, UNHCR should of course seek to meet them. However, experience suggests that the most serious threats and incidents occur as a result of a deliberate attempt to force UNHCR to change its position and accede to the protesters' demands. Resettlement is perhaps the most common demand. Some demands may be in UNHCR's power to meet; others will not, though this is frequently not accepted by the protesters.

21.   Experience shows that compromising in the face of such protests often leads to further demands and exacerbates the underlying problem. UNHCR should not change its position in response to threats or actual violence, whether towards UNHCR and its partners or self- or otherwise inflicted on refugees. Headquarters should be informed as soon such protests occur or are likely. If a field office is in doubt, advice should be sought from Headquarters on the most appropriate response to the demands. The security and law-and-order aspects of threats and violent protests are a matter for the authorities and police, and UNHCR offices should not hesitate in seeking their early involvement and assistance. Measures to ensure staff security are not covered herein. In the absence of a Field Staff Safety Officer, the advice of the Field Staff Safety Section at Headquarters should be sought without delay.

12 December 1997